Family Communication at the End of Life

Special Issue Editor

Maureen P. Keeley

MDPI • Basel • Beijing • Wuhan • Barcelona • Belgrade

MDPI

Special Issue Editor
Maureen P. Keeley
Texas State University
USA

Editorial Office
MDPI AG
St. Alban-Anlage 66
Basel, Switzerland

This edition is a reprint of the Special Issue published online in the open access journal *Behavioral Sciences* (ISSN 2076-328X) in 2017 (available at: http://www.mdpi.com/journal/behavsci/special_issues/family_communication).

For citation purposes, cite each article independently as indicated on the article page online and as indicated below:

Author 1, Author 2. Article title. *Journal Name.* **Year**. Article number/page range.

First Edition 2017

ISBN 978-3-03842-518-2 (Pbk)
ISBN 978-3-03842-519-9 (PDF)

Table of Contents

About the Special Issue Editor

Maureen P. Keeley Professor in the Department of Communication Studies, Texas State University. She earned her PhD (1994) from the University of Iowa, her MA (1987) and BA (1983) from the University of Arizona, all in Communication. Dr. Keeley has a sustained program of research on communication, grief, health and relationships; for over a decade she has been exploring Final Conversations in the familial context. Her work has resulted in an award-winning book (2007), over thirty professional articles in National/International journals, book chapters, and encyclopedia entries. In 2016, she was awarded the Health Communication Distinguished Article of the Year Award from the National Communication Association, as well as the Article of the Year Award from the Journal of Family Communication. She has been quoted in National and State media on death and dying. She is the preeminent expert on final conversations and is at the forefront of end-of-life communication research.

Preface to "Family Communication at the end of Life"

As the Guest Editor for this special issue on "Family Communication at the End of Life" I hope to accomplish numerous goals: to emphasize the important role that family members play at the end of life; to highlight the significant work of communication scholars that have been studying end of life communication; and, to reach more people with the knowledge available regarding family communication at the end of life. With so much out of people's control in the midst of a death journey, communication is one thing that the terminally ill and their family members can control and improve for better outcomes. Thus, bringing academic research in an accessible manner to people looking for answers about communication at the end of life is vitally important. Too much academic research is read only by other scholars reading academic journals; with an open access journal such as Behavioral Science, any person who can search their questions pertaining to death, dying, family, communication, and end of life, will find new answers available to them. I also realize that it is the right time to underscore the need for more effective communication given the aging population in the world in this era of mature baby boomers.

Baby boomers, the largest segment of the U.S. population, are coming to the age where they must cope with their parents' deaths or declining health, as well as face their own mortality. A lot of middle-aged Americans have their parents living with them and many of them are becoming care givers for their parents who are in increasingly poor health. The number of people dying at home and in the care of family members escalates dramatically when considering other countries and cultures that live with multi-generations in their homes. With medical advances in the treatment of cancer and other degenerative diseases, it is becoming more likely that an ailing loved ones will live longer with their terminal illness and then will die at home or in hospice care. The extended period of time that the family will be dealing with the terminal illness makes communication a focal point; starting with whether or not the approaching death is acknowledged and talked about amongst family members and with outsiders, continuing with the multiple conversations that are held with a wide variety of healthcare professionals, and all of the conversations that transpire during the journey.

Why is it important to focus on family communication at the end of life? The death journey is taken together by the terminally ill and their family members. All participants are greatly impacted by the communication that occurs during this time period that I call "terminal time." Terminal time begins from the moment of diagnosis of a terminal illness and ends at the moment of death. It is a time period where people often prioritize their relationships with one another because of the acute awareness that their time left together is limited. Terminal time activates family members' journey with their dying loved one. Their path will usually take them to numerous healthcare and palliative care professionals looking for answers to challenges that come with the end of life. Furthermore, family members often spend more time with one another than they have in years; time that may be filled with the creation of new memories, with laughter and tears, with the sharing of stories, beliefs, even fears and/or conflict.

This end of life journey may take days, weeks, months, or even years, but however long between the diagnosis and the inevitable death, the terminally ill and their family members begin looking for answers to questions about their impending challenges. These questions may include but are not limited to the following: How and when should people get honest about talking about death and dying? Who is going to make the difficult end of life decisions? What are the best choices for care at the end of life? How do family members deal with and communicate about the often challenging symptoms that come with age and disease? How can family members communicate with the terminally ill when illness impedes verbal communication? How can family members communicate effectively with professional healthcare professionals so that the needs of the terminally ill be dealt with quickly and correctly? How can professional healthcare workers improve communication with the terminally ill and their family members to lead to better outcomes with less pain and fewer unnecessary treatments? What can all pertinent parties (i.e., terminally ill, family members, healthcare professionals) do to improve their communication to fulfill important goals at the end of life? How can family members communicate with their dying loved ones in ways that will leave them without regret or without things left unsaid? How can communication with the dying loved one better prepare individuals who must go on living following the death, deal with their loss, grief and ability to move on with life after the death of their loved one? All of these questions and more will be answered by experts in this special issue.

It is the collective goal of the experts that have written articles for this special issue to increase awareness about the important role that communication plays at the end of life. These communication scholars have spent years exploring and examining the impact of communication of the terminally ill, family members, and healthcare professionals to improve care, compassion, and connection at the end of life. Authentic, honest, and open communication provides a way to concentrate on the person rather than the illness at the end of life. It is my hope that this special issue on "Family Communication at the End of Life" begins more conversations about death and dying for the terminally ill and family members; and triggers new research focusing on family, communication and the end of life from all participants' perspectives.

Maureen P. Keeley
Special Issue Editor

behavioral
sciences

MDPI

Article

Upstreaming and Normalizing Advance Care Planning Conversations—A Public Health Approach

Maryjo Prince-Paul * and Evelina DiFranco

School of Nursing, Case Western Reserve University, 2120 Cornell Road, Cleveland, OH 44106, USA;
evelina.difranco@case.edu
* Correspondence: mxp42@case.edu

Academic Editor: Maureen P. Keeley
Received: 27 February 2017; Accepted: 7 April 2017; Published: 12 April 2017

Abstract: As a society, we simply don't talk about this universal experience called dying and death; in fact, we ignore it until we have to face it. Thus, it is often in a crisis experience when we have to make decisions while we are laden with uncertainty and intense emotions. Sixty percent of people say making sure their family is not burdened by tough decisions is extremely important, yet 56% of them have not held a conversation about its context. Instead of waiting to make end-of-life decisions, let us begin to think about what matters most while we are living, what we value most, and how we translate these values into conversations about what is important. As a public health concern, if we can upstream the advance care planning discussion into usual health promotion activities, perhaps, as a society, we can begin to normalize and reshape how we make decisions about the last chapters of our lives.

Keywords: advance care planning; death education; public health

1. Introduction

The inevitability of death encompasses us all. We are all born with the disease of mortality. We all die. And yet, to many of us, the details of dying and death are a mystery. It is an abstraction we would rather not think about. Contemplating our own death and doing the necessary preparatory work is a rarity in modern America. In fact, most all people in modern America think the time to decide about health care choices is "later." Furthermore, having end-of-life discussions are rarely considered during the routine days of living; rather, these types of conversations and health care decisions are made during a time of crisis, when both patients and families are laden with anxiety, fear, and the lack of time to make mindful, reasonable, and logical decisions. This lack of openness has affected the quality and range of support and care services available to patients and their families. It has also affected our ability to die where or how we would wish. As Americans, we should learn how to make a place for death in our lives and learn how to plan for it.

A 2013 national survey of nearly 2100 Americans aged 18 and older found that, while 90% said that talking about end-of-life decisions was important, fewer than 30% had actually done so [1]. In another survey, 82% of people said it was important to put their wishes in writing, yet only 23% had actually done it [2,3]. The fact is that when patients with serious and life-threatening illness are prepared, they die well and their families and caregivers tend to grieve better. When people have done the work of considering their own goals and values and have documented those preferences, they make different choices.

Modern medicine in America saves many people from acute illness, who then go on to live longer with chronic illnesses whose disease trajectories are associated with declining physical and mental functioning over months and years, often punctuated by episodes of acute illness and decompensation. Unfortunately, unnecessary suffering, as well as dissatisfaction with and poor health care resource utilization result from a mismatch between the patients and family's needs and the current health care system environment. In most cases, the suffering could be avoided, or at least mitigated, by some education on dying and death and informed conversations about it. Ultimately, this will involve a fundamental change in society in which dying, death, and bereavement will be thought about, seen, and accepted as a natural part of life's cycle. Upstreaming Advance Care Planning (ACP) and its accompanying discussions provides a means of ameliorating this mismatch, but is yet to be embedded in America's public consciousness.

2. What is Advance Care Planning

Advance care planning (ACP) is a process of communication between individuals, families, and others who are considered important to the discussion, as well as health care providers, to understand, discuss, and plan future health care decisions, not only to lay preparations in the event that an individual loses decision-making capacity, but also to offer detailed instruction about values and wishes. ACP is about planning and talking about the "what ifs" that might occur across the entire lifespan. The goal is to try to engage in conversations more proactively rather than just reacting to changes in health conditions.

Advance directives are one part of the advance care planning process; that is, a formal, legal document that addresses plans about what treatment people wish to have or not have when they near death. These statements can include expectations about what people may wish to refuse to have, such as cardiopulmonary resuscitation, artificial ventilation, or artificial nutrition/feeding; they can be positive preferences such as what they would like to experience when they are near death, such as being at home with a loved one, preserving dignity and worth, and leaving a legacy. In addition, this process should involve the identification of a decision-maker, or surrogate decision-maker, who will honor, uphold, and respect a person's preferences. However, this document goes into effect only when a person is incapacitated and loses the ability to speak for him/herself. Most importantly, this document should be viewed as a "living document"—one that can be revised and adjusted over time, as situations change, including change in health status.

3. Advance Care Planning as a Process

In the past, ACP has often been focused on the completion rates of actual advance directive documents, despite the lack of evidence to support that such documents improve end-of-life care or correspond with future care preferences [4]. Although evidence remains insufficient that ACP documentation leads to engagement of health care professionals in end-of-life discussions, we argue that upstreaming these conversations into lay communication may heighten the "normalization" of the topic into mainstream dialogue [5].

Perhaps a more superior focus will encourage widespread dialogue about ACP as a process for iteratively identifying and facilitating what people constitute as a "good death", including identifying what factors are considered important (i.e., achieving a sense of control, leaving a legacy, maintaining a sense of dignity, being without pain or symptoms, relieving financial burdens, strengthening close relationships, and saying important things), and for informally communicating their future wishes [6]. Fried and colleagues suggest that ACP should be recognized as a health behavior and that the most effective way to engage people in this process is to tailor the information to a person's readiness for engagement [7].

Conceptually, this comprises five distinct phases, from pre-contemplation to action and maintenance, which includes the completion of a written advance directive (a living will and a durable power of attorney for health care, otherwise known as a surrogate decision-maker). Three necessary components are germane to this discussion. First, there must be a willingness of the individual to reflect. This involves a discussion aimed at defining values, life goals, and wishes about the future. Commonly, this is grounded in how one sees a "life well lived". Second, there is need for an organized "coming together" of all persons who will be involved in honoring the wishes. Plain language, timing, and trust are key elements of the success of this meeting. Third, an ongoing discussion about the preferences, especially in light of the complexity of life-limiting and serious illness, must be engaged in [8,9]. Conversations take time and effort and cannot be completed as a single checklist; they need to take place on more than one occasion.

As outlined in the standards of the National Framework and Preferred Practices for Palliative and Hospice Care Quality (NQF) optimal advance care planning is not a one-time event, but an ongoing discussion at critical milestones throughout the life cycle (e.g., when a person turns 18 years of age) [10,11]. Initiating these conversations earlier in the life cycle, at key maturation points, presumes that the person is generally healthy and has decision-making capacity. This can normalize discussion about values and life goals that can be revisited overtime, as part of primary health care, or simply when having conversation within the family context during sentinel life events. Ideally, these discussions would start early in adulthood, addressing global values and the selection of potential proxy decision-makers. With changes in health status, they would reflect more specific instructions.

Challenges of ACP derive from both a sociological and technological perspective. From a sociological context, there is a pervasive reluctance to publicly and personally engage in discussion about how people want to live with a serious illness, how they want to personally engage in discussion about dying and death, and how they would prefer to be cared for at the end of their lives. In addition, there are diverse ethnic and religious understandings, teachings, and preferences about individual autonomy. From a technological lens, different types of diseases have different disease trajectories and treatment options often have varying purposes with often contrasting consequences. And, while some older adults remain healthy and robust until very close to death, it is more likely that an older individual will have lived for two or more years with one or more chronic diseases and will have experienced substantial disability before dying. Along the way, he or she, and the family, will have to make what are sometimes difficult choices about health care.

4. Our Aging Population in the USA

Throughout our lives, but especially when we are older and facing increased risk of serious illness, we need a plan about what services are essential to living well and meaningfully. Medical advancements have contributed to increased life expectancy for Americans. The number and proportion of older persons in the United States is rapidly increasing. Persons 65 years or older numbered 46.2 million in 2014 (the latest year for which data is available). They represent 14.5% of the U.S. population, which is about one in every seven Americans. By 2060, there will be nearly 98 million older persons, more than twice their number in 2014. People 65+ represented 14.5% of the population in the year 2014, but are expected to grow to be 21.7% of the population by 2040 and the youngest members of the Baby Boomer generation will reach 65 years of age in 2030 [12]. Taken together, the unprecedented numbers of aging adults coupled with the corresponding likelihood of chronic conditions, such as heart disease, diabetes, dementia, depression, frailty, and end-of-life issues, will challenge the existing health care system. As the face of America ages, holding conversations about preferences for care is therefore paramount. Most often with family present, elders do engage in ACP conversation, if given the opportunity to reflect and share. Those who have had this conversation are almost three times as likely to have their end-of-life wishes both known and followed, and their family members demonstrate less anxiety, stress, and depression during bereavement [13].

5. ACP and Public Health, Education, Engagement

Internationally, death awareness and death literacy are not only more culturally transparent, but seem to be integrated into the context of everyday living. Through community engagement and social action, conversations about death and dying are commonplace and have set the stage for the development of a public health approach, specifically in such countries as the United Kingdom and Australia [5]. Death literacy, defined as a set of knowledge or skills that help persons gain access to, understand, and then act upon end-of-life and death care options, is positioned within a public health framework [14]. It is a resource that people and communities use to strengthen their capacity for future caring. Embedded in this framework is death education, and its role is to moderate the relationship between death awareness and knowledge about society as a death system. Taken together, this public heath approach, commonly practiced in the aforementioned countries, is operationalized through community engagement, collaboration, and empowerment, and creates a template for an American public health approach to ACP.

The Centers for Disease Control and Prevention (CDC) recognizes the public health opportunity to educate Americans, especially older adults, about ACP in order to improve their quality of care at the end of life [15]. ACP also meets other criteria that define a public health issue. According to the CDC, ACP can potentially affect a large number of people, can reduce unwanted, futile, and expensive treatment, and can meet public demand to change the way care has been addressed in the past. Just as health care is not solely the responsibility of the sick but also the healthy, so too, dying and death are the responsibility of everyone, not simply those who are old or have serious illness. In order to provide a context for the role of public health engagement, it is critical to first establish what must happen before this movement gains momentum.

A public health education approach to death and dying can upstream the conversation about ACP squarely in the domain of a broader death education context. Not disseminating general education about death and dying (having open discourse about this inevitability) and/or encouraging conversations about ACP, and then leaving a loved one to make critical decisions for their sick family member, is like asking people to eat healthier (planning meals, recognizing healthier options) without providing education on the nutritional value in the food products they are purchasing or resources on planning meals and better habits around eating. By engaging schools, workplaces, service clubs, recreation facilities, churches and their leaders, and other venues (see Box 1), death education becomes a population health approach for health promotion. This action has the momentum to not only change social attitudes, but also the behaviors and qualities of experiences of living until death.

Box 1. Venues to consider for public education and conversation about advance care planning.

- Churches, synagogues, temples, and other places of worship (and their leaders)
- Service Clubs (Rotary International, Kiwanis, Lions)
- Local public library forums
- Girls Scouts and Boys Scouts of America meetings (Merit badges—e.g., public health, family life, communication, law)
- Book Clubs
- Senior Centers
- Local fitness centers
- Barber shops/beauty salons
- High school curricula (http://www.dyingmatters.org)
- Undergraduate courses at public and private schools of higher education
- Death cafes (http://www.deathcafe.com)
- Wellness programs at places of employment
- Progressive dinners/Death Over Dinner (http://deathoverdinner.org)
- National Healthcare Decisions Day (http://www.nhdd.org)

Recommendation 5 of the Institute of Medicine's report on Improving Quality and Honoring Individual Preferences Near the End of Life highlights the importance of public education and engagement [16]. It states: "Civic leaders, public health and other governmental agencies, community-based organizations, faith-based organizations, consumer groups, and professional societies, should engage their constituents and provide fact based information to encourage ACP and informed choice based on the needs and values of individuals. Public education and engagement efforts should aim to normalize these difficult conversations and to assist people in achieving the necessary information to have meaningful discussions about the values and goals of care" [16] (p. 370). Like all modern public health initiatives, the pursuit of death education and engagement programs in the community should seek to create social changes that promote healthy behaviors, reduce harm, and maximize well-being and quality of life.

6. One Avenue: The Influence of Community Clergy

As the baby boomer generation ages, increased numbers of persons will inevitably be forced to cope with illness and end-of-life issues, bringing diverse cultural and spiritual beliefs and practices into making decisions about how they want to live until they die. Religious and/or spiritual beliefs remain central to most Americans; they provide a sense of continuity of self and a sense of belonging, especially in the face of serious illness [17]. Today, the role of religion and spirituality has become an increasingly salient component as people aim to find a sense of connectedness and purpose before life's end [18]. America's current population not only reflects an aging population but one with multigenerational family members combined with an array of spiritual practices. Unfortunately, spiritual practice and its integration in the health care delivery system is often overlooked [19]. Evidence suggests that many people want spirituality incorporated as a component of health care, but most report that spiritual needs are often neglected by the medical community [20]. A sense of meaning and purpose in life, supported by spirituality is related to lower death anxiety, death avoidance, and depression, and an overall sense of greater subjective well-being [21]. Community clergy, spiritual leaders, and places of worship have a unique opportunity to engage constituents, including families, into conversations about ACP before illness strikes [22]. Spiritual leaders are situated in a relationship of trust with covenants and they have an important role to help clarify ways in which people's beliefs and values might influence their health care preferences and decisions.

7. National Movements at the Community Level

Unfortunately, we live in a society that largely denies death or at least attempts to avoid it. Yet, it is the case that most Americans will age and die; there is a finitude of living. The reluctance to examine this experience shapes the way we view and think about dying well. However, many Americans tell stories about death gone wrong and how their parents or other family members received care that was inconsistent with their values and wishes. This has activated consumers and generated an approach about not accepting care that violates their own wishes. By sharing these very personal stories in the public domain, people have started a national conversation that is creating a dynamic, social shift.

Community engagement programs have the capacity to mobilize and maximize family, community, and workplace supports in an effort to reorganize a culture of denial toward a culture of acknowledgement of this universal experience. The current national conversation to encourage the general public to talk more about death and dying or, more specifically, what is valued the most, should greatly facilitate ACP. Two recent, national efforts have largely propelled the dialogue—The Conversation Project and the Stanford Letter Project [1,23].

The Conversation Project is a public engagement campaign that advocates "kitchen table" conversations with family and friends about wishes and preferences for health care [1]. The Conversation Project, in collaboration with the Institute to Improve Health Care (IHI), offers people the tools and guidance by way of the Conversation Starter Kit—a resource organized by a "get ready, get set, go, keep going" approach that reflects the Transtheoretical Model outlined by Fried and colleagues [7]. Intended to specifically gather individuals' preferences for end-of-life care, the Conversation Project's campaign may be casting a larger net, from a public health perspective. Social support has been shown to have the greatest influence on health- related quality of life outcomes [24]. By gathering loved ones, friends, and people who matter most around a kitchen table or a common meeting area, social engagement and support occur organically. Perhaps these difficult discussions will become easier and more comfortable when taking place with important others, before a crisis, and in the comfort of a natural surrounding—not the intensive care unit.

Another effort, the Stanford Letter project, began in 2015 under the direction of Dr. Vyjeyanthi Periyakoil from Stanford University School of Medicine [23]. Dr. Periyakoil and her team spent years conducting interviews and focus groups in multiple languages with people in the community and talking to numerous patients and their families about the challenges of having and preparing for discussions about the last phase of life. Their research has shown that most Americans find it extremely difficult to discuss this important topic with both their family members and friends, as well as their health care providers. Furthermore, people simply do not quite know how to initiate these conversations [25]. To that end, the Letter Project and its accompanying tools were specifically designed to help people voice key information needed to prepare for the future. Three letter templates exist and include: "The What Matters Most" template—a document that provides anyone the space to write about what matters most to them and what treatments they want in the future; the "Letter Project Advance Directive"—a valid advance directive and a supplemental letter that describes preferences for medical care at the end of life and is submitted to the health care provider; and the "Friends and Family Letter"—a life review document that acknowledges important people, treasured moments, and allows for sharing relational-based conversation including gratitude, love, and forgiveness. The Stanford Letter Project goal is to help, empower, and support all adults to prepare for their future and to take the initiative to talk to their doctors and their friends and family about what matters most to them at life's end. All tools are free and available in print, as an online fillable form, and as a mobile app.

8. Conclusions

For most people in the United States, until a loved one is actually facing a serious, life-threatening illness, interest in engaging in ACP discussions is often low. The demands of everyday living coupled with our pervasive societal denial of death in the United States, provide a ready excuse to not engage. Upstreaming ACP conversations will require a broad participation of multiple stakeholders, not limited to health care providers. We must stretch to the public health, social and supporting services sector, such as faith based communities where Americans and their families often rely on assistance for practical issues, information, and advice. As a result, we can potentially transform our culture so that more people can have their values and preferences about what matters most to them honored at life's end. Perhaps then, as a society, we will have the courage to confront the reality of mortality and to seek the truth about our hopes and our fears.

Author Contributions: Maryjo Prince-Paul conceived of and designed the article, collected data, and wrote the paper. Evelina DiFranco provided critical revision of the drafted article. Maryjo Prince-Paul and Evelina DiFranco provided the final edits and approval of the version to be published.

Conflicts of Interest: The authors declare no conflict of interest.

References

1. The Conversation Project Your Conversation Starter Kit. Available online: http://theconversationproject.org/wp-content/uploads/2017/02/ConversationProject-ConvoStarterKit-English.pdf (accessed on 26 February 2017).
2. California Health Care Foundation. Final Chapter: Californians' Attitudes & Experiences with Death & Dying. Available online: http://www.chcf.org/publications/2012/02/final-chapter-death-dying (accessed on 26 February 2017).
3. Rao, J.K.; Anderson, L.A.; Lin, F.C.; Laux, J.P. Completion of advance directives among U.S. consumers. *Am. J. Prev. Med.* **2014**, *46*, 65–70. [CrossRef] [PubMed]
4. Weathers, E.; O'Caoimh, R.; Cornally, N.; Fitzgerald, C.; Kearns, T.; Coffey, A.; Daly, E.; O'sullivan, R.; McGlade, C.; Molloy, D.W. Advance care planning: A systematic review of randomised controlled trials conducted with older adults. *Maturitas* **2016**, *91*, 101–109. [CrossRef] [PubMed]
5. Lewis, E.; Cardona-Morrell, M.; Ong, K.Y.; Trankle, S.A.; Hillman, K. Evidence still insufficient that advance care documentation leads to engagement of healthcare professionals in end-of-life discussions: A systematic review. *Palliat. Med.* **2016**, *30*, 807–824. [CrossRef] [PubMed]

6. Steinhauser, K.E.; Christakis, N.A.; Clipp, E.C.; McNeilly, M.; McIntyre, L.; Tulsky, J.A. Factors considered important at the end of life by patients, family, physicians, and other care providers. *JAMA* **2000**, *284*, 2476–2482. [CrossRef] [PubMed]

7. Fried, T.R.; Redding, C.A.; Robbins, M.L.; Paiva, A.L.; O'leary, J.R.; Iannone, L. Development of personalized health messages to promote engagement in advance care planning. *J. Am. Geriatr. Soc.* **2016**, *64*, 359–364. [CrossRef] [PubMed]

8. Wittenberg-Lyles, E.; Goldsmith, J.; Oliver, D.P.; Demiris, G.; Kruse, R.L.; Van Stee, S. Using medical words with family caregivers. *J. Palliat. Med.* **2013**, *16*, 1135–1139. [CrossRef] [PubMed]

9. Fried, T.R.; Bullock, K.; Iannone, L.; O'leary, J.R. Understanding advance care planning as a process of health behavior change. *J. Am. Geriatr. Soc.* **2009**, *57*, 1547–1555. [CrossRef] [PubMed]

10. National Quality Forum (NQF). A National Framework and Preferred Practices for Palliative and Hospice Care Quality. Available online: http://www.qualityforum.org/Publications/2006/12/A_National_Framework_and_Preferred_Practices_for_Palliative_and_Hospice_Care_Quality.aspx (accessed on 26 February 2017).

11. Benson, W.; Aldrich, N. Advance Care Planning: Ensuring Your Wishes Are Known and Honored If You Are Unable to Speak for Yourself. 2012. Available online: https://www.cdc.gov/aging/pdf/advanced-care-planning-critical-issue-brief.pdf (accessed on 24 February 2017).

12. U.S. Department of Health & Human Services Administration for Community Living. Available online: https://aoa.acl.gov/Aging_Statistics/Index.aspx (accessed on 26 February 2017).

13. Detering, K.M.; Hancock, A.D.; Reade, M.C.; Silvester, W. The impact of advance care planning on end of life care in elderly patients: Randomised controlled trial. *BMJ* **2010**, *340*, c1345. [CrossRef] [PubMed]

14. Noonan, K.; Horsfall, D.; Leonard, R.; Rosenberg, J. Developing death literacy. *Prog. Palliat. Care* **2016**, *24*, 31–35. [CrossRef]

15. Center for Disease Control and Prevention. Give Peace of Mind: Advance Care Planning. Available online: https://www.cdc.gov/aging/advancecareplanning/about.htm (accessed on 24 February 2017).

16. Pizzo, P.; Walker, D.; Bomba, P. *Dying in America: Improving Quality and Honoring Individual Preferences near the End of Life*; Institute of Medicine: Washington, DC, USA, 2014.

17. Puchalski, C.M.; Blatt, B.; Kogan, M.; Butler, A. Spirituality and health: The development of a field. *Acad. Med.* **2014**, *89*, 10–16. [CrossRef] [PubMed]

18. Puchalski, C.; Ferrell, B.; Virani, R.; Otis-Green, S.; Baird, P.; Bull, J.; Chochinov, H.; Handzo, G.; Nelson-Becker, H.; Prince-Paul, M.; Pugliese, K.; Sulmasy, D. Improving the quality of spiritual care as a dimension of palliative care: The report of the Consensus Conference. *J. Palliat. Med.* **2009**, *12*, 885–904. [CrossRef] [PubMed]

19. Balboni, M.J. A theological assessment of spiritual assessments. *Christ. Bioeth.* **2013**, *19*, 313–331. [CrossRef]

20. Peteet, J.R.; Balboni, M.J. Spirituality and religion in oncology. *CA Cancer J. Clin.* **2013**, *63*, 280–289. [CrossRef] [PubMed]

21. Krause, N.; Pargament, K.I.; Ironson, G. In the Shadow of Death: Religious Hope as a Moderator of the Effects of Age on Death Anxiety. *J. Gerontol. B Psychol. Sci. Soc. Sci.* **2016**. [CrossRef] [PubMed]

22. LeBaron, V.T.; Smith, P.T.; Quiñones, R.; Nibecker, C.; Sanders, J.J.; Timms, R.; Shields, A.E.; Balboni, T.A.; Balboni, M.J. How Community Clergy Provide Spiritual Care: Toward a Conceptual Framework for Clergy End-of-Life Education. *J. Pain Symptom Manag.* **2016**, *51*, 673–681. [CrossRef] [PubMed]

23. Stanford Medicine Letter Project. Available online: https://med.stanford.edu/letter.html (accessed on 24 February 2017).

24. Fayers, P.M.; Machin, D. *Quality of Life: The Assessment, Analysis and Interpretation of Patient-Reported Outcomes*; John Wiley & Sons: Hoboken, NJ, USA, 2013.

25. Periyakoil, V.S.; Neri, E.; Kraemer, H. No easy talk: A mixed methods study of doctor reported barriers to conducting effective end-of-life conversations with diverse patients. *PLoS ONE* **2015**, *10*, e0122321. [CrossRef] [PubMed]

behavioral sciences

MDPI

Article

Death Cafés: Death Doulas and Family Communication

Paula K. Baldwin

Department of Communication Studies, Western Oregon University, Monmouth, OR 97361, USA;
baldwinp@wou.edu; Tel.: +1-503-838-8065

Academic Editor: Maureen P. Keeley
Received: 28 February 2017; Accepted: 19 April 2017; Published: 26 April 2017

Abstract: The Death Café is part of the Death Positive movement, and as such, is uniquely positioned to bring the dialogue about death and dying to the public. Participants in a Death Café typically have two different perspectives. Some participants have not experienced death in their family and friends' circle and wish to converse with others about their beliefs on death and dying. Others are those who have experienced death somewhere in their circle of friends and families. One of goals of the Death Café facilitators is to help attendees reconcile their family narratives regarding death using the broader lens of the Death Café. Using the insights provided by interviews from 15 Death Café facilitators, this manuscript discusses the role of the Death Café facilitators as the death doulas of family communication.

Keywords: Death Café; communication; family communication; end of life; death doulas; death

1. Introduction

The experience of death in contemporary American society is frequently divided along racial, ethnic, and religious lines [1]. Although the American death culture cannot be categorized easily, American individualism, our unwillingness to accept aging and death, and the "keep them alive at all costs" medical system has a very strong influence on our perception of end of life [2].

Death Café (DC), the Death Salon, and the Order of the Good Death are all part of the Death Positive movement that seeks to counter a collective reluctance to embrace mortality [3,4]. The Order of the Good Death and its event, Death Salon, focus on bringing together professionals to discuss the broader cultural impacts of death; DC focuses on one's personal interactions with mortality. Death Café is a grassroots organization driven by volunteers who feel strongly about creating a safe space for people to meet, eat cake, drink tea or coffee, and discuss death with no agenda, objectives or themes [5]. Rather than a grief support or counseling session, DC is a private, group-directed discussion.

Death Cafés

Jon Underwood and Sue Barsky Reid developed the Death Café model based on the ideas of Bernard Crettaz, Swiss sociologist [3]. DC's objective is to "increase awareness of death with a view to helping people make the most of their (finite) lives" [3,4]. Death Cafes spread quickly across Europe, North America and Australasia (Australia, New Zealand, the island of New Guinea, and neighboring islands in the Pacific Ocean). As of this writing, 4096 Death Cafes in 42 countries have been held since September 2011, all run by volunteers [4].

Holding a DC requires a host and facilitator, a venue with refreshments, and people who want to talk about death. A host is not necessary to the process, but the facilitator is essential. Both roles can be combined, but the facilitator only performs their role during the actual DC session. The DC facilitators (DCF) welcome the attendees to the DC and share the guidelines. Anyone can host a DC, but the DC facilitators and the DC attendees (DCA) must agree to follow the DC guidelines: not-for-profit, held in an accessible, respectful, and confidential space, with no intention of leading people to any conclusion, product, or course of action, and serving refreshing drinks and cake [6]. Rarely do the DCA violate these rules, but if they do, the DCA are reminded of the rules and then redirected. If the attendee chooses not to comply, then they would be asked to leave.

Becoming a DCF is informal. The founders of the DC movement ask that a potential DCF read and download their DC Guide, which includes suggestions for holding a DC [5,6]. They ask that potential facilitators read and adhere to the DC guidelines and post their DC date and information on the DC website.

The DC is an interesting phenomenon to study because the organization is entirely run by volunteers. These volunteers find and reserve the venue, design, print and distribute the fliers, purchase the refreshments, run the DC session, debrief the participants, and clean up afterwards. Many of the DCF hold their DC at least once a month, if not more frequently.

Death Café attendees typically have two different perspectives. Some attendees have not yet experienced death in their family and friends' circle and wish to converse with others about their beliefs on death and dying. Other DC attendees are those who have experienced the death of a loved one and are driven to make sense of the experience, particularly if the attendee has had a less than satisfying experience with a loved one's death. Our families are the initial sources for all our beliefs, including our attitudes and opinions, about death and dying [7]. Either directly or indirectly, to some degree, most of the DC attendees have a common goal of reconciling their family narratives regarding death during a Death Café where talking about death is welcomed. As a comparatively new phenomenon, there is relatively little existing academic research on this topic [8,9]. To date, the current scholarship on Death Café focuses on its history and the lack of diversity among attendees, but they do not tell us about the volunteers, the DCF, and why they do this work. Therefore, the purpose of this study was to examine the DCF motivations for holding DC.

2. Methods

In order to begin to understand DCF's motivations for volunteering, interviews were selected as the primary means of data collection. Semi-structured interviews allow the researcher to ask the same basic questions of all interviewees, yet allow for flexibility if topics arise that require additional probing or inquiry. Interviews are also beneficial because they allow participants to reflect upon and make sense of their experiences [10]. In addition to investigating motivations, interview questions further attempted to understand the DCF through a close examination of their personal goals in holding DC, and their observations about themselves and the DCA (see Appendix A for interview questions).

After receiving approval from the author's institutional review board, participants were recruited through the Death Café website with permission from its founder. A second recruitment solicitation was also sent by email inviting a select group of DCF considered particularly active by having hosted at least six DCs per year. Eligibility criteria also required all participants to be age 18 years or older and able to speak English. A total of 15 facilitators were recruited from the United States (14) and Italy (1). Phone interviews were digitally recorded, transcribed verbatim, and analyzed, resulting in 176 pages of data. To protect the confidentiality of the DCFs, all identifying information was removed from the data presented here. Interviews were conducted until thematic saturation was reached and no new information was found.

Death Café facilitator transcripts were reviewed and analyzed using an iterative process of thematic analysis [11]. The author trained two upper division undergraduate students in the process of coding, using an emergent strategy to identify themes. An intercoder reliability of 92% was reached on approximately 20% of the data. At the conclusion of the coding, the resulting themes were shared with two DCF interviewees for membership check validity, resulting in positive confirmation of the themes. Open coding was used to identify comments suggesting themes, and association into more compact categories reduced to three themes related to family communication about dying and death and the role of the Death Café facilitator in helping DC participants make sense of their musings about mortality.

3. Results

The majority of the DCF were ages 55–64 (67%). The DCF were White Non-Hispanic (100%), female (93%), and college educated (80%). Sixty-seven per cent of the DCF were married or in a committed partnership (Table 1 shows a summary of DCF characteristics). Demographic information was not collected about the DCF nuclear or extended family, unless that information was shared during the interview process. The following sections include exemplars of the study themes of advocacy, validation, and personal identity, which illuminate the DCF's motivations for doing this work.

Table 1. Death Café (DC) Facilitator Characteristics.

Characteristic	*n* = 15 (%)
Age	
24–34	1 (7%)
35–44	1 (7%)
45–54	3 (20%)
55–64	10 (67%) *
Sex	
Female	14 (93%)
Male	1 (7%)
Hispanic Ethnicity	
No	15 (100%)
Education	
Some College	2 (13%)
Bachelor	6 (40%)
Master	4 (27%)
PhD	2 (13%)
No Answer	1 (7%)
Relationship Status	
Single	2 (13%)
Divorced	1 (7%)
Married	9 (60%)
Committed Partnership	1 (7%)
Widowed	2 (13%)
Employment	
Unemployed	1 (7%)
Employed	5 (33%)
Self-employed	5 (33%)
Semi-retired	1 (7%)
Retired	2 (13%)
Student	1 (7%)
Religious Affiliation	
Agnostic	1 (7%)
Buddhist	2 (13%)
Spiritual	5 (33%)
Jewish	3 (20%)
Wiccan	1 (7%)
Did not identify	1 (7%)
None	2 (13%)
Employment and Experience with Death	
Work(ed) in the death industry (e.g., social workers, hospice volunteers, thanatologists, hospice nurses, funeral directors, hospice social workers)	12 (80%)
Experienced multiple deaths in family and friends	9 (60%)
DC facilitators (DCF) who work(ed) in the death industry and experienced multiple deaths in family and friends	12 (80%)

Note: Percentage total varies due to rounding.

Table 2 shows the three themes, how they were defined and their saturation.

Table 2. Thematic Information.

Theme	Definition	Data Counts (Instances Where DCF Mentioned a Theme)
Advocacy	Raising Awareness, Educating, Changing the Narrative	202
Validation	Affirmation for themselves and attendees, bonding with the DC attendees (DCA), Building community	201
Personal Identity	Personal growth, personal calling to be of service in this area	144

Nearly 80% of the DCF interviewed work or have worked in some aspect of the death industry, in funeral homes, as grief counselors, social workers, and thanatologists to name a few. That such a large percentage of the DCF interviewed for this study are members of the death industry suggests that they are exceptionally sensitive to the impact that little to no communication has on the surviving family members. As one facilitator remarked,

> I work in a cemetery; I am a family service advisor. And I know everyday I've met people who have things they want to say but they never get to. Or they don't have somebody at home to talk with until devastating happens and then they are having to have to deal with grief and that they don't totally understand the information. So I saw a need for it. I think people just need to talk some of these things out in a non-bereavement setting and since I work with death everyday, it just felt very natural for me to do this. I'm also a cancer survivor and I had to face death at 40. And it made me realize, it just doesn't escape anybody (T6).

Another DCF remarked: "The goal is really just creating this environment where more people can turn to because they don't feel comfortable talking to their friends and family ... And the goal is really to just keep the conversation flowing and make more and more people aware of what DC is." (T7) Perhaps having witnessed so much pain and discomfort around end-of-life events, this is one of the sources of the advocacy noted among the study interviewees.

3.1. Advocacy

Raising awareness, education, and promotion of change in people's abilities to communicate openly about issues relating to death and dying comprise the theme of advocacy. All 15 of the DCF commented on their strong commitment to changing the narrative about death and dying by also encouraging the Death Café attendees to continue the communication process with their families. As one DCF says, "Conversation in that DC setting enables them to go to their families and have the kind of conversation they need to have about death, that's why we have DC." (T8).

The DCF recognize that expanding the conversation about death is critical in a time when people often actively avoid talking about death until that conversation is thrust upon them. One DCF put it thus:

> My goal is to bring that conversation that we have at our DC at each table to bring the conversation home to their table. This is something that needs to be discussed rather than ignored because it is inevitable that we are all going to experience multiple losses, not only our loved ones, but our friends! We just can't ignore it anymore (T3).

Having experienced death and dying within their own families, and understanding the pain of loss, the DCF are fiercely committed to DC and recognize their role in shaping participants, but also influencing the broader culture that frequently denies the inevitability of death: "I feel like it is important to change, or be an agent of change and I feel like with DC that fits in . . . changing society's views on death and dying and bringing that back into everyday life" (T1).

By taking on the role of coordinating and facilitating a DC, DCF take particular ownership or responsibility for advocating or shaping the culture. They also recognize that communication during a DC affirms the concerns that others have about living in a society unwilling to openly discuss dying and mortality.

3.2. Validation

Validation for the DCF is about both, the DCF and the attendees, with the larger view of bonding with the participants while building communities within communities. Some DCF had experienced horrific death experiences within their own families. As one facilitator commented, "I did not want people to go through that and [for] people to have those terrible deaths (her family's experiences with uncle)" (T1). Other DCF recognized that DC offers safe spaces for the attendees: "I think it is an opportunity and a place for people to talk about certain subjects where they don't have these opportunities in their social lives, or with their families" (T4). DC offers the DCF the outlets to experience validation of the time and effort they expend:

> The people. The people just amaze me and the ones that come back and the new ones amaze me and their stories amaze me and I always see that we have a need to come and they have much to say and then I feel like we are providing a service for them and it's my only way in life to give back, and I've been blessed to still be here and its ok to do that (T6).

One of the rewards for the DCF is when the attendees come back with feedback on the positive effect that the DC experience had for their family. A DCA approached one DCF and said, "I just want you to know that I have, with my family, sat down last week and we worked out our will. We did it with our entire family and it's because of the DC that I had the courage to do that and I want to thank you" (T11).

The same DCF also said, "I have had a mother, a daughter, and an aunt all come to the DC and they came up to me afterwards and they said, 'You have done such a service for our family'" (T11). Sometimes, it is the DCF family that directly benefits from the DCF participation: "Well it was interesting the first one I had my parents came to, and afterwards they said, 'Okay come over. We are going to show you where all the papers are.' And so that was an a-ha for me that it did open within my own family a sharing of information that might not have happened otherwise" (T8).

Serving as a DCF allows both attendees and the facilitator to validate their concerns, while creating opportunities for initiating dialogue with families. This validation contributes positively to DCF's personal identity formation, which is the third and final theme.

3.3. Personal Identity

Identity is confirmed and reinforced for the DCF through what they perceive to be their calling and their personal growth. As one DCF put it,

> I benefit a lot from it, from you listening to the conversations and participating in the conversations, and you know there is a superstition that if you talk about death you invite it close . . . . I feel like talking about death and being part of the DC makes me more alive, it makes me feel very alive and that's very rewarding and that's why I keep doing it (T1).

Oftentimes, DC have repeat attendees and they offer the DCF important feedback:

> Repeat attendees come back, with things that they tell me they are doing. 'I got my directive I talked to my husband, daughter about directives.' They come back like they are giving me gifts of what they have done, like you would with your favorite teacher and I figured if that helps make the process easier, that's fine (T10).

Behav. Sci. **2017**, *7*, 26

Many of the DCF view this as a calling:

> My goal is to be of service. And it's a way for me to give back to my community and I think I was probably looking for a way. I see a need in people to search for more meaning, to search for answers. It's kind of a spiritual thing to me (T6).

Furthermore, as another interviewee said: "We celebrate life, and death is part of that. It's the end game of everybody's path. I began to realize so many people didn't want to talk about it or they didn't know what to do when the death occurred" (T10). One DCF explains it: "I think a way to really help the planet and the people who are living on it who will die is have them explore this topic with each other, especially their families" (T11) and as another DCF says about holding a DC: "That's my purpose; it's my joy" (T10).

4. Discussion

The three themes from interviews with DCF indicate that family plays an important role in communication about dying and death. The first place where many learn about death and develop related attitudes and beliefs is in the family, therefore, it is important to consider communication in this context [12]. Bereavement following the loss of a family member can help or hinder family communication. Our families may also make our healthcare and after death care decisions. Thus, attending and participating in a DC can help minimize the silence surrounding mortality and mitigate or even prevent negative reactions.

DCF consistently reported that DCs were helpful to initiating family communication about dying. "What I say at the end of every DC is to bring that conversation that we have at our DC at each table to bring the conversation home to their table" (T3). Furthermore, in most cases, it was the DCFs' own high levels of personal experience with death, either through work or deaths in their families, which seem to be the impetus for their volunteerism with DC. It is reasonable then, that interviewees would talk about the ways in which they and the conversations they facilitated influenced DC attendee's family communication. Like the doulas that help birth new lives into the world, the DCF breathe new life into our communication about death and dying into the world; the DCF have become the doulas of death communication. One DCF recognized and remarked: "I feel there is just another kind of honoring the dead in sincere sadness without the regret because I have had the opportunity to dialogue. Nothing is left undone. And people can start really embracing death the way we do birth you know" (T10).

5. Conclusions

Death Café seeks to disrupt the proscription around death talk. This study specifically seeks to understand what motivates Death Café facilitators to volunteer. One DCF said it best: "based on my own experience, I really believe that if we speak about death, that we will ease the suffering of those we leave behind" (T3) and through that communication, the DCF and the DC continue to fulfill their personal mission of continuing the conversations around death and dying. Future directions include continuing research on this movement and its ability to shape our end-of-life communication.

Acknowledgments: I would like to thank Jillian A. Tullis, Assistant Professor, University of San Diego for giving so generously of her time and her valuable insights to this manuscript. I would also like to acknowledge the valuable contributions of my two undergraduate research assistants on this project, Kendall Rehn and Tatianna Olivare.

Conflicts of Interest: The author declares no conflict of interest.

Appendix A

Death Cafes: Death and Dying with a Side of Coffee, Tea and Cake

Interview Questions

1. How long have you been a facilitator?
2. How did you come to get involved in Death Cafes (DC)?

  a. If someone close to them died, ask what the communication about death and dying with/around that person died was like?
  b. How many Death Cafes have you facilitated yourself or assisted?
  c. What is your goal in hosting meetings like this?

3. What have you observed occurring in the Death Cafes?

  a. Are there one or more particular topics that you have noticed occurring regularly?

    i. If so, why do you think that is?

  b. If the person has given more than one DC ask: do you follow the recommended open format or do you set topics ahead of time?

    i. Why did you make that choice?
    ii. Have you notice repeat attendees?
    iii. If yes, why do you think that is?

  c. Do you use some format to have people write their responses on, such as a blackboard, a blank poster, a book, with questions such as, "Before I die, I want to ... " or "To me, death means ... ?"
  d. Do you have a favorite conversation starter or icebreaker that you use to get the conversations started?
  e. What was the atmosphere like at the beginning and the end of the DC?
  f. Where was your DC located? (Coffee shop, etc.)
  g. What is your favorite a-ha moment from the participants?
  h. What is your personal favorite a-ha moment?

4. How has your involvement in Death Cafes affected your own communication about death and dying?

  a. Do you have an advanced directive?
  b. Did you have an advanced directive before you began hosting DCs?

5. What keeps you doing DC?
6. If you could offer the living one piece of advice about talking about dying, what would it be?
7. Any final thoughts about death, dying, or Death Cafes?

References

1. Koenig, B.A.; Gates-Williams, J. Understanding Cultural Difference in Caring for Dying Patients. *West. J. Med.* **1995**, *163*, 244–249. Available online: https://www.ncbi.nlm.nih.gov/pmc/articles/PMC1303047/ (accessed on 1 April 2017). [PubMed]
2. Institute of Medicine (US) Committee on Care at the End of Life. *Approaching Death: Improving Care at the End of Life*; Field, M.J., Cassel, C.K., Eds.; National Academies Press: Washington, DC, USA, 1997. Available online: https://www.ncbi.nlm.nih.gov/books/NBK233601/ (accessed on 1 April 2017).
3. Underwood, J. Death Café. What Is Death Café? Available online: http://deathcafe.com/what/ (accessed on 14 February 2017).
4. Underwood, J. Death Salon. About Us. Available online: https://deathsalon.org/about-us/ (accessed on 14 February 2017).

5. Miles, L. The First Death Café in the USA , 10 May 2012. Available online: https://www.kickstarter.com/project/lizzymiles/the-first-death-café-in-the-usa (accessed on 4 April 2017).
6. Underwood, J. Holding Your Own Death Café. Available online: http://deathcafe.com/how/ (accessed on 1 April 2017).
7. Olson, L.N.; Baiocchi-Wagner, E.A.; Wilson-Kratzer, J.M.; Symonds, S.E. *The Dark Side of Family Communication*; Polity: Cambridge, UK, 2012.
8. Miles, L.; Corr, C.A. Death Café. *OMEGA J. Death Dying* **2015**. Available online: http://journals.sagepub.com/doi/abs/10.1177/0030222815612602 (accessed on 2 April 2017). [CrossRef]
9. Green, L.; Daley, A.; Ward, A.; Wilcock, T. P-34 If death cafes are the answer, what is the question? *BMJ Support. Palliat. Care* **2016**, *6*, A21. Available online: http://spcare.bmj.com/content/6/Suppl_1/A21.2?rss=1 (accessed on 1 April 2017).
10. Lindlof, T.R.; Taylor, B.C. *Qualitative Communication Research Methods*, 2nd ed.; Sage Publications: Thousand Oaks, CA, USA, 2002.
11. Creswell, J.W. *Qualitative Inquiry and Research Design: Choosing among Five Traditions*; Sage Publications: Thousand Oaks, CA, USA, 1998.
12. Bowlby-West, L. The impact of death on the family system. *J. Fam. Ther.* **1983**, *5*, 279–294. Available online: http://onlinelibrary.wiley.com/doi/10.1046/j.1983.00623.x/full (accessed on 14 February 2017). [CrossRef]

behavioral sciences

MDPI

Article

Contradictions and Promise for End-of-Life Communication among Family and Friends: Death over Dinner Conversations

Andrea Lambert South [1,*] and **Jessica Elton** [2]

[1] Department of Communication, Northern Kentucky University, Highland Heights, KY 41099, USA
[2] Department of Communication, Eastern Michigan University, Ypsilanti, MI 48197, USA; jelton@emich.edu
*   Correspondence: lamberta3@nku.edu; Tel.: +1-859-572-6615

Academic Editor: Maureen P. Keeley
Received: 16 February 2017; Accepted: 18 April 2017; Published: 20 April 2017

Abstract: The free, open-access website called "Let's Get Together and Talk about Death", or Death over Dinner (DoD), provides resources for initiating end-of-life conversations with family and friends by taking the frightening—talking about death—and transforming it into the familiar—a conversation over dinner. This qualitative, descriptive study uses grounded theory and thematic analysis to answer the following research question: How do friend and family groups communicate about death and dying in DoD conversations? To answer this question, 52 dinner groups were recruited and conversations were conducted, which consisted of a facilitator and volunteers. The facilitators were the researchers or research assistants who allowed dinner participants to control the conversation and identify topics of interest, and participants were free to share as much or as little as they wanted. Our analysis revealed that family and friend groups communicated similarly in that they talked about similar topics and used similar communication strategies to discuss those topics. Three major themes emerged: *Desire for a good death*, which juxtaposed people's perceptions of a "dreaded" death with those of a "desirable" death; *tactics for coping*, which consisted of the subthemes of humour to diffuse tension or deflect discomfort, spiritual reassurance, and topic avoidance; and *topics that elicit fear or uncertainty*, which consisted of the subthemes of organ and whole-body donation, hospice and palliative care, wills and advance directives. Ultimately, however, participants felt their experiences were positive and DoD shows promise as a tool for families to engage in end-of-life conversations.

Keywords: end-of-life; family; friends; communication; death; dying

---

1. Introduction

Death is an important stage in the life cycle and, like birth, is an inevitability for all human beings [1]; however, in many cultures death and dying are stigmatised, taboo, or fear-inducing topics [2–6]. This makes communicating about death challenging [7,8], and there are several negative implications of avoiding talking about death. Countries that are the most death-averse, and therefore the least likely to communicate about the end of life, tend to rank lowest in end-of-life care quality [6]. In many countries, the majority of people report that they would like to die at home; however, most people die in hospitals [5,9,10], and the Australian Medical Association reports that most Australians want palliative care, yet few actually receive it [11]. Failure to communicate about end-of-life preferences has been identified as one of the reasons people do not receive the care they prefer [6]. Thus, avoiding end-of-life communication results in greater health care spending, more unwanted hospital admissions, and less patient and family satisfaction [9,12].

Although avoiding communication about death has negative repercussions, engaging in it has many benefits. For example, talking about death may help people work through their fears and better understand what they want during the end of life and also makes one's care preferences known to others [13]. It might also make people aware of end-of-life services, like palliative care and hospice, of which they previously had little to no knowledge [6], and sharing positive stories about end of life may change people's attitudes toward death and dying, thus making it easier for people to prepare for the end of life. Communication about the end of life also results in better care for the patient and offers stress relief and support for families and friends [5,14].

Noting the importance of communicating about end-of-life issues, many countries, from Hong Kong to Hungary, are working to destigmatise death and encourage people to discuss and plan for it [12,15–17]. Organisations like the National Health Service in the United Kingdom, and the Institute of Medicine in the United States, encourage people to speak with their families and care providers about their end-of-life wishes in order to normalise these conversations [18,19].

2. Death over Dinner

In response to health professionals' and policy makers' calls for people to communicate more about death and dying, a number of resources have been created that seek to help people engage with others in these conversations. In addition to both community- and web-based resources that encourage conversations about death, such as Death Café, the Conversation Project, and the Before I Die Festivals, is "Let's Get Together and Talk about Death" (e.g., Death over Dinner or DoD), a free, public website created by Michael Hebb to facilitate discussions of death and dying with family and friends [20]. DoD strives to create a space where people can consider and share their thoughts about death and their preferences for end-of-life care by transforming the frightening—communicating about death—into the mundane—a conversation with family or friends over dinner—by creating a familiar and comfortable space to begin discussing preferences for end-of-life care and final arrangements before it is too late [21]. One study found that people expressed a desire to talk about dying, but they wanted someone else—e.g., a family member, physician, or friend—to initiate the discussion [22]. DoDs do exactly this—they allow a person to gather family and friends and initiate a conversation people may be uncomfortable initiating themselves.

Anyone with a computer and internet connection can access the DoD website. Thus, virtually anyone can host a DoD conversation. The free and open-access website, in which the researchers have no personal stake or connection, is maintained by a Seattle-based web design company called Civilization and the content was created by Michael Hebb in collaboration with a number of people, including academics, health care providers, artists, and health care CEOs [21]. When one goes to the DoD website, he/she completes a short questionnaire that asks about the person's goals for hosting a dinner. Goals or reasons for hosting a dinner range from wanting to discuss end-of-life issues because the host, or the host's loved one, has a terminal illness to believing that having difficult conversations can be liberating [21]. "Homework" assignments such as TedTalks or short news articles are suggested based on these goals, which the host can share with dinner guests to read or watch before gathering for dinner as a way to get guests to think about end-of-life issues [21]. The site also provides language that the host can use in email invitations to guests, which make the purpose of the dinner—to discuss death and dying—clear. Once guests are gathered, the host acts as both a facilitator and participant, and the conversation is allowed to flow according to the topics that interest the facilitator and/or the dinner guests.

This study uses the DoD conversation as a framework for exploring conversations about death and dying because it provides an informal space for discussing what many consider an uncomfortable topic. In this study, the dinner conversations were conducted similar to focus groups. In a DoD conversation hosted by a lay person, the facilitator would participate in the discussion along with dinner guests. In this study, however, the host acted as a conversation facilitator and only joined the conversation to ask a prompt question if the conversation waned.

To date, no studies have empirically analysed DoD conversations. Hence, the aim of the study was to gather friend and family groups to engage in DoD conversations for the purpose of understanding how these groups communicate about death and dying, and whether the DoD approach offers a useful framework for having these conversations. The over-arching research question guiding this study is: How do friend and family groups communicate about death and dying in DoD conversations? To this end, we identified prominent themes that emerged during DoD conversations.

3. Grounded Theory

This qualitative, descriptive study uses a constructivist grounded theory approach [23] to understand communication in DoD conversations. Grounded theory uses a systematic approach that guides qualitative researchers to constantly and reflexively code the emerging interactions of interview participant responses. As noted by Glaser and Strauss, this is a process that continues throughout the investigation, from beginning until the end [24]. Additionally, a constructivist approach concedes that our relationships and perceptions are built in and through our interactions with others. When utilizing a constructivist grounded theory approach, the researcher is a part of the research process and a part of the research product. Thus, concepts and themes emerge from the data; however, this approach acknowledges that these concepts are the researcher's interpretation [25].

4. Methods and Materials

The study used the DoD framework to conduct informal, unstructured focus groups among friend and family groups. The following section describes the study's research setting, procedure, participant recruitment and inclusion criteria, and analysis.

4.1. Research Setting

The DoD dinners took place in three primary settings: a participant's home, a research assistant's home, or a public restaurant. In public settings, other diners may have been nearby during the conversation; however, in dinners held in private homes, the participants and research assistants were the only individuals present.

The research assistants scheduled the meetings and arranged the meeting place (and/or dinner plans). Dinners hosted in homes were potluck style and participants were invited to bring a dish to share, if they wished. Participants were not required to bring a dish, however. For dinners held at non-meal times, coffee, tea and a snack (e.g., crackers and cheese) were provided by the facilitator. Dinners hosted at restaurants were paid for by the participants themselves, and participants were notified ahead of time that each participant would be responsible for paying for his/her meal.

4.2. Procedure

The basic format of the dinners was similar to a focus group; however, the dinner conversations were unstructured. Participants were free to determine which topics they wished to discuss, and the facilitator only used general topic prompts if the conversation waned. Staying true to the DoD design, participants were free to choose when they contributed to the conversation. The DoD design allows dinner guests to share as much or as little as they wish. Facilitators did not call on particularly silent participants and ask them to speak out of respect for their choice not to contribute. Additionally, dinner conversations were transcribed by research assistants who did not facilitate that particular dinner and, during transcription, pseudonyms replaced participant names to ensure confidentiality.

4.3. Participants

To qualify for this study, participants had to be 18 years or older and they were recruited by the research assistants. The primary means of recruitment was network (or snowball) sampling. Research assistants asked friends and/or family members if they were willing to participate in a DoD. Given the relationship of participants to the research assistants, every effort was made to avoid coercing participants to participate. Invitations to participate in a DoD conversation used the stock language provided by the DoD website; however, they also included information that the event was for research and participation was voluntary. The consent form was attached to the email, and prior to the conversation, consent forms were reviewed in depth, reiterating the voluntary nature of participation. Data were collected until saturation was achieved. As noted by Strauss & Corbin, saturation occurs when the coding yields no new information [26].

4.4. Analysis

Emergence is at the heart of grounded theory, and this study used inductive thematic analysis [24,25]. More specifically, the data were analysed manually using the six-step thematic analysis technique outlined by Braun and Clarke [27]. First, both authors familiarized themselves with the data by reading and re-reading the transcripts and writing down initial ideas. Next, both authors generated initial codes independently. After the initial codes were discussed, the authors searched for themes independently and reviewed the themes together. Working together, the authors completed the fifth stage of the analysis, defining and naming themes, entailed "identifying the 'essence' of what each theme is about, and determining what aspect of the data each theme captures" [27] (p. 92). The last step of the outlined thematic analysis technique includes writing the report. In an effort to reduce bias, only the research assistants facilitated DoD conversations. Thus, the co-authors did not participate in any of the dinners they coded and analysed.

5. Results

Given the sensitivity of the topic, the researchers believed that the group setting of DoD conversations allowed participants to participate as much or as little as they wished, and the informality of the dinner conversations shifted control from the facilitator/host to the participants/guests, allowing all who participated to ask each other questions and probe for more information while also sharing their thoughts, ideas and experiences.

Following institutional review board (IRB) approval, 52 DoD conversations were conducted. The dinners were facilitated by the researchers or research assistants who were extensively trained and IRB-certified. Facilitators began by reading a short welcome note and reviewing the consent form, which each participant signed prior to participating in the DoD discussion. All participants were informed that they could leave the conversation at any point if they wished, and their contributions would be redacted. Of the 240 participants in this study, none chose to withdraw from the study. Conversations were allowed to develop organically; however, facilitators had unstructured question prompts they could use if the conversation waned. The length of the dinners ranged from 32–184 min, and all of the dinners were audio-recorded. Research assistants transcribed the recordings. Once the dinners were transcribed, the audio recordings were erased.

Each dinner consisted of 4–8 participants and resulted in 240 participants ranging in age from 18–76. There were 109 men (Mean age = 27.85) and 118 women (Mean age = 31.00) who participated in the study. Thirteen participants indicated that they were transgender or selected "other" on the demographic questionnaire. Of the 46 DoDs, 27 were friend and/or colleague groups and 19 were primarily family groups. Participants were recruited from a metropolitan area in the mid-western states of the United States of America (USA).

The analysis revealed that there were more similarities than differences in how friend and family groups communicate death. One difference that did emerge was that in friend groups, which also included work colleagues, the participants were more likely to state that they were unable or uncomfortable talking about death with family or that they could be more candid talking about death to friends than family members. Participants in friend groups would often report "I would never tell my family this", "my family would never approve of this", or "I think it's difficult to talk with family about it". The opposite statement was not made of family groups about their friends.

The analysis also revealed three main themes (with various subthemes) that illustrated how participants communicated about death: Desire for a Good Death, Tactics for Coping, and Topics that

Confuse or Elicit Fear. (Note: in the following paragraphs, direct participant quotes are cited with the DoD identification number first and the transcript line numbers second. For example, 123: 45–46 would be DoD number 123 and transcript lines 45–46).

5.1. Desire for a Good Death

The first theme relates to reported desirable and undesirable outcomes when it comes to what people want at the end of their lives. When asked what they perceived to be a "good" or "acceptable" death, depending on the facilitators' word choice, participants were more likely to first report what they did not want at the end of life before they were willing or able to elucidate how they would prefer to die.

5.1.1. Dreaded Death

When describing their perception of a "good" death, participants were most likely to first respond with what they did not want at the end of their life. Many participants responded that they "don't want to be a vegetable" or did not want to "live on machines with no hope of recovery". Also, many participants reported that they "dread drowning" or dying by "fire." As one male in his 40s succinctly stated, "I don't wanna drown. And I don't wanna burn" (230: 481), and his brother retorted, "Yeah, true dat" (230: 482).

The most notable theme related to what participants did not want at the end of their lives was to "be a burden". However, when probed by DoD facilitators, most participants were unable to explain what would differentiate as burdensome versus unburdensome to their families. Many expressed that the mere dependence on friends or family members at the end of life was more than they could bear. However, many family members and also friends retorted that it would not be a burden and would, in fact, be an honour to take care of them in their time of need. Also, the mention of not being a burden was especially prevalent among men:

> Man 2: But I personally, speaking for myself, would feel like I am a burden.
> Man 1: I think that is a pride thing for anybody.
> Man 2: I don't want to have to have my butt wiped.
> Woman 4: I think it is harder for a man to be dependent than for a woman.
> Woman 5: I agree.
> Man 3: I can see that.
> Woman 1: Because men are more about not burdening their family and women are, like, well, it would be nice to be able to take care of you and see you in your final moments, in that kind of way.
> Man 2: But, I feel like if I am at the point where I can no longer provide and protect my family, you know, as a man, I would want to go home with God (230: 497–507).

Additionally, many participants identified an untimely death as a dreaded or even feared death. Untimely death was discussed as one that comes before a person has the opportunity to accomplish what he/she/they wishes to accomplish. For example, a male participant said:

> Man 1: I fear what things I haven't done that I should have done.
> Woman 1: Haven't finished.
> Man 1: Yeah, finished up. And If I don't feel I like I got anything done or finished am I going to come back as a spirt or you know.
> Man 2: Mmm-hmm.
> Man 1: That's basically it. That's how I feel about that (123: 94–100).

5.1.2. Desirable Death

When expressing what they desired at the end of life, participants' descriptions were somewhat more vague and ambiguous. For example, participants said that they would prefer their death "to be inexpensive for the family", have a "quick and painless death", or to "go out with a bang". Many participants expressed a desire to "die peacefully in their sleep". As one father, humorously expressed in a family DoD:

> Man 2: I would prefer to be in my sleep.
> Woman 1: Yes, I would agree with that I would want to be in my sleep too. I would like to die comfortably, quickly, not painfully or long term (232: 60–63).

If being a burden to one's family was considered an undesirable death, having some quality of life before or during death was described by many participants as a desirable death. This related to people's wishes to have painless and quick deaths. However, how participants described quality of life in the conversations varied. Some participants referred to it generally, simply stating that they wanted to have "quality of life" at the end of their lives or "quality over quantity" of life. Other participants described it more specifically as being able to do some of the things one enjoys. For example, one woman said, "I feel like as long as I can read and not be bored out of my mind, I would be okay dying" (134: 159–160).

Another participant conceptualized a desirable death as one that was positive for survivors: "Well, it seems to me that a good death is when the people that survive you, uh, have a role to play in your care, and uh, see you at your best at the end, whatever that happens to be" (119: 280–281). This also reflects participants' insistence that caring for the dying is an honour and privilege, despite fears that it makes one a burden to family and friends. Related to this was a desire to be remembered, which was expressed by some participants. In the words of one man, "I want to be remembered, I mean everybody wants to be remembered" (124: 209).

5.2. Tactics for Coping

As noted earlier in this article, discussing death can be uncomfortable. The analysis revealed that participants in this study used several coping tactics for dealing with the discomfort of discussing or thinking about death. Coping tactics included communication strategies that moved the conversation away from tension or uncomfortable interactions; invoking one's spiritual beliefs to reassure or comfort them when talking about death, or separating oneself from death or aging in order to not think about it.

5.2.1. Humour to Diffuse Tension or Deflect Discomfort

Regardless of friend or family group, humour was prevalent throughout the DoD conversations. The humour was used in two ways. First, it was used as a release valve for a difficult part in the conversation to diffuse tension. For example, in one family DoD when a mother and daughter engaged in an emotional exchange in which the daughter told her mother to complete an advance directive because she (the daughter) would be "selfish" and choose to keep her mother on life support indefinitely, another family member interjected and said, "How about them cowboys?" (130: 607), after which everyone laughed and the tense moment was diffused.

Second, humour was used to deflect the discomfort of thinking about death, particularly preferences for final arrangements. For example, one male mentioned that he wants his funeral "to be a party, and I want to be taken out in the cheapest pine box available" (131: 94), and a female queried whether "Viking funerals are still allowed" (121: 168). Another male dyad quipped to each other "you can just leave me out in the garbage" (135: 196), and "I just want to be composted" (135: 196). Participants were particularly creative when describing what they wanted to have happen to their bodies with one male saying he wanted "my femur turned into a sword" (131: 114), another male mentioned that his family can "skin me and turn me into a football" (121: 373), and a female asking if she could "do like an Eskimo version, just push me out on a block of ice and let the polar bears take care of it" (120: 525–526).

5.2.2. Spiritual Reassurance

A vast majority of participants took solace in their spiritual beliefs when it comes to death. Many felt that it was important to take care of the issues related to their earthly life, but felt that everything would work itself out and they would be happy and saved by a higher power. As an older female mentioned, "if I die, according to scripture I feel great that I would be in paradise" (125: 280–281). Another female participant explained that her amalgam of religions give her solace:

> Yea, so like I said earlier I'm Romani but I'm also part Native American, which you would never tell by my skin tone but oh well. And I'm also Wiccan so, uh, and being raised in a Roman Catholic setting just, the spirituality has always been in me so I know what the Roman Catholics believe, and what the Wiccan believe, and what the Romani believe, and what the natives believe, and I just kinda mix it all together and it gives me a real strong sense that there is, uh, a better place out there. Like it's not gonna be worse than this, and it's not just gonna be this. There actually is a place better than this (126: 406–416).

In contrast, individuals who did not express a spiritual association were sometimes envious of those who did. As one young female expressed:

> For me like, death is inevitable, there's nothing we can do to get away from it. I know that's ugly and scary. It's natural to be scared of things like that we don't understand or, like, the "unknown". But at the same time, like for me I don't have faith either, so, like, we gotta make the most of it while we're here 'cause this is all we have. For me, I envy people with faith 'cause it would be nice to, like, believe in something on the other side, something for you, something better (126: 399–403).

5.2.3. Separating Oneself from Thinking about Death

Many participants expressed that "I don't really think about [death]" (221: 152), or "death doesn't really bother me, um, I never really put a lot of thought into it" (224: 90). These participants tended to be younger. Most admitted that they had thought about their parents' (or especially) their grandparents' death, but the likelihood of their own death was beyond their grasp. As one young female mentioned:

> Because I don't see myself growing old. Like I really don't see myself growing old. So like dying of an illness or dying of natural causes doesn't seem like something that's going to happen to me (223: 161–163).

This theme often overlapped with the previous theme as many participants who confessed that not knowing is the best way of knowing also cited a spiritual preference, or lack thereof, as the impetus of their not knowing. One young female participant illustrates this in the following quote:

> Well I would argue, as the person in the room without any faith (if you weren't aware), as the person in the room without any faith, I don't worry about it. I was just fine before I was born and I'll be just fine after I'm dead. I won't know the difference (228: 104–106).

5.3. Topics that Elicit Fear and/or Uncertainty

The third theme describes the topics that elicited fear or uncertainty among participants. The main sources of fear and/or uncertainty issues related to organ and whole-body donation, hospice and palliative care, and wills and advanced directives.

5.3.1. Organ and Whole-Body Donation

Although a majority of participants expressed that they thought organ donation was important, many rebutted those notions with negative comments. As a middle-aged female revealed, "it's like if you were in a car accident and pronounced dead for two minutes, I don't want them to just rip them [internal organs] out or anything" (131: 209–210). There were many examples of participants bantering back and forth about organ donation. First, two young females dialogued with a male who thought that medical professionals were likely to end an organ donor's life early because of their donation decision:

> Woman 1: I don't like it to be known [organ donation], because what if somebody was like....
> Man 1: Think they kill you off quick just to get your organs.
> Woman 2: That is a genuine concern for a lot of people (130: 780–784).

Another woman in her late 50s expressed her fear that organ donors, if they ended up in the hospital, are misled by health care providers:

> They might think that they are saving their life and bringing 'em back later, but they can harvest their organs or whatever, which is so someone can use it (123: 233–235).

In addition to some participants feeling wary of organ donation, some participants also felt that donating their bodies to medical science was financially detrimental:

> Man 1: But I found out through my insurance agent that one, it costs a lot of money to donate your body to science.
> Woman 1: What?!
> Man 2: To donate it? (134: 225–228).

5.3.2. Hospice and Palliative Care

Although many participants expressed positive feelings about hospice, hospice and palliative care were also topics that elicited uncertainty among the participants in this study. Those who had experience with hospice often spoke authoritatively about what hospice does and does not do. As a woman in her fifties expressed:

> That's why we brought my mom home. We didn't put her in the hospice for that reason. Until the day they said well . . . her lung was filled up with fluids and they [hospital staff] said . . . "Was she in hospice?" And I said, "No". And they said, "If she was in hospice they would leave that fluid in there and you would sit there and watch her suffocate". So we, I said, "No, we don't have that she's not in hospice". "Well you can sign it now". I said, "No I don't, I'm not signing it" (123: 214–218).

Another man held that hospice does not provide antibiotics and that by choosing hospice, he was choosing death for his parents:

> My mother actually called the hospital at one point to have dad taken to the emergency room and hospice found out and wanted him sent back home, because they are not trying to do anything that is helping keep him alive basically. Until I had the personal experience I never realized what all was included in going to hospice. Even if you get a cold, you do not get any antibiotics, they let it go into pneumonia (135: 488–495).

5.3.3. Wills and Advanced Directives

The use of a will is complex. Many of the younger participants talked about the fact that they didn't care "who gets my blender" (221: 56) or as one young women illuminates, she doesn't feel the need to complete a will or advanced directive because "I don't even have anything to give, like who gets to keep my cat" (128: 206–207). In the following excerpt, a man in his late 20s explained when he thinks someone should complete a will:

> That's one thing like I don't like about wills. I mean, I don't want to have a will. Like if I had a will, it's going toward something, like, positive ... If I have children I want that to go towards their college ... I'll make sure that goes towards their college or anything ... and like not want them to have it to waste or anything like that. But, like, if I'm single ... like if I'm like a forty-year-old man or something like that dying early, like an early death or something like that, and I have a will ... I'll give it to charity or something like that because ... I believe a will should be ... your final thoughts with your family. Like you wanted them to know this, like, before you died, and it's like it shouldn't be a material thing. It should be a closure (127: 446–455).

One middle-aged female talked about how making end-of-life decisions for someone else is still difficult, even when there is an advance directive:

> It's still hard because you got a piece of paper and possibly have to let go of someone you love or make a decision not to give them food, and you still have to watch the result. So, um, that's why I think, yeah, yeah, you're trying to honour their wishes, but at the same time... (129: 217–225).

Participants also had some uncertainly about their family members' willingness to honour their wishes, even if they were to express them through advance directives. As two participants noted, "I don't think they would, or take me off it [life support] I think they'd put me on for as long as I can go," and in response, "Yea I feel like our parents would probably fight for as long as possible" (125: 208–209).

6. Discussion

This study sought to understand how family and friend groups communicate about death and dying during DoD dinners and whether the DoD approach offers a useful framework for having these conversations. The analysis revealed that friend groups displayed more candidness than family groups when discussing death; overall, how family and friend groups communicate about death and dying in the DoD context is more similar than different. While it was the researchers' initial thought that there would be substantial differences between the communication in family and friend groups, those differences were not evident in most cases. Many family groups did not talk about specific family instances but rather their own views of death. Spouses and/or significant other pairs tended to quip back and forth between each other about wishes, but those quips were similar in same-sex and opposite-sex (close) friendship pairs.

The only difference that the analysis revealed was that participants in friend groups said that they were being more candid than they would be with family members. The candidness among friend groups may be the result of the study sample. Participants in this study were younger adults, and younger adults tend to disclose more to friends than to family members [28,29]. This may be problematic when it comes to end-of-life decisions as friends have no legal rights, but may in fact know what the person actually wants at the end of their life.

From the analysis of over 240 participants, it is clear that there are many misunderstandings about death that have yet to be dispelled and are quite prevalent in contemporary discussions about death. The results of this study highlighted topics that made participants uncomfortable or fearful, which suggests that the participants have some cognitive contradictions about death. The results revealed four contradictions. First, participants whole-heartedly trusted that family would equitably distribute personal items (especially if a will did not lay out the distribution of property), but they did not believe that family members could be trusted to follow end-of-life wishes. Although the research on the effectiveness of advance directives varies, studies that suggest the presence of advance directives results in end-of-life care that more closely aligns with a patient's preferences [30,31].

Second, the topic of wills and advance directives contradicts what many participants said about what constitutes a good death. Participants intellectually believe in wills and advanced directives but felt these documents/processes were not necessarily for them. Participants also wanted their family to be comfortable and not to be burdened by the loose-ties of their lives, but it often wasn't significant enough for them to consider the need to plan ahead. This is consistent with other research that noted that although people think advance directives, like living wills, are good, they do not complete them [32]. In particular, younger participants expressed indifference with wills and advance directives, which is consistent with research [33–35].

The third contradiction was that participants claimed that they did not want them or their loved ones to die in the hospital, yet participants expressed deep distrust in hospice and/or palliative care. Based on their expressed concerns with hospice, participants were clearly uninformed about the differences between palliative and hospice care. Whereas palliative care, which focuses on quality of life and the whole patient, is available to people at any stage in an illness, hospice care is only for people with a terminal illness diagnosis, a life expectancy of six months or less, and who have accepted palliative (for comfort and pain management) instead of curative care [36]. This misunderstanding is not unusual, however, and Cagle et al. found that although many of the participants in their study had heard of hospice, many of them were unaware of the parameters of receiving hospice care [37].

Lastly, contradictions related to organ donation were prevalent. Participants thought that, intellectually, organ donation can be seen as a societal good, but they did not trust the organ donation process. This mistrust may be the result of mass media representations of organ donations [38], which tend to portray the organ donation process as negative and morally corrupt [39].

Although the results reveal several contradictions related to participants' desires, perceptions, fears, and uncertainty about death and dying, the DoD format provided a space for participants to share their thoughts, feelings and experiences. Overall, participants communicated various feelings about their DoD experience including: "thought-provoking", "overwhelmed", "confused", "mind-blowing", "a little depressed", "the same", "empowered", and "relieved". Moreover, a majority of participants found the experience positive and noted similar sentiments to a participant who claimed that "I think we just have more of this. I think having more conversations about it makes it less hard to take" (133: 942–943). Thus, although the communication that occurs in DoD conversations is at times contradictory, for many it is a positive experience nonetheless.

7. Limitations

This study was limited in three ways. First, we relied on a convenience/snowball sample. Although this sampling method in and of itself is not overtly negative, in this case it could be that family and friend groups that agreed to participate were more open and willing to talk about death. Second, participants were aware that the dinner conversations were part of a larger research study, which could have influenced what they said. Third, a majority of family and friend DoDs were conducted in one geographical area. As a qualitative project, our goal is not to generalize to other audiences, it is important to remind the reader that the project is descriptive and not prescriptive. In the future, it will be important to expand the study and examine end-of-life discussions nationally and internationally.

8. Conclusions

This study asked how DoD participants communicated about their end-of-life choices and also empirically analysed DoD experiences. The results revealed three prominent themes that at times contradicted each other; however, given the importance of communicating about the end of life, the conversations provided a space for participants to share their experiences, feelings, fears and hopes.

Hosting a DoD among family members allows participants to share their preferences with those who may become their surrogate decision makers, whereas DoDs involving friends may provide a context for exploring one's thoughts about death or expressing concerns not easily shared with family members. However, DoDs may also serve to perpetuate misinformation as friends and family members can express uncontested untruths during the dinners and, as a result, may contribute to people's anxiety about death. Despite the potential drawbacks, however, based on predominantly positive feedback participants share, DoD events offer a promising method to encourage people to talk about their end-of-life wishes and feelings about death.

Author Contributions: Andrea Lambert South and Jessica Elton conceived and designed the study, analyzed the data; contributed reagents/materials/analysis tools. The paper was written by both authors.

Conflicts of Interest: The authors declare no conflict of interest.

References

1. Goldsmith, J.; Wittenberg-Lyles, E.; Ragan, S.; Nussbaum, J.F. *The Routledge Handbook of Health Communication*; Thompson, T.L., Parrott, R., Nussbaum, J.F., Eds.; Routledge: New York, NY, USA, 2011; pp. 441–468.
2. Abdel-Khalek, A.M. Why Do We Fear Death? The Construction and Validation of the Reasons for Death Fear Scale. *Death Stud.* **2002**, *26*, 669–680. [CrossRef] [PubMed]
3. Neimeyer, R.A.; Moser, R.P.; Wittkowski, J. Assessing Attitudes toward Dying and Death: Psychometric Considerations. *OMEGA J. Death Dying* **2003**, *47*, 45–76. [CrossRef]
4. Yick, A.G.; Gupta, R. Chinese Cultural Dimensions of Death, Dying, and Bereavement: Focus Group Findings. *J. Cult. Divers.* **2002**, *9*, 32–42. [PubMed]
5. World Health Organization Regional Office for Europe. Better Palliative Care for Older People. 2004. Available online: http://www.euro.who.int/__data/assets/pdf_file/0009/98235/E82933.pdf (accessed on 24 March 2017).
6. Economist Intelligence Unit. The Quality of Death: Ranking End-of-Life Care across the World. Available online: http://graphics.eiu.com/upload/eb/qualityofdeath.pdf (accessed on 24 March 2017).
7. Ohs, J.E.; Trees, A.R.; Gibson, C. Holding on and Letting Go: Making Sense of End-of-Life Care Decisions in Families. *South. Commun. J.* **2015**, *80*, 353–364. [CrossRef]
8. Yingling, J.; Keeley, M. A Failure to Communicate: Let's Get Real about Improving Communication at the End of Life. *Am. J. Hosp. Palliat. Med.* **2007**, *24*, 95–97. [CrossRef] [PubMed]
9. National Audit Office. End of Life Care. 2008. Available online: https://www.nao.org.uk/wp-content/uploads/2008/11/07081043.pdf (accessed on 24 March 2017).
10. Office for National Statistics. National Survey of Bereaved People (VOICES): UK, 2015. Available online: https://www.ons.gov.uk/peoplepopulationandcommunity/healthandsocialcare/healthcaresystem/bulletins/nationalsurveyofbereavedpeoplevoices/england2015#support-for-relatives-friends-or-carers-at-the-end-of-life (accessed on 24 March 2017).
11. Australian Medical Association. Time to Talk Openly about Death and Dying. Available online: https://ama.com.au/media/time-talk-openly-about-death-and-dying (accessed on 24 March 2017).
12. Economist Intelligence Unit. The 2015 Quality of Death Index Ranking Palliative Care Across the World. Available online: https://www.eiuperspectives.economist.com/sites/default/files/2015%20EIU%20Quality%20of%20Death%20Index%20Oct%2029%20FINAL.pdf (accessed on 24 March 2017).
13. Keeley, M.P.; Koenig Kellas, J. Constructing Life and Death through Final Conversations. In *Narratives, Health, and Healing: Communication Theory, Research, and Practice*; Harter, L.M., Japp, P.M., Beck, C.B., Eds.; Lawrence Earlbaum Associated: Mahwah, NJ, USA, 2005; pp. 365–390.
14. Keeley, M.P. Family Communication at the End of Life. *J. Fam. Commun.* **2016**, *16*, 189–197. [CrossRef]
15. Caughlin, J.P.; Mikucki-Enyart, S.L.; Middleton, A.V.; Stone, A.M.; Brown, L.E. Being Open without Talking about it: A Rhetorical/Normative Approach to Understanding Topic Avoidance in Families after a Lung Cancer Diagnosis. *Commun. Monogr.* **2011**, *78*, 409–436. [CrossRef]
16. Considine, J.; Miller, K. The Dialectics of Care: Communicative Choices at the End of Life. *Health Commun.* **2010**, *25*, 165–174. [CrossRef] [PubMed]
17. Keeley, M. Turning toward Death Together: The Functions of Messages during Final Conversations in Close Relationships. *J. Soc. Pers. Relat.* **2007**, *24*, 225–253. [CrossRef]
18. National Health Service. What to Expect from End of Life Care. Available online: http://www.nhs.uk/Planners/end-of-life-care/Pages/what-to-expect-from-care.aspx (accessed on 24 March 2017).
19. Institute of Medicine. *Dying in America: Improving Quality and Honoring Individual Preferences Near the End of Life*; The National Academies Press: Washington, DC, USA, 2015.

20. McClurg, L. Let's Talk About Death Over Dinner: The Salt: NPR. Available online: http://www.npr.org/sections/thesalt/2015/05/07/405003161/lets-talk-about-death-over-dinner (accessed on 14 February 2017).

21. Hebb, M. How Death Came to Dinner. Available online: http://deathoverdinner.org/about (accessed on 14 February 2017).

22. Schrader, S.L.; Nelson, M.L.; Eidsness, L.M. Dying to Know: A Community Survey about Dying and End-of-Life Care. *OMEGA* **2010**, *60*, 33–50. [CrossRef]

23. Charmaz, K. *Constructing Grounded Theory: A Practical Guide through Qualitative Analysis*; Sage Publications: London, UK, 2006.

24. Glaser, B.G.; Strauss, A.L. *The Discovery of Grounded Theory: Strategies for Qualitative Research*; Aldine Publishing Company: Chicago, IL, USA, 1967.

25. Charmaz, K. Grounded Theory as an Emergent Method. In *Handbook of emergent methods*; Hesse-Biber, S.N., Leavy, P., Eds.; Guilford Press: New York, NY, USA, 2008; pp. 155–170.

26. Strauss, A.L.; Corbin, J.M. *Basics of Qualitative Research: Techniques and Procedures for Developing Grounded Theory*; Sage Publications: London, UK, 1998.

27. Braun, V.; Clarke, V. Using Thematic Analysis in Psychology. *Qual. Res. Psychol.* **2006**, *3*, 77–101. [CrossRef]

28. Mathews, A.; Derlega, V.J.; Morrow, J. What Is Highly Personal Information and How is it Related to Self-Disclosure Decision-Making? The Perspective of College Students. *Commun. Res. Rep.* **2006**, *23*, 85–92. [CrossRef]

29. Pulakos, J. Young Adult Relationships: Siblings and Friends—ProQuest. *J. Psychol.* **1989**, *123*, 237–244. [CrossRef]

30. Silveira, M.J.; Kim, S.Y.H.; Langa, K.M. Advance Directives and Outcomes of Surrogate Decision Making before Death. *N. Engl. J. Med.* **2010**, *13362*, 1211–1218. [CrossRef] [PubMed]

31. Teno, J.M.; Gruneir, A.; Schwartz, Z.; Nanda, A.; Wetle, T. Association between Advance Directives and Quality of End-of-Life Care: A National Study. *J. Am. Geriatr. Soc.* **2007**, *55*, 189–194. [CrossRef] [PubMed]

32. Fagerlin, A.; Ditto, P.H.; Hawkins, N.A.; Schneider, C.E.; Smucker, W.D. The Use of Advance Directives in End-of-Life Decision Making: Problems and Possibilities. *Am. Behav. Sci.* **2002**, *46*, 268–283. [CrossRef]

33. Rao, J.K.; Anderson, L.A.; Lin, F.-C.; Laux, J.P. Completion of Advance Directives Among U.S. Consumers. *Am. J. Prev. Med.* **2014**, *46*, 65–70. [CrossRef] [PubMed]

34. AARP Bulletin Poll Getting Ready to Go Executive Summary. Available online: http://assets.aarp.org/rgcenter/il/getting_ready.pdf (accessed on 14 February 2017).

35. Lyon, M.E.; Mccabe, M.A.; Patel, K.M.; D'Angelo, L.J. What Do Adolescents Want? An Exploratory Study Regarding End-of-Life Decision-Making. *J. Adolesc. Health* **2004**, *35*, 1–6. [CrossRef]

36. US Centers for Medicare and Medicaid Services. Your Medicare Coverage: Hospice and Respite Care. Available online: https://www.medicare.gov/coverage/your-medicare-coverage.html (accessed on 14 February 2017).

37. Cagle, J.G.; Van Dussen, D.J.; Culler, K.L.; Carrion, I.; Hong, S.; Guralnik, J.; Zimmerman, S. Knowledge About Hospice: Exploring Misconceptions, Attitudes, and Preferences for Care. *Am. J. Hosp. Palliat. Care* **2016**, *33*, 27–33. [CrossRef] [PubMed]

38. Feeley, T.H.; Servoss, T.J. Examining College Students' Intentions to Become Organ Donors. *J. Health Commun.* **2005**, *10*, 237–249. [CrossRef] [PubMed]

39. Morgan, S.E.; Harrison, T.R.; Chewning, L.; Davis, L.; Dicorcia, M. Entertainment (Mis) Education: The Framing of Organ Donation in Entertainment Television. *Health Commun.* **2007**, *22*, 143–151. [CrossRef] [PubMed]

behavioral sciences

MDPI

Article

Designing Effective Interactions for Concordance around End-of-Life Care Decisions: Lessons from Hospice Admission Nurses

Carey Candrian [1,*], Channing Tate [2], Kirsten Broadfoot [3], Alexandra Tsantes [4], Daniel Matlock [2,5,6] and Jean Kutner [1]

[1] Division of General Internal Medicine, Department of Medicine, University of Colorado School of Medicine, Aurora, CO 80045, USA; jean.kutner@ucdenver.edu
[2] The Adult and Child Consortium for Outcomes Research and Delivery Science, Department of Medicine, University of Colorado School of Medicine, Aurora, CO 80045, USA; Channing.Tate@ucdenver.edu (C.T.); daniel.matlock@ucdenver.edu (D.M.)
[3] Center for Advancing Professional Excellence, Department of Medicine, University of Colorado School of Medicine, Aurora, CO 80045, USA; kirsten.broadfoot@ucdenver.edu
[4] The Denver Hospice, Denver, CO 80246, USA; alexandratsantes@gmail.com
[5] Division of Geriatric Medicine, Department of Medicine, University of Colorado School of Medicine, Aurora, CO 80045, USA
[6] VA Eastern Colorado Geriatric Research Education and Clinical Center, Denver, CO 80220, USA
* Correspondence: carey.candrian@ucdenver.edu; Tel.: +1-303-724-7892

Academic Editor: Maureen P. Keeley
Received: 4 February 2017; Accepted: 11 April 2017; Published: 18 April 2017

Abstract: Near the end of life, hospice care reduces symptom-related distress and hospitalizations while improving caregiving outcomes. However, it takes time for a person to gain a sufficient understanding of hospice and decide to enroll. This decision is influenced by knowledge of hospice and its services, emotion and fear, cultural and religious beliefs, and an individual's acceptance of diagnosis. Hospice admission interactions, a key influence in shaping decisions regarding hospice care, happen particularly late in the illness trajectory and are often complex, unpredictable, and highly variable. One goal of these interactions is ensuring patients and families have accurate and clear information about hospice care to facilitate informed decisions. So inconsistent are practices across hospices in consenting patients that a 2016 report from the Office of Inspector General (OIG) entitled "Hospices should improve their election statements and certifications of terminal illness" called for complete and accurate election statements to ensure that hospice patients and their caregivers can make informed decisions and understand the costs and benefits of choosing hospice care. Whether complete and accurate information at initial admission visits improves interactions and outcomes is unknown. Our recent qualitative work investigating interactions between patients, caregivers, and hospice nurses has uncovered diverse and often diverging stakeholder-specific expectations and perceptions which if not addressed can create discordance and inhibit decision-making. This paper focuses on better understanding the communication dynamics and practices involved in hospice admission interactions in order to design more effective interactions and support the mandate from the OIG to provide hospice patients and their caregivers with accurate and complete information. This clarity is particularly important when discussing the non-curative nature of hospice care, and the choice patients make to forego aggressive treatment measures when they enroll in hospice. In a literal sense, to enroll in hospice means to bring in support for end-of-life care. It means to identify the need for expertise around symptom management at end-of-life, and agree to having a care team come and manage someone's physical, psychosocial, and/or spiritual needs. As with all care, hospice can be stopped if it is no longer considered appropriate. To uncover the communication tensions undergirding a hospice admission interaction, we use Street's ecological theory of patient-centered communication to analyze a case exemplar of a hospice admission interaction. This analysis reveals diverse points of struggle within hospice decision-making processes around hospice care and the need for communication techniques that promote trust and acceptance of end-of-life care. Lessons learned from talking about hospice care can inform other quality initiatives around communication and informed decision-making in the context of advance care planning, palliative care, and end-of-life care.

Keywords: hospice decision-making; concordance; end-of-life communication

---

1. Background

Near the end of life, receiving hospice care is associated with less distress, fewer hospitalizations, and improved caregiver outcomes [1–4]. However, the decision to enroll in hospice while dependent on an individual's knowledge of hospice and its services is also heavily influenced by diverse emotions and fears, cultural and religious beliefs, and levels of acceptance around the diagnosis [5,6]. The more interactions an individual has with nurses, physicians, chaplains and social workers, family and friends, the greater their understanding of hospice. One key interaction in this chain of influence around hospice enrolment is the hospice admission consult [6]. While this unpredictable, nonstandard, and highly variable interaction often occurs late in the illness trajectory, it plays a significant role in shaping decisions regarding end-of-life care. Because hospices hold an obligation to provide accurate information to their patients (beneficiaries) about the hospice benefit, election statements and the clarity of information provided in admissions consults has been recently examined by the Office of Inspector General (OIG) [7].

The OIG 2016 Report, "Hospices should improve their election statements and certifications of terminal illness," states that resolving disparities and vulnerabilities in election forms is crucial to ensuring patients and caregivers make informed hospice care decisions. It calls for hospices to provide complete and accurate information at the initial consult [7]. However, outside of a clear election statement, how else can we improve initial admission interactions? Our own qualitative pilot research on these complex consultations is guided by two objectives: (1) enhance clinician understandings of patient and caregiver expectations and needs around hospice admission conversations and (2) identify communication techniques to facilitate concordance, or a point of commonality between individuals' preferences (what they want), concerns (what are they against), and circumstances (the facts of their life), that incorporates patients' and caregivers' perspectives. The pilot data highlights diverse and often diverging stakeholder-specific expectations and perceptions based on setting, situation, diagnosis, and patient, caregiver, and nurse perspectives. What becomes clear in both observation data and the analysis of in-depth interviews with hospice nurses, patients, and caregivers, is that participants are often on different pages when they enter these interactions, endangering concordance and requiring nuanced communicative efforts from first contact to establish trust and credibility with each other.

Not only do parties in the interaction carry with them diverse and often diverging interests and motivations, the interaction itself occurs in a stress-laden context. The hospice admissions nurse or social worker must balance the intersecting needs of patients often too ill and fatigued to participate, overburdened caregivers who fear that choosing hospice means giving up on loved ones, and referral sources or other healthcare providers anxious for a quick hospice transition. These tensions and competing needs necessitate clear, tailored communication during the consult [6]. Reaching concordance is critical for any type of informed decision-making around advance care planning and other end-of-life care conversations [8,9].

Hospice admission nurses in particular are at the forefront of facilitating quality interactions geared towards concordance around hospice care. To illustrate the nature of this interaction and address the research gap surrounding it, we present a detailed narrative case of a hospice admission interaction and critically analyze the communicative practices used by the hospice nurse and caregiver using the social ecological model. Of note, in the initial hospice consult, we talk generally about palliative care as a program of care that is appropriate when patients are facing advanced illness and have symptom management needs (or maybe just extra psychosocial support needs), but are still continuing treatment of their disease. On the other hand, we talk generally about hospice as meaning the patient is receiving symptom management support, but is not treating their disease. Moreover, palliative care programs are not standardized (or paid for) like hospice is, so palliative programs can look different depending on where individuals are receiving care.

2. Analyzing Hospice Admissions from an Ecological Perspective

The primary goals of the hospice admission interaction are (1) to exchange information between provider, patient, and caregiver about health-related concerns; (2) make decisions about medical care; and (3) in the best of cases, establish or maintain a relationship characterized by rapport, trust, and respect [6]. As such, it is a dynamic, creative, and complex event. How the interaction unfolds depends on how participants select, adapt, and coordinate responses to accomplish their individual and mutual goals.

Street's ecological theory of patient-centered communication focuses on the complex interplay between individual, relational, community, and societal influences on interactions around health [10]. This theoretical framework approaches the hospice admission interaction not as an isolated event, but as embedded within a number of contexts. In doing so, it enables an in-depth understanding of the range of factors that put pressure on individuals when making decisions (see Figure 1):

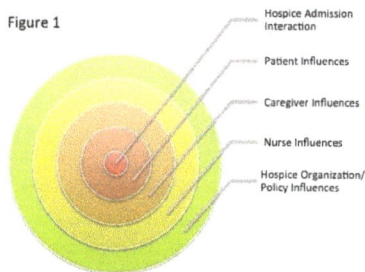

Figure 1. Ecological model of hospice admission interactions.

Interpersonal context: includes predisposing influences of the provider, patient, and family (e.g., communication style, attitudes, beliefs, personality, and linguistic resources), as well as cognitive-affective influences of participants (e.g., perceptions, communicative strategies, and emotional state).

Political-legal context: includes Medicaid/Medicare coverage and conversations around medication discontinuation and payment.

Cultural context: includes influences of ethnicity, socioeconomic status, philosophy of care, and religion.

Organizational context: includes standards of care, services offered, facility restrictions on where interaction takes place, hospice admission training, and hospice organization goals.

Although the hospice admission encounter may be contextualized, influenced, and understood in a number of ways, the one within which the hospice admission encounter is most fundamentally embedded is the interpersonal context.

Behav. Sci. **2017**, *7*, 22

3. Research Setting and Sample

The project grew out of a long-standing community-academic partnership between a local hospice and university. Monthly agendas for this partnership meeting included an item titled, "what bugs you." During a meeting in 2015, in response to this agenda item, the president of the hospice talked about the significant variability and non-standardization of hospice admission visits and the desire to have evidence, or a core set of best practices, surrounding admission visits so that patients and families who would like to benefit from hospice are able to do so while fully understanding what their decision to enroll means. The local hospice is a large, urban, non-profit organization that has served more than 70,000 patients and their families since its founding in 1978. It is the fifth longest-established hospice in the United States and remains a well-respected leader at local and national levels. Patient census reported 506 hospice patients and 214 palliative care patients under their care each day in 2014. In 2015, the numbers climbed to 532 and 227, respectively. Services are provided by teams of professionals and volunteers focused on individualized, integrative care in patient homes, skilled nursing facilities, or in their own Inpatient Care Center. No patient is ever turned away regardless of ability to pay.

In 2015, the president of the hospice put the first author in contact with the admissions manager (A.T.) to talk about the project and the opportunity to "shadow" hospice admission nurses on their initial visits with patients and caregivers. The admissions manager developed a schedule that assigned specific days and times with different admission nurses and settings over a three-month period. Because admission visits were often scheduled the day before, the admissions manager would email the first author (C.C.) in the morning with the schedule for visits and text during the day as others were scheduled or cancelled. The schedule included home, nursing home facilities, and hospital room visits across an area in the Rocky Mountain region of the United States.

When visits were scheduled, A.T. would email C.C. and the assigned nurse with a brief overview of the visit including the patient's age, diagnosis, and anything important to know before the visit (e.g., this was the patient's second admission visit; do not use the word hospice; family is struggling with this decision); C.C. did not access medical charts. C.C. would then confirm a meeting place with the nurse before the interaction started so they could walk in together and as needed, be briefed about the patient, family situation, and project beforehand. The admission visits lasted between 30 min to 2 h. There were visits that had as little as three people present, and as many as nine, including the hospice nurse and C.C. To ensure a diverse sample, participants included: African Americans, Latino, undocumented, Russian, Caucasian, tribal, homeless, religious, non-religious, gay, straight, married, and widowed. Additionally, nurses that were shadowed were also diverse in terms of years at hospice and experience before coming to hospice.

On site, C.C. was introduced to the patient and family as a researcher from the local university studying hospice communication to define best practices. In all cases, patient and/or caregivers verbally consented to researcher presence before starting. During these conversations, C.C. sat next to the nurse, or in some cases, wherever the family encouraged her to sit based on the arrangement of the room/setting. Ethnographic field notes were minimally taken to capture key words or phrases used during the interaction, and sometimes not at all depending on the situation. In these cases, C.C. would write them directly after the visit. Note taking was not considered obtrusive, as the admissions nurse also had a notebook and took notes during the conversation. C.C.'s role in these interactions was solely to observe, and patient and family interaction was limited to polite greetings and good-byes.

At the end of each admission visit, and always dependent on the situation and comfort of participants, C.C. asked the patient and/or caregiver if they would be willing to answer five questions related to the visit. There were five instances where C.C. did not ask the participants given the perceived distress or known circumstances that would have impinged participation. For the other 20 visits, all who were asked to voluntarily participate agreed to so do.

4. Data Collection and Analysis

C.C. conducted nonparticipant observations of hospice admission visits between hospice admission nurses and patients and their caregiver(s) over a three-month period during 2016–2017. The setting of these interactions varied from hospice home visits, skilled nursing facility visits, and hospital room visits. The resulting data set included 60 h of observation, including interviews with 15 caregivers, 6 patients, and 9 hospice admission nurses ($n = 30$). All interviews were audio-recorded. Because of the health of participants, circumstances around each visit and ethical considerations guiding every stage of this project, interviews lasted no longer than 15 min to respect the comfort of participants and the time with their loved ones, if present. Of the observed admission visits, 20 enrolled in hospice, 3 were undecided, and 2 declined hospice.

C.C. also attended hospice admission monthly staff meetings where "defining best practices," was a standing agenda item ($n = 3$). Before observations began, C.C. provided a short presentation at the staff meeting about the project: what was required of admission nurses, the goals of the observation and interviews, how results would be shared back with the organization, and answered any questions they had. None of the admission nurses chose to opt-out of participating. Ethnographic field notes of these meetings were written and typed single-spaced for a total of 250 pages (8–12 pages per visit).

Interviews were transcribed verbatim and then analyzed alongside the ethnographic field notes using thematic discourse analysis in an inductive, data-driven approach. Each observed admission conversation was broken down and coded, allowing the researcher to establish a pattern by relating codes/categories to one another. The Colorado Multiple Institutional Review Board approved the study (protocol # 16-1897).

5. Ethical Considerations

This project would not be possible without a strong ethical foundation. Ethics have been incorporated from initial study design to the sharing of results. The skill of introspection and the ability to accept and process feedback regarding very personal aspects of this work are important attributes of any researcher doing end-of-life research [11]. The instrument in ethnographic qualitative research is a human instrument: the researcher as a whole person in the midst of a culture being studied. Therefore, a profound awareness and understanding of the nature of the constructed boundaries of one's own identity and personal experience is critical to being an effective human instrument.

This project has specifically been guided by post-colonial ethics of accountability, context, truthfulness, and community. More specifically, through a felt need of endorsing other models of reflexivity, we have looked to others who have done similar work, like Ellingson, Broadfoot, Foster, Hirschmann, de la Garza, and Eisenberg [12–16], documenting the ethical tensions that arise and how they worked through them. An ethical concern and models of reflexivity extend the challenge of speaking for others, which is interrelated with the politics of representation and the crisis of legitimation around qualitative work [17,18]. In order to work with this tension and challenge, Alcoff encourages researchers to not speak for, but to speak with participants by engaging them in conversation and representing the writing in a way that is meaningful and accessible to the ones who have shared and created their stories at extremely fragile times in their lives [17]. In an effort to work through the challenges of representation, alternative forms of writing, such as narrative styles and case studies have been used to escape the constraints of traditional writing as well as respond to the ethical tensions of speaking for others in qualitative research. Further, pseudonyms have been used throughout this paper to protect participants' identities.

For these reasons, we have chosen a case study exemplar for this paper, as a powerful example of the many issues associated with hospice admissions [19]. Although we have pages of observations and conversations documented in field notes (conversations were not audio taped, just the interviews), we chose this particular narrative because it is a comprehensive exemplar of our larger data set and it effectively highlights the ecological nature of these interactions. Through this lens, our analysis highlights critical communicative acts and turning points and demonstrates the inherent complexities of hospice admission interactions.

Establishing concordance is necessary to coordinate communication and decision-making, as it sets the tone for all future interactions around hospice [8]. Pilot data illustrates that what unfolds in these interactions ultimately depends on the communicative actions that emerge directly from interactants' goals, linguistic skills, perceptions, emotions, and knowledge, as well as the constraints and opportunities created by the responses of others (i.e., caregiver, patient, and hospice nurse). Using an ecological lens to view these interactions shifts analytical attention beyond focusing on relationships between providers and patients and the various outcomes resulting from the interaction (e.g., satisfaction with care, commitment to treatment, health improvement) to describing concrete processes within the admission interaction that affect communicative action [8,20].

6. Real Case Exemplar: "I Don't Want to Go Back and See Her, Just Tell Me If It's Time for My Mom to Start Hospice"

6.1. Background and Context to the Interaction

It is cold but sunny and glass doors open onto a dark lit room in the Alzheimer's Care Center. The facility walls are decked out in holiday decorations, and Christmas music can be heard playing in the background. James, the hospice admission nurse and I (C.C.) have an appointment to meet with the patient's daughter, but first we need to look through her record and talk with her nurse. There is no one in the halls as we enter, save a patient trying to exit. It smells of feces, urine, and artificial cleaning products. It is hard to breathe. Several residents sit in their wheelchairs at the entryway of their rooms, lined up as though they are waiting for a delivery. Some look up as we walk by, while others are sleeping with their heads cocked to one side. Other residents meander through the hall, scuffing their feet across the carpet to move their wheelchairs. The smell gets stronger the further we go. We pass the "living room" filled with about 15 residents gathered in a semi-circle around the TV in their wheelchairs. Every head is bowed with eyes closed.

We arrive at the nurse's station and, upon request, receive a large blue binder containing the patient's record. As we open it, another resident approaches the desk. James greets her and asks if he can help, and she says there is a lot he can help with before walking away. A patient yells at a nurse as they walk out of the dining room because she is holding his arm (to prevent a fall). I hear a conversation between another nurse and patient involving a nail gun, as the patient complains that it sounds like someone has been kicking the wall. "Lunch is in an hour", another nurse says to a patient sitting in the hall as she walks by a nursing aide wheeling a woman backwards into the shower room.

6.2. Notes from Hospice Organization to the Admissions Nurse

Patient and family are undecided on whether to enroll patient into hospice services or not. Dr. Hanks has expressed to them that he does not think patient is hospice appropriate at this time, but is open to reconsidering this based on hospice's evaluation. Family is also wanting more information and an evaluation to determine whether patient is appropriate or not. Daughter has many concerns about admitting patient to hospice, and several questions on why or why not her mother would qualify. Daughter would like hospice nurse to lay eyes on patient, then meet with her in the lobby after.

6.3. The Patient

The patient's nurse tells us that Judy is a "very pleasant 93-year-old. She has congestive heart failure (CHF) and had a change of condition a few days ago: fluid in her lungs. Her appetite is good and she is ambulatory. She has a little pain, does not talk much, just general facial expressions. She had antibiotics to help treat the fluid and has gotten a little better". James gets her medications and confirms that there is only one medication with the nurse. He asks about a note in the record that outlines the family's request to not call the house before 8 am for non-urgent matters and asks how this affects the nurse's interactions with them. There does not seem to be any concern, but the nurse shares that the family used to come every week but that lately no one has been around. James closes the binder, puts it back on the shelf, and signals me to follow. We make our way back up to the lobby to meet Emily, Judy's daughter. Four patients in wheelchairs are lined up looking at the front door. It seems they are going out to Applebee's. They wait for a staff member to pull their transport around, only to find that it is not operational. They are devastated by this news.

6.4. Interaction with Emily the Family Caregiver (Daughter)

We find Emily in the lobby after she dropped a stack of clothes at the receptionist's desk. We introduce ourselves and head somewhere to talk.

J: "Before I give you a bunch of information, can you tell me your understanding of hospice?"
E: "I understand it as two levels of care. Palliative being less hands-on, and hospice being more involved."

(James takes a pause and elaborates on the meaning of both, underscoring the additional support of hospice and the benefits of both for her mother.)

J: "I saw your mom very briefly earlier today and she is doing well. She got up by herself and walked about the room. She's continent."
E: "She's continent? She has been in a diaper every time I have seen her."
J: "Sometimes around here they put diapers on almost like a security blanket so the patients can be relaxed if they have an accident or can't get up quickly enough to the restroom. We can go see her after we finish our conversation."
E: "I don't want to go back."

[*Turning point #1*: In this moment, James is having this conversation without the patient in the same room because the daughter does not want to go back to see her. One of her expectations for James today is to evaluate her mother, but not being able to see her while speaking with the daughter makes providing recommendations challenging for James. While James saw her very briefly that morning, he is not sure the last time the daughter has seen her. Thoughtfully and openly, James knows they will not be going back, and also knows the daughter is not yet ready to hear details about her mother's health condition, so James turns the conversation.]

J: "What are your goals today?"
E: "We want an honest assessment of where she is to determine if we should enroll in palliative or hospice care. You are the experts. We are leaning more towards palliative care, but we just don't know. Is she eligible for hospice? Would her doctor support that decision?"

[*Turning point #2*: James has already asked and suggested they go back so he is able to provide what the daughter wants: an honest assessment. However, having the conversation in the mother's room is not an option. Another layer of complexity is added when she introduces two competing perspectives, stating that James and hospice are "the experts" before quickly asking, "would her doctor support that decision?" It is unclear who carries more credibility. This makes it difficult for James to know what role he needs to play. In response to the question "What are your goals?" Emily redirects decision-making responsibility to James by effectively stating, "tell me what to do."]

J: "Yes, he said he would support that decision."
E: "I'm confused—I thought he didn't feel she was appropriate?"'
J: "Initially, Dr. Hanks said he didn't think she was appropriate for hospice, but in the chart from November it states he would support the decision to enroll in hospice if we felt she met criteria, which I feel she does. After seeing your mother, I think she can benefit from palliative or hospice

care, and I have information and paperwork on both options today. But this decision is ultimately for you and your family to make. Do you know what she wants?"

E: "No, I mean she can't communicate."

[*Turning point #3*: Emily is navigating some inconsistencies—the doctor was originally unclear about her mother being hospice appropriate, but now it appears that she is. James asks another question to try and elicit the degree to which they have discussed her mother's preferences around end-of-life care options.]

J: "Did you talk with her before about what she would want?"

E: "Not really. But I think she's ready for palliative care and until the doctors feel absolutely certain she is ready for hospice, we will go from there. Is that reasonable?"

J: "Yes, absolutely."

E: "Can you re-evaluate her in 90 days? It's risky, I know, since she could go downhill quickly and maybe need more help."

J: "It's a very difficult decision, and we want to help you in whatever way we can. We can fill out both paperwork, and you can think more about it and let us know within a few days."

E: "Do you think she is ready for hospice?"

J: "I think she is, but the decision to enroll is really up to you. She is eligible and would certainly have more eyes on her with a larger care team."

E: "Would she have more interaction and would your team interact with the team here okay?"

J: "Yes, she would have more frequent visits on our hospice program, as our palliative team serves more in a consultative capacity. But know that both programs provide an extra layer of support to our patients. Hospice also works hard to provide support to you as her family member … we know this is a challenging time."

E: "I don't know what to do. This is really hard and you're not giving me any guidance!" (Emily gives her first brief smile.)

[*Turning point #4*: James has outlined several options for Emily about going forward (signing both papers and making a decision later), but during this exchange it is clear that Emily is struggling with what to do and keeps asking reassuring and guidance-seeking questions to James. In James's mind, he is helping her: asking questions about goals of care, asking what the mother would want, supporting her concerns, clarifying her understanding of hospice and palliative care, and leaving the decision very open. Ultimately, James is encouraging Emily to weigh the options. At this point in the interaction, Emily feels stuck and fearful of making the wrong decision. James astutely recognizes that not all family members feel comfortable making decisions or choosing between options, and that some interactions require more direct, less open-ended communication to help with the decision-making.]

J: "We just want you to be prepared as possible should things get worse, and we want to be able to best support you all. So often patients and families wait until they are close to dying before enrolling in these services, whereas signing up earlier could really benefit not only your mom, but you and your siblings as well. If I could make a recommendation, I would encourage you to sign your mom up for palliative care today and then we can move her onto hospice services when you feel more comfortable with that transition. If you change your mind, just give us a call; these decisions are not set in stone. Your palliative team will also help you understand when the time is right for a transition to hospice."

(Emily takes a deep breath, uncrosses her arms, and leans in towards the table.)

E: "You know, my father died 10 years ago. My mom insisted he get cancer treatment until the day he died while living at home. It was a Saturday and my mother wanted us to haul him to the hospital for another treatment. He was so sick and so weak. And my family and I finally intervened and told my mother no. He died that following Monday." (pauses) "I want hospice. Let's go directly to hospice. I don't want to have her be on hospice for 4–5 years, but I also don't want to ignore something she might really need and benefit from. This is so hard."

[*Turning point #5*: James's patience and use of silence allows Emily to open up and tell this story about her father, which has had a significant impact on how she is navigating this decision for her mother. Moreover, as James plays the role of expert in this moment, it opens things up for Emily to say something different (e.g., remembering her experience with her father). James's silence also allows Emily to come back and answer his first question about goals of care.]

E: "I want her as comfortable as possible and free of pain, with an extra set of eyes." (Emily's eyes fill with tears. James pulls out the paperwork.)
J: "Just remember that no matter what you decide, you can always change your mind at any point."
E: "You can re-evaluate her at 90 days, right? This is so hard."
J: "Yes, we can, and I will put that in the notes."

(James starts to go through the enrollment paperwork Emily needs to sign to get her mom enrolled in hospice. Emily has no questions.)

[*Turning point #6*: Organizationally, this is an effective interaction because there is a plan in place: to sign up for hospice care with the understanding that if it is not the right fit, Emily can discontinue services at any time. However, psychosocially, did Emily get the help she needed? This is the more challenging question to answer. Is it James's fault if she did not? Many times, families cannot reach a decision for a number of reasons—societal norms around the meaning they have assigned to hospice, deep family dynamics that still need to be addressed and dealt with, acceptance of the illness, acceptance of the reality of caregiving needs, uncertainty what their loved one wants, fear of financial burden keeping their loved one home, even if it is what they want, and so on. The interaction comes to a close in the next lines when James is filling out paperwork and having Emily sign the consent forms, when he notices Emily's birthday on the power of attorney form.]

J: "Your birthday is coming up!"
E: "And so is my mom's."
J: "Are you having a party for her?"
E: "No, actually. I will be in Chicago.

(Judy's nurse Katie comes in to have Emily sign a paper.)

E: "Hi, Katie, how is she doing?"
E: "Is she still on oxygen?"
K: "No, just as needed."
E: "I left some clothes for her at the front. Can you take them back to her?"
K: "Sure."

(Emily signs the last document. She takes her copies, grabs her bag.)

E: "Thank you, and I will talk with you soon, ok? I would like to know more about that bereavement program for children you spoke of because my mother's granddaughter has a lot of emotional issues and would benefit from that support. Can you put that in the notes?"
J: "You got it. Thanks for coming, Emily."

The hospice admission encounter, like the one outlined above, reveals a variety of reoccurring patterns of communication and struggle. Looking at the narrative, there are clear communication challenges, as well as opportunities to assess each unique situation, connect, clarify, and create new meanings. Identified turning points illustrate how the outcomes of these interactions ultimately depends on the communicative actions of participants and their goals, linguistic skills, perceptions, emotions, and knowledge, as well as the constraints and opportunities created by the responses of others (i.e., caregiver, patient, and hospice nurse). Examining this interaction through an ecological lens, the following points become apparent:

Interpersonally: In not wanting Emily to feel forced into a decision, James initially struggles to provide a recommendation for one service over the other. Emily struggles to understand why James is not playing the role of expert and telling Emily what she should do. On a personal level, James struggles to understand why Emily does not want to go back and see her mother, and wonders what dynamics are at play. Emily is struggling to accept the new normal of her mother, including not wanting the same thing that happened to her father to happen to her mother. Emily is overwhelmed being her mother's primary caregiver.

Organizationally: Entering skilled nursing facilities to talk about hospice adds an extra layer of complexity to the encounter, as hospice nurses navigate the organization's controls and rules, gaining access, finding the chart, and finding the patient's nurse prior to starting the interaction. James's experience working in skilled nursing facilities (and not always having a positive experience) as well as the training he has received at his particular organization regarding admissions conversations and communication strategies also shapes how he thinks and feels during admissions interactions and decisions. Emily's presence inside the skilled nursing facility (and her wishes to not go past the front door) also influences the interaction. Furthermore, this is James's second of four visits for the day. Visits can last between 30 min and 2 h, and often James does not have a lot of time between cases to debrief from the last one and prepare for the next.

Culturally: Emily and James navigate several cultural subtleties in their conversation. Broadly, both dealt with the culture of the nursing facility where the conversation took place. The cultural tensions of nursing home care are often dictated by insurance reimbursements and staffing shortfalls. These challenges frequently create a culture of apathy or indifference, which is difficult to manage. Further, the culture of the nursing home directly influences the ability of hospice to enter the facility and provide care. Emily, a retired US Parks Worker, entered this interaction looking for guidance and for someone to tell her what choice to make. She viewed James as the medical expert with an exclusive knowledge base who could quickly make the decision for her. The term "expert," is used by groups and individuals to legitimize claims of expertise or competence. As a term and 'position' in society, the 'expert' is also able to influence how people understand and act in social realms and their world.

This is a common paradigm in the culture of medicine in which paternalism and physician choice in medical decisions is the longstanding cultural norm [21]. As a hospice admissions nurse, James comes from a culture of information giving and decisional autonomy. A cultural tension exists in whether it is appropriate for James to exercise some paternalism and influence Emily's decision as the expert or let her own cultural values and beliefs guide the discussion. Ultimately, Emily reflecting on her experience with her father allowed her to clarify what decision was best for her mother and family. Thus, the interaction and its decisions rest on the intersection of two forms of expertise and the struggle over who should determine next steps. Emily defers decision-making to whom she perceives to be the only expert (as verified by society and training)—James. James, however, wishes the decision-making would be guided by the person who has lived experience and is therefore expert—Emily.

What we learned from analyzing this interaction ecologically:

- *First, participants play multiple roles*: Hospice nurses are asked to play many different roles at any given moment (e.g., medical professional, social worker, therapist, end-of-life-care expert, facilitator, advisor, educator, etc.). It is important to have these roles defined and understood from the outset and re-confirmed throughout the interaction.

- *Second, participant goals vary*: Patient and caregiver goals can vary, change, and evolve visit-to-visit. Clarifying the goal of the interaction enhances the likelihood of establishing trust at the beginning of the encounter and reaching concordance.
- *Third, understanding intersection(s) is key to adaptation*: Understanding that roles and goals may come into opposition, but finding intersections where concordance, or points of commonality between people's purposes, concerns, and circumstances exists and remaining focused and adaptive leads to better shared decision-making. Finding intersections quickly and returning to them frequently helps discern between what patients/caregivers want, what they do not want, and what role the nurse must play to help the patient and family achieve those goals in light of their unique circumstances.

Although we agree with the assertion in the OIG report that patients require complete and accurate information about the hospice benefit to make an informed decision, we have shown the impracticality of one standardized method of hospice enrollment. The competing demands and expectations of the patient, family, and provider all need to be tempered to maximize the effectiveness of these interactions. Analyzing hospice admission interactions through an ecological lens demonstrates how the OIG's mandate for clear election statements for informed decision-making is tempered and mediated by the complexity and heterogeneity of each individual hospice admission interaction. Moreover, this case study demonstrates that achieving concordance and informed consent is far more nuanced than verbiage on election forms. It demands real-time interpretation of a patient's goals of care, patience, adaptability, and awareness of the interpersonal, organizational, and culture tensions that impact effective communication and interaction design.

7. Conclusions

Patients and families enter into hospice admission interactions with varying degrees of comfort and knowledge, having to make a significant decision at a time when their loved one is extremely ill and the family is often very fatigued. This is deep and profoundly difficult caring work for admission nurses, who often conduct multiple consults a day and are responsible for explaining the hospice benefit, completing consents and advance directives, holding a goals of care conversation, and coordinating care of each patient. Analyzing this interaction reveals the different spaces patients, families, and nurses can inhabit, and why finding concordance from the outset is integral to facilitating a meaningful interaction.

The critical function of communication studies is to improve dialogue and decision-making processes. In palliative and hospice care interactions, understanding the impact of particular communicative practices on patients and families in the extremely vulnerable terrain of advanced illness requires detailed, scientific, and theory-driven explanations and constructions of alternative meaning and discourses [6,8,10,20]. Applying Street's ecological theory of patient-centered communication to these interactions allows us to see how different communicative practices in real time can impact the ability to reach concordance and shared decision-making. A qualitative methodological approach to these interactions uncovers the complexities of discourse around the end of life and the nuances of meaning surrounding illness and care options. How individuals experience hospice, and the ways in which social, political, and cultural contexts impinge upon parts of the hospice admission interaction further contribute to these complexities. Advancing the rigor of studies of communication in hospice care settings using a qualitative methodological approach can illuminate the communicative techniques and practices necessary to improve decision-making, as well as evaluate the causes and effects of meaningful communication in improving care [22]. Developing communication guidelines built around a sensitized, rather than standardized attitude, should be an immediate next step.

Acknowledgments: This project was funded in full through a small grant from The University of Colorado School of Medicine, Division of General Internal Medicine, USA.

Author Contributions: Carey Candrian and Alexandra Tsantes conceived and designed the study; Carey Candrian performed the experiments; Carey Candrian and Kirsten Broadfoot analyzed the data; Carey Candrian,

Kirsten Broadfoot, Channing Tate and Alexandra Tsantes wrote the paper; Daniel Matlock and Jean Kutner contributed materials.

Conflicts of Interest: The authors declare no conflict of interest.

References

1. Casarett, D.J.; Crowley, R.; Stevenson, C.; Xie, S.; Teno, J. Making difficult decisions about hospice enrollment: What do patients and families want to know? *J. Am. Geriatr. Soc.* **2005**, *53*, 249–254. [CrossRef] [PubMed]
2. Casarett, D.J.; Crowley, R.; Hirschman, K.B. How should clinicians describe hospice to patients and families? *J. Am. Geriatr. Soc.* **2004**, *52*, 1923–1928. [CrossRef] [PubMed]
3. Candy, B.; Holman, A.; Leurent, B.; Davis, S.; Jones, L. Hospice care delivered at home, in nursing homes and in dedicated hospice facilities: A systematic review of quantitative and qualitative evidence. *Int. J. Nurs. Stud.* **2009**, *48*, 121–133. [CrossRef] [PubMed]
4. Johnson, C.B.; Slaninka, S.C. Barriers to accessing hospice services before a late terminal stage. *Death Stud.* **1999**, *23*, 225–238. [PubMed]
5. Myers, G.E. Can illness narratives contribute to the delay of hospice admission? *Am. J. Hosp. Palliat. Care* **2002**, *19*, 325–330. [CrossRef] [PubMed]
6. Wittenberg-Lyles, E.M.; Thompson, S. Understanding enrollment conversations: The role of the hospice admissions representative. *Am. J. Hosp. Palliat. Med.* **2006**, *23*, 317–322. [CrossRef] [PubMed]
7. Office of Inspector General Report. Available online: https://oig.hhs.gov/oei/reports/oei-02-10-00492.asp (accessed on 1 December 2016).
8. Street, R.L.; O'Malley, K.J.; Cooper, L.A.; Haidet, P. Understanding concordance in patient-physician relationships: Personal and ethnic dimensions of shared identity. *Ann. Fam. Med.* **2008**, *6*, 198–205. [CrossRef] [PubMed]
9. Marinker, M. Personal paper: Writing prescriptions is easy, but to come to an understanding of people is hard. *BMJ* **1997**, *314*, 747–748. [CrossRef] [PubMed]
10. Street, R.L. Communication in medical encounters: An ecological perspective. In *Handbook of Health Communication*; Thompson, T., Dorsey, A., Parrott, R., Miller, K., Eds.; Lawrence Erlbaum: Mahwah, NJ, USA, 2003; pp. 63–89.
11. González, M.C. The four seasons of ethnography: A creation-centered ontology for ethnography. *Int. J. Intercult. Relat.* **2000**, *24*, 623–650. [CrossRef]
12. Ellingson, L. *Communicating in the Clinic: Negotiating Frontstage and Backstage Teamwork*; Hampton Press: Cresskill, NJ, USA, 2005.
13. Broadfoot, K.J. "She's come undone!": Engaging scholarship and viral research. In *Engaging Communication, Transforming Organizations: Scholarship of Engagement in Action*; Simpson, J.L., Shockley-Zalabak, P., Eds.; Hampton Press: Cresskill, NJ, USA, 2005; pp. 98–112.
14. Hirschman, K. Blood, vomit, and communication: The days and nights of an intern on call. *Health Commun.* **1999**, *11*, 35–57. [CrossRef] [PubMed]
15. Foster, E. Lessons we learned: Stories of volunteer-patient communication in hospice. *J. Aging Identity* **2002**, *7*, 245–256. [CrossRef]
16. Eisenberg, E.; Murphy, K.; Wears, R.; Schenkel, S.; Perry, S.; Vanderhoef, M. Communication in emergency medicine: Implications for patient safety. *Commun. Monogr.* **2005**, *72*, 390–413. [CrossRef]
17. Alcoff, L. The problem of speaking for others. *Cult. Crit.* **1991–1992**, *20*, 5–32. [CrossRef]
18. Lindlof, T.R.; Taylor, B.C. *Qualitative Communication Research*, 2nd ed.; Sage: Thousand Oaks, CA, USA, 2002.
19. Flyvbjerg, B. Five misunderstandings about case-study research. *Qual. Inq.* **2006**, *12*, 219–245. [CrossRef]
20. Street, R.L.; Makoul, G.; Arora, N.K.; Epstein, R.M. How does communication heal? Pathways linking clinician-patient communication to health outcomes. *Patient Educ. Couns.* **2009**, *84*, 795–301. [CrossRef] [PubMed]

21. Lupton, D. Toward the development of critical health communication praxis. *Health Commun.* **1994**, *6*, 55–67. [CrossRef]
22. Steinhauser, K.E.; Barosso, J. Using qualitative methods to answer key questions in palliative care. *J. Palliat. Med.* **2009**, *12*, 725–730. [CrossRef] [PubMed]

behavioral sciences

MDPI

Article

Family Communication about End-of-Life Decisions and the Enactment of the Decision-Maker Role

April R. Trees *, Jennifer E. Ohs and Meghan C. Murray

Department of Communication, Saint Louis University, 3733 West Pine Blvd, Xavier 300, St. Louis, MO 63108, USA; johs@slu.edu (J.E.O.); mmurra28@slu.edu (M.C.M.)
* Correspondence: atrees@slu.edu; Tel.: +1-314-977-3144

Academic Editor: Maureen P. Keeley
Received: 1 March 2017; Accepted: 2 June 2017; Published: 7 June 2017

Abstract: End-of-life (EOL) decisions in families are complex and emotional sites of family interaction necessitating family members coordinate roles in the EOL decision-making process. How family members in the United States enact the decision-maker role in EOL decision situations was examined through in-depth interviews with 22 individuals who participated in EOL decision-making for a family member. A number of themes emerged from the data with regard to the enactment of the decision-maker role. Families varied in how decision makers enacted the role in relation to collective family input, with consulting, informing and collaborating as different patterns of behavior. Formal family roles along with gender- and age-based roles shaped who took on the decision-maker role. Additionally, both family members and medical professionals facilitated or undermined the decision-maker's role enactment. Understanding the structure and enactment of the decision-maker role in family interaction provides insight into how individuals and/or family members perform the decision-making role within a cultural context that values autonomy and self-determination in combination with collective family action in EOL decision-making.

Keywords: end-of-life decision-making; family roles; surrogate decision maker

1. Introduction

In the United States, when an individual is incapacitated at the end of life and cannot make a decision for him or herself, family members often are called upon to make decisions for the individual. End-of-life (EOL) care decisions encompass decisions to initiate, withhold, continue, or end life-sustaining treatment. Making a decision for a family member at the end of life is one of the most emotionally difficult decisions families will ever face [1,2]. How this decision is managed has important implications for the patient's quality of life at the end [3] and affects family members' emotional well-being long after the decision has been made [1,2]. During decision-making, families encounter various dilemmas and challenges, including uncertainty about what to do and how to behave [4].

As they navigate this emotionally-charged experience and coordinate action together, family members take on roles in the decision-making process that may be supported or challenged by others in the interaction. One particularly important role in this context is the decision-maker role itself [5]. The U.S. legal and medical systems encourage the use of an advance care directive (ACD) to designate a formal decision maker, although many individuals do not engage in EOL planning [6]. In contrast to other legal systems (e.g., the United Kingdom where clinicians serve as default decision makers based on best interests), in the U.S., a family member typically takes on the decision-maker role in cases where a patient can not make decisions for him or herself, using substituted judgment or best interests to guide the decision-making [7,8]. The decision-maker role, however, is rarely enacted in isolation. Multiple family members, for example, often participate in the decision-making interaction [9,10].

Given the interdependence of the family and the value of family engagement in the decision-making process, expectations and behaviors for the decision-maker role likely emerge in and are shaped by interaction with others in the family. Understanding the enactment of the decision-making role in family interactions about EOL decisions provides insight into how family members coordinate EOL interaction together and either support or undermine the performance of the decision-maker role.

1.1. Family Communication and End-of-Life Decision-Making

In the U.S., the legal and medical systems emphasize individual autonomy in health-care decision-making, expecting decision makers to follow the wishes of the individual [11]. Individuals are encouraged to engage in EOL planning and complete formal documentation that specifies preferences regarding life-sustaining treatment and names a surrogate decision maker [12]. Despite this emphasis on advance care planning, the percentage of U.S. adults completing an advance care directive (ACD) is relatively low [6]. Several different surveys have demonstrated that many individuals feel that talking to family members about EOL wishes and having written documentation of wishes are both important, but a low percentage of respondents have actually had conversations with family and even fewer have legal documentation in place [13,14].

Most often, in situations where a surrogate decision maker has been established, the individual identified as a surrogate is a family member (e.g., spouse, child or grandchild) [15,16]. This reflects a dominant preference across cultural groups in the United States for family to be involved in surrogate decision-making [3,17,18]. Additionally, regardless of whether or not a formal decision maker has been identified in an ACD, multiple family members usually participate in decision-making conversations when a decision must be made [9,10,19], and some families may expect consensus in the decision [20].

The complexity of EOL decision situations creates a number of dilemmas for family members required to make a decision for a loved one at the end of life. Family members may face challenges in obtaining the information needed to make a good decision [21] or knowing when a decision point is nearing [22]. Without adequate information from health care providers to inform the decision, families can experience resentment and emotional burden after a decision is made [21,22]. Family members also may be uncertain about the right decision to make [10], even when there is an ACD in place [4]. Living wills, for example, do not always provide insight into the specific decision that must be made [23]. Additionally, when family members are aware of the patient's wishes, they still may encounter a contradiction between their own desires and the patients' desires [24], often experienced as a tension between holding on and letting go [25]. Family members also may struggle to make sense of the decision and of a loved one's likely death. In interaction during clinician-family conferences in an intensive care unit, for example, family members grappled with understanding withdrawing or withholding life support as killing a loved one versus seeing it as letting him or her die [24]. They also experienced a contradiction between perceiving death as a burden or as a benefit.

As family members make decisions, they can experience challenges in effectively coordinating family decision-making and working with medical professionals. Families, for example, sometimes experience conflict and disagreement as multiple family members participate in the decision-making process. Family members may disagree over who should be included in the decision-making [24] or, ultimately, what decision to make [5]. A history of family conflict prior to the EOL decision, communication in which family members try to assert control over the decision, and families having difficulty talking with each other about the situation all predict greater family conflict when making an EOL decision [26]. Family conflict in EOL decision-making can lead to more aggressive treatment [27] and reduce the degree to which decisions match the preferences of the patient [28]. Conflict in the family during decision-making also may undermine the quality of family relationships after a decision has been made [29].

1.2. Family Roles and End-of-Life Decision-Making

Clearly family interaction around EOL decisions is fraught with complications that affect the well-being of both the patient and the family. As families negotiate this unfamiliar communicative terrain, members take on a variety of informal roles in the decision-making process [5]. Roles refer to communicatively negotiated understandings of behavior to be enacted by family members in particular positions [30,31]. Roles are communicatively created and recreated in interaction with others [30]. Roles both develop in and then guide interaction as family members form expectations about how someone holding a particular role will act. As a family faces an EOL decision, family members in both formal (e.g., designated surrogate decision maker) and informal decision-making roles must work out what their roles mean for family communication and decision-making behaviors.

Within family interaction, the behaviors of others shape how a role is enacted. Role appropriation is shaped by role expectations and others in the family can facilitate or undermine the enactment of a particular role, which may need to be negotiated among family members [32]. Additionally, Salazar [31] recognizes that roles that develop in groups are shaped by both past and present interaction and have environmental constraints. In EOL decision-making, roles likely build on past family interactional histories, formal familial roles (e.g., spouse, child), and gender role expectations [30,33], but also adapt to the unique decision-making situation facing the family. The larger medical and legal systems in the U.S. also add an extra layer of expectations for formal role assignments that shape interaction within the family and between the family and medical professionals [21]. Although there might be a variety of different informal roles that develop in the family system when making an EOL decision for a loved one [5], of particular interest for this project is the decision-making role itself. More specifically, we pose the following research question:

RQ: How do family members enact the decision-making role in EOL decision-making interactions?

2. Materials and Methods

2.1. Participants

Individuals who participated in family decision-making for a loved one at the end of life, either as a surrogate decision maker or as a family member involved in the communication about the decision, were interviewed about their family communication during the decision-making process. Participants were recruited via an announcement in a University newsletter, announcements on Facebook, researchers' social networks, and referrals from participants. We interviewed 22 participants, 19 women and 3 men. Participants had an average age of 44 (range = 18 to 70). Fourteen participants identified as Caucasian, four as African American, two as Asian, one as Dominican, and one as Indian. Eight participants indicated that their family member at the end of life had formally designated a surrogate decision maker. Seven participants reported that their family member had not designated a surrogate, and six were unsure. One person reported on a decision involving a family member who did not reside in the United States at the end of life and was unsure of legal means and options to designate a surrogate decision maker for the person at the end of life.

Many of the decisions faced by families in this study involved decisions about initiating or withdrawing life support. Others included decisions about pursuing specific interventions (e.g., surgery, chemotherapy), stopping treatment and going on hospice, and whether or not a patient could return home or must remain in the hospital. In many cases, decision makers and families faced a number of different decisions as they navigated the end of life with their loved one. All of the decisions except one were made within the context of the health-care and legal system in the United States. However, decision narratives involved families of mixed citizenships and cultures. In one case, the family member at the end of life had moved from her lifelong residence in Singapore to the United States to be with her family during her final days. Thus, the experiences reported here represent a variety of cultural and familial backgrounds that are influenced by the communication surrounding EOL care within the U.S. medical and legal system.

Three participants had made more than one EOL decision on behalf of a family member, yielding 25 different decision situations in the data. In two cases, family members represented a patient who was not entirely incapacitated. Decisions were made for parents (15), siblings (4), grandparents (3), a mother-in-law (1), an aunt (1), and a nephew who was fictive kin (1). Respondents reported on decisions that were made between 1 and 10 years prior to the interview, with an average time between the decision and the interview being 3.75 years. Respondents reported on various roles in the decision. Eight individuals reported that they were one of the persons who made the EOL decision in the family. Six reported that they were the sole surrogate decision maker. Three people indicated they were consulted about the decision, three witnessed the process of decision-making, and one was told about the decision after it was made. One person indicated that her role was that of the spokesperson for the family.

2.2. Procedures and Analysis

The Saint Louis University Institutional Review Board approved the study. Prior to the interview, participants were asked a series of questions to gather demographic information and information about the nature of the decision-making situation. Interviews were conducted either face-to-face or over the phone and were audio-recorded. The interview protocol invited participants to tell the story of their family communication surrounding a care decision made on behalf of a loved one at the end of life, starting at the point that they became aware that an EOL decision might need to be made.

The research team consisted of four individuals: three Caucasian women and one Indian-American woman. Interviewers identified as young or middle-aged adults. The two primary investigators trained the other members of the research team to follow the semi-structured interview protocol. Interviews proceeded as a guided conversation, asking a variety of questions about family communication during the process, including what was talked about or avoided, who interacted with whom in what contexts, and how decisions were made. Interviewers were prepared for the emotional nature of the interviews and were attentive to cues of respondent distress. If a respondent became distressed, interviewers were prepared to offer resources and professional referrals for care. Interviews ranged in length from 22 to 94 min. After interviews were completed, they were transcribed, and participants and family members referenced in the interview were given pseudonyms to protect their identities.

To analyze the interview data, the second two authors independently reviewed each transcript, specifically looking for places in the data where participants talked about the behaviors and expectations associated with the decision-making role in their family interaction and how others supported or challenged that role. Honoring an emic perspective focused on the point of view of interviewees, the authors engaged in open-coding, identifying common patterns and themes in the data related to enactment of decision-making roles. All three researchers then met to compare and contrast the emerging themes, determine points of overlap and similarity and to reconcile differences between the two analyses. After identifying the relevant themes in the data, the second two authors also engaged in axial coding, noting the relationships among the different themes.

After arriving at a preliminary set of themes, the three authors met again to engage in investigator triangulation [34]. They discussed points of commonality and reconciled differences, finding that they had converged in their analysis. They then read through the transcripts to identify additional themes or negative cases. No new themes emerged and given that the properties and dimensions of each theme were well-developed and that the relationships among the categories were well-established, theoretical saturation was concluded [35]. Two key areas of analysis emerged in this thematic analysis of the interview transcripts, with subthemes within each area that help to develop a clearer understanding of how EOL decision-making roles are enacted in the family.

3. Results

3.1. The Structure of Decision-Making Roles within the Family System

When making EOL decisions for a loved one, one or more family members took on the decision-making role. Three different patterns of role enactment were identified in the interview data. The first two patterns of consulting and informing emerged in families with a single designated decision maker who received collective family input. Within these patterns of role enactment, family and gender roles shaped decisions regarding who took on decision-making roles. The third pattern of collaborating emerged in families in which the collective family unit took on the decision-maker role.

3.1.1. Single Designated Decision Maker with Collective Family Input: Consulting or Informing

In many cases, one individual was designated, formally or informally, as the official decision maker for a loved one's end-of-life care, but there was also collective family involvement. In these cases, there was a clear expectation that a specific individual would make the decision for the loved one. For a number of families, this role was established by formal legal documentation. Phyllis, for example, had health care power of attorney for her mother and noted, "Throughout the whole decision-making process, obviously, my dad and my sister, we kind of always conferenced as a family, but I was the one making the ultimate decisions on her end-of-life care."

In other families, a decision-maker was not specified through legal documents, but family members understood who should make the decision based on legal and cultural understandings of family roles (e.g., spouse rather than children) as well as gender role expectations. For example, Laura indicated that in her Dominican family "it is usually the elder daughter who always makes the decision, but she does not make the decision on her own." Age also emerged as a factor shaping who took on the decision-making role in the absence of formal documentation. Sheila, for example, noted that "the younger people deferred all of the decision-making to the older people."

Less commonly, the decision-maker role emerged through decisive behaviors on the part of a family member in the absence of formal, legal documentation. Beatrice, for example, observed that her mother "wasn't prepared for the situation because it had occurred so quickly." Her mother and her brother were in denial about her father's end of life, and when Beatrice arrived, she took over, asking questions and making arrangements. According to her, "I protected him; I mean I literally felt like his guard dog . . . . if I hadn't had been there they would have just kept treating him. Even though there was no treatment."

Family roles (e.g., spouse, child), gender roles, and age all emerged as existing roles in the family that shaped expectations regarding who would take on the decision-making role. Specifically, if a spouse was living, he or she was expected to take on the decision-making role, and participants provided explanations for why that did not happen in situations where a child or sibling took on the role instead. The need to protect the husband or wife given his or her emotional distress often emerged as an explanation for role enactment by a child instead. Beatrice, for example, indicated, "My mother, God bless her soul, she was just a bystander . . . . She could not communicate well with the doctors or the nurses, you know, she just . . . it was almost as if she was in shock." Although the gendered nature of the role varied from family to family, descriptions of who should take on decision-making roles intersected with gendered expectations regarding children's influence and support. Expectations regarding age and family roles were apparent in the data as well. Beatrice, for example, specifically noted that her role in the decision-making was unexpected to her because she was the youngest child and female. In situations where the decision-maker role was held by someone unanticipated (e.g., the youngest sibling), participants typically rationalized the role. For example, some participants pointed to the expertise of the chosen individual (e.g., "I'm the nurse so everyone turned and looked to me," Sheila), closeness and trust in the relationship with the patient, or their willingness to make difficult decisions. Jackie, for example, said that her mom chose her to be the decision maker even though she was the youngest "because the rest of my siblings were all sissies. She chose the tough one."

Regardless of the formality of the decision-maker role, collective family input was an important part of the decision-making process. How individuals enacted the decision-maker role in relationship to this collective input, however, varied across situations. In some cases, like Phyllis's described above, family conferences and other types of group interaction offered an opportunity for a number of different family members to have input into and, at times, get on board with the decisions that were going to be made. The behaviors of the decision maker involved consulting other family members as a way to enact the decision-maker role. Caroline, for example, talked about her sisters offering different suggestions to her dad about what to do, which he took into consideration as he made decisions for her mom. John's brother-in-law included his wife's family in conversations about his wife's EOL decisions prior to making decisions. In these types of role enactments, the individual in the formal decision-making role integrated the input of family members into the decisions made.

In other cases, the decision-maker role in family interaction involved informing more than consulting. Both listening and explaining were a part of the behaviors enacted in this type of decision-maker role. For example, individuals in the decision-maker role used family interactions to create a space for family members to express themselves before the decision maker made the decision he or she already knew would honor the loved one's wishes. This offered an opportunity to recognize and hear other family members' thoughts and opinions. Jackie, for example, said "I would tell them, 'Hey guys, this is where we are, this is the outlook, this is what things are.' And it was always ... the discussion was always ... we'll do everything possible to keep her alive. And which ... I had to always ... had to hear them out and allow them to express themselves and allow them to say what their desires were." Even though Jackie was officially recognized in her mother's medical record as the surrogate decision maker and knew that her mother should be taken off of life support, she included her family in a collective discussion to give them an opportunity to share before telling them what needed to happen.

At times, the decision maker used collective interaction as an opportunity to inform the family members of what the loved one would want and explain what the decision should be. Amy, for example, described her mom telling her adult children "this is what's going on, this is what the best decision was for him, and him and I talked about it before" at their family conference around the kitchen table. When her father had a stroke, Maria said that "my mother looked to me and my son ... she said 'no that is not what we had discussed .... you know, your father and I already discussed it.'" These conversations offered an opportunity for the decision maker to demonstrate knowledge of what was best and provide an argument for it grounded in the desires of the patient.

3.1.2. The Collective Family Unit as Joint Decision Makers: Collaborating

Although most families indicated that one person specifically took on the decision-maker role, a few families did not display this type of role enactment. Instead, family members jointly took on the decision-maker role together as a unit and collaborated together. In the families where this happened, there was a designated surrogate decision maker or a spouse who might have been expected to take on the decision-making role given the formal expectations of the legal and medical systems. That person, however, preferred to structure the interaction around collaborative group decision-making rather than take on the decision-making role individually. Catherine's mom, for example, had given her sister medical power of attorney. All seven siblings, however, regularly consulted one another as a group on decisions related to her mother's Alzheimer's. "It was always really understood that unless we were all on board, we weren't doing it ... So it was all or nothing. Like we weren't just going to leave one person feeling guilty about something." Similarly, although Molly's mother had power of attorney to make decisions for her father after her father's stroke, Molly's family had "an official family meeting" around the kitchen table at which her brother read her father's living will. Each family member then expressed their opinion about life support decisions that needed to be made. Molly noted that even her brother-in-law, whom she had originally felt should have no say, had proven himself to be a strong support and was asked to participate and voice his opinion. In contrast, Teresa's sister had no advance care directive in place. Her sister's husband was reluctant to take the decision-maker role on by himself, however, although Teresa noted that "we respected the fact that Justin was her husband and he had the final say." At one point, he called Teresa and said, "the kids and I want you to come up and help us make a decision about Alice." Although she initially indicated reluctance to be a part of the decision-making, Teresa, Justin, and her sister's three children had a family meeting and discussed extensively what they all thought Alice would want and made a decision as a group.

In these family situations, there was no clear surrogate decision-maker role given to a specific family member in the interaction. Family members were called upon to help make a decision together as a unit rather than one person taking on the decision-maker role alone. Coming together to discuss the loved one's wishes and focusing on the "we" aspect of the family emphasized the collective role the family enacted.

3.2. Facilitating and Undermining the Enactment of the Decision-Maker Role

Regardless of whether a single decision-maker was designated or emerged during family interactions or the family collectively made a decision, the communication choices of others either facilitated or challenged the decision-maker's role enactment. Both other family members' response to the role and the behavior of physicians and medical professionals made a difference in how the decision-maker role was enacted.

3.2.1. Family Members and Role Enactment

Given the importance of family interaction for the decision-making process, it is not surprising that family members' responses shaped the decision-maker role. This primarily occurred through two means. First, family members sometimes offered supportive behavior that bolstered the decision-maker's influence and helped him or her cope with the decision to be made. Alternately, conflictual behavior that challenged the decision maker's right to make the decision or the wisdom of his or her decision-making behavior was also evident.

One way in which families facilitated decision-making roles was by supporting one another's suggestions. Agreeing with the decision reinforced the decision maker's rights and responsibilities in that role. Family support was particularly important for decision makers who took on the role through decisive behavior. Sheila's sister did not have a surrogate decision maker, and Sheila reported that, "when I told them that enough is enough, don't put her through surgery, my other sister, she was supportive of that. And then my mom was kind of supportive of that. So, it was really us trying to tell the rest of the family that this is probably the best." Others' acceptance of that decision contributed to Sheila's enactment of the decision-maker role in the absence of legal documentation and/or a family role that would position her as next-of-kin. Support also became important in the context of family conflict. Charlotte's sister-in-law, for example, did not approve of the choices that her brother-in-law was making for her sister and was calling people in the family about it. Charlotte said everybody else in the family "told her basically we trust Adam's choices." Showing support could be seen as a sign of collective solidarity reinforcing the decision-maker role.

Additionally, family communication also provided an opportunity for other family members to reinforce the decision-maker's formal role by reminding the designated surrogate decision maker about the EOL care that had already been discussed or the wishes of the patient. Phyllis, for example, noted that "I just had to be the one to sign the paper. And I was always a little hesitant. Umm . . . And my dad would just kind of chime in and say, 'You know, remember what you and your mom had discussed last week. Remember what the three of us talked about the week before.'" Edna talked about sitting with her best friend Patty, whose son had been in a car accident. At one point, Patty was talking about how she could not let her son go, and she said, "I get to make the decisions." Edna said, "And I said 'yes you do.'" At the same time, Edna pointed out that this is not what he would want. In this moment, Edna supported Patty's right to make the decision while also encouraging her to consider what her son would want when that was a very difficult thing to face. Family members who were not considered primary decision makers acted as a support system to reinforce the decision that was made and to show support for the surrogate decision maker.

The decision-maker's role enactment was undermined when family members engaged in conflict around who should take on the role or what the right decision should be. In Jackie's situation, for example, family conflict emerged around whether or not the baby of the family should get to make decisions, even though she had legal standing as the surrogate decision maker. In contrast, Lynn, who was caring for a mother with dementia, indicated that her siblings were divided over the decision to keep her mother in her home, with four supporting the decision and three not supporting it. At one point, she said "we were one man down for a while, could you help us and all three of them said 'if you need help, put her in a nursing home.'" Family members were not always consistently unsupportive in their response to the decision-maker's behavior. Phyllis, for example, reported that her dad "was very argumentative with me and using a lot of foul language and kind of yelling at me" when she made the decision to decline a pacemaker for her mom. At other times, however, he had been supportive and encouraging given the difficult decisions she faced.

3.2.2. Physicians and Medical Professionals and Role Enactment

Other family members were not the only ones to influence the enactment of the decision-maker role. Physicians and medical professionals played an important part in supporting the decision maker in his or her role or in supporting the family as a collective. In addition, physicians were an essential source of information for the decision-making process, and how they responded to questions also shaped the enactment of the decision-maker role.

For the most part, physicians respected multiple voices in the family decision and encouraged family meetings about the decision, regardless of whether or not a designated surrogate decision maker had been named. In other cases, physicians played a role in ensuring that the family as a decision-making unit was honored. For example, Molly reported that her mother was the formally designated decision maker when her father had a stroke. However, she indicated that the physicians engaged all of the family members in discussion about her father's care at the end of life, helping the family to make a decision collectively. She said, "When the doctors talked to us, they looked at everybody ... " In the end, all of the family members came together to play a part in the decision, which, according to Molly, was supported by the hospital staff. "Everybody got equal amount of respect from the doctors and the nurses, "she said. This support provided space for the kind of collective interaction that was important for families, regardless of the type of decision-making role being enacted.

If, however, families engaged in conflict or hesitated in making a decision, the physician often encouraged the formal surrogate to step in to make the decision and reinforced the centrality of his/her legal position for taking on that kind of decision-making responsibility. Similarly, if families were not following the formalized wishes of the person at the end of life, physicians seemed to encourage those family members who were committed to following the formal wishes of the person at the end of life to take a lead. Jackie, for example, was faced with making a decision to withdraw treatment that was consistent with her mother's wishes but conflicted with her siblings' preferences. This conflict motivated the physician to encourage her, as the designated decision maker, to take the lead: "It came to uh ... the point of the physician talking to me one on one. And telling me it was my duty and it was my responsibility .... He said, 'This is not about them; this is about your mom.' And he said, 'You need to regain your focus.'"

In very few situations, participants also indicated that physicians engaged in behavior that undermined their ability to effectively perform the decision-making role. Most often, this revolved around failing to provide important information. Across interviews, it was clear that physicians provided key information that helped decision makers and family members understand the nature of the decision that they faced and orient to the possible consequences of different decisions. Questioning medical professionals was an important part of the decision-maker role. Molly, whose family reflected the collaborating pattern of role enactment, described everyone [in the family] asking questions "like a round table". When physicians were ambiguous or avoided sharing difficult information, this made decision-making more difficult. Beatrice, for example, was frustrated with her father's physician who did not provide important information for deciding whether or not to shift to hospice. Due to his reluctance to share difficult information, her persistent questioning of the doctor became a part of her enactment of the decision-maker role.

4. Discussion

The primary decision-maker role is a key role in EOL decision-making [5]. This study offers insight into the expectations and behaviors that constitute that role in families when decisions must be made. The findings of this study highlight the importance of collective family interaction as a part of the decision-makers' role enactment and the significance of family interaction for facilitating or inhibiting the enactment of the role. Additionally, this study provides insight into the ways in which the larger cultural, legal, and medical contexts intersect with specific family interaction to shape the structure and performance of the decision-maker role.

4.1. Family Interaction and the Enactment of the Decision-Maker Role

Across decision situations, interaction with other family members was an important part of the role enactment. This is consistent with research indicating that families in the United States often prefer family conversations about decisions over individual decision-making [9,10,20]. The findings demonstrate, however, that there can be important variation in the nature of that family interaction in relation to the decision-making role. In some families, the collective input was a key component of the decision-making, and in other family contexts, collective conversations were an opportunity for the decision maker to help other family members understand what decision should be made.

Although the U.S. legal system emphasizes the role of an individual surrogate decision maker, some families chose to construct the role as either a collaborative or consultative process rather than individual action. This occurred even in decision situations in which the patient had designated a specific person to be the legally recognized decision maker. For families who enacted a collective group decision-maker role or who had an individual decision maker who actively consulted other family members and adapted to their perspectives, collaborating and consulting created a more distinctive shared responsibility for the decision. Making an EOL decision for a family member carries a significant emotional burden [3,36], and diffusing the responsibility for the decision across family members may be one way to mitigate or share the emotional weight of the decision.

Additionally, a desire to develop a shared understanding might help explain the informing approach to decision-maker role enactment. In those families, individual decision makers used the family's collective interaction to explain the decision to other family members. In these cases, the surrogate decision maker's responsibilities extended beyond making a decision for the patient to also ensuring that the family understood the rationale for the decision. Family interaction was oriented around educating other family members about what the patient would want, rather than jointly reaching a decision together.

Regardless of the type of role enactment, the construction of the decision-maker role as one that engages collective family input reflects the complexity of making a decision in the context of an on-going, interdependent relational system. As long as it is not conflict laden, family interaction in EOL decision-making may help to create a shared perspective on whether or not we are "doing the right thing", something that family members struggle with as they face EOL decisions [3,24]. In addition, incorporating collective family interaction in the decision-making role, regardless of the form that it takes, may be one way in which families coordinate interaction so that they are able to go on together after a loved one has died. It is likely that what occurs in family interaction at the end of life, including the way in which the decision-maker role is enacted, has important consequences for how family members relate to each other after the death of their loved one.

4.2. Enactment of the Decision-Maker Role within the Cultural, Legal, and Medical Context of the United States

4.2.1. Understanding the Patients' Wishes and the Enactment of the Decision-Maker Role

Debate exists about whether or not family members are the best people to make decisions at the end of life. Whereas some scholars argue that their lack of medical expertise and/or emotional distress might undermine their decision-making capacity (e.g., [37]), others contend that they are uniquely positioned to know the values and preferences of the patient (e.g., [17]). Family members in this study, however, did not question whether or not a family member was the appropriate person to be making a decision for a loved one. The few conflicts that were reported oriented around the specific decision being made or who in the family was making the decision, but did not challenge the legitimacy of a family member as the appropriate decision maker. At the same time, however, the patients' wishes were clearly essential to knowing how to be a good decision maker for many of the participants in this study and their family members. This family emphasis on what the patient would want reflects a cultural emphasis on autonomy and patient self-determination that has appeared in other EOL studies in the United States [3,19].

The importance of a person's EOL wishes for families to know what to do as well as the significance of family support and collective interaction in decision-making point to the value of ensuring that family members other than the designated decision maker know one's EOL preferences. Researchers have encouraged families to have informal discussions among family members about EOL preferences in addition to formal planning [29]. Findings from this study clearly support that need, given the influence of informal family discussions on decisions regardless of whether or not a formal decision maker was designated. Engaging family members, broadly defined, in collective discussions about patients' EOL care needs, ensures that all involved parties are more likely to understand and respect patients' preferences.

4.2.2. Medical Professionals and the Enactment of the Decision-Maker Role

Based upon the pattern of findings in this study, medical professionals helped to bolster and support decision makers and reinforce the legitimacy and importance of that role to the family. Past research in the U.S. indicates that medical professionals can find family involvement in decision-making to be problematic, particularly when multiple different family members expect to participate in decision-making interaction [38]. Group interaction contradicts a medical model that emphasizes the relationship between the physician and the patient and/or a single surrogate decision maker [20,39]. Family members in this study, however, described ways in which physicians' behaviors helped to support the inclusion of collective family input in the performance of the decision-maker role. Research has demonstrated that physicians and other medical professionals serve as an important source of information for families facing a difficult decision [21]. In serving as a source of information for families, physicians are in a position to support collective family discussions about EOL decisions through their communication with the family as a whole during this time. When family members experience conflict around who should be making EOL decisions, physicians also offer support for surrogate decision makers, reinforcing the legitimacy of their role as a decision maker.

4.2.3. Family Roles, Age, Gender and the Decision-Maker Role

The decision-making role was clearly enacted within a familial context that carries with it a hierarchy of influence and responsibility in relationship to decision-making. Family, age and gender roles all appeared in family members' explanation for who took on the decision-making role in the family. This hierarchy of influence is culturally grounded. Research, for example, indicates variation across ethnic and racial groups in the U.S. in what individuals identify as the preferred formal family role (e.g., spouse, child, sibling) to draw on for a surrogate decision maker [18]. In situations where the person taking on the decision-making role in this study did not fit cultural or legal expectations for who should be making a decision (e.g., an adult child instead of a spouse), participants offered explanations for why unexpected role performances occurred.

5. Conclusions

The findings of this work offer valuable insight regarding how family members enact the decision-making role in family interactions surrounding the end-of-life decisions. However, the study is limited in several ways. First, the sample of this study was partially drawn from snowball methods, which limits the perspectives included. In contrast to other research interviewing surrogate decision makers (e.g., [40]), our participants had generally positive experiences with medical professionals and reported very little conflict with physicians. The influence of the physician in role enactment would be very different in contexts of disagreement around treatment decisions. Additionally, no participants who volunteered for the study reported on EOL decision-making for a spouse. Given the importance of the spousal role for EOL decision-making, the absence of the spousal perspective limits the transferability of findings.

Future research should attend to both cultural and familial factors that shape family interaction during EOL decision-making. The intersection of autonomy and interdependence that emerges in work attending to family processes in EOL decision-making [39] reflects a particular cultural understanding of families and their relationship to EOL decisions. Cross-cultural comparisons regarding family structure and expectations [41] as well as beliefs about decision-making responsibility [42] would offer additional insight into family processes related to EOL decision-making. The relational processes and expectations that family members bring to the decision-making situation also likely shape the patterns that emerge in the family [41]. Molly, for example, suggested that the cohesiveness that characterized relationships within her immediate family network helped to explain why everyone was involved actively in making the decision together. Future research should explore the ways in which the relational dynamics that the family brings to the decision-making situation shape the roles that emerge.

The end of life of a family member is an emotionally challenging and complex site of family decision-making. How family members socially construct the decision-maker role is critical for the decisions that are made and the coordination of family members in the decision-making process. Given the importance of collective interaction for role enactment and the significance of family members' responses for supporting or undermining that role enactment in EOL decisions, researchers and practitioners need to attend carefully to the interdependent family context when considering the process of EOL decision-making.

Author Contributions: April R. Trees and Jennifer E. Ohs conceived and designed the interview study and collected the data (with the assistance of graduate and undergraduate research assistants). Jennifer E. Ohs and Meghan C. Murray analyzed the data. April R. Trees wrote the introduction, April R. Trees and Jennifer E. Ohs wrote the materials and methods section, Jennifer E. Ohs, Meghan C. Murray, and April R. Trees wrote the results section, and April R. Trees wrote the discussion section, and all three authors edited the manuscript once complete.

Conflicts of Interest: The authors declare no conflict of interest.

References

1. Buckey, J.W.; Molina, O. Honoring Patient Care Preferences: Surrogates Speak. *OMEGA* **2012**, *65*, 257–280. [CrossRef] [PubMed]
2. Wendler, D.; Rid, A. Systematic Review: The Effect on Surrogates of Making Treatment Decisions for Others. *Ann. Int. Med.* **2011**, *154*, 336–346. [CrossRef] [PubMed]
3. Tilden, V.P.; Tolle, S.W.; Nelson, C.A.; Fields, J. Family Decision-Making to Withdraw Life-Sustaining Treatments from Hospitalized Patients. *Nurs. Res.* **2001**, *50*, 105–115. [CrossRef] [PubMed]
4. Lopez, R.P.; Guarino, A.J. Uncertainty and Decision Making for Residents with Dementia. *Clin. Nurs. Res.* **2011**, *20*, 228–240. [CrossRef] [PubMed]

5. Quinn, J.R.; Schmitt, M.; Baggs, J.G.; Norton, S.A.; Dombeck, M.T.; Sellers, C.R. Family Members' Informal Roles in End-of-Life Decision Making in Adult Intensive Care Units. *Am. J. Crit. Care* **2012**, *21*, 43–51. [CrossRef] [PubMed]
6. Morhaim, D.K.; Pollack, K.K. End-of-Life Care Issues: A Personal, Economic, Public Policy, and Public Health Crisis. *Am. J. Public Health* **2013**, *103*, e8–e10. [CrossRef] [PubMed]
7. Kitzinger, J.; Kitzinger, C. The "Window of Opportunity" for Death after Severe Brain Injury: Family Experiences. *Soc. Health Ill.* **2012**, *35*, 1095–1112. [CrossRef] [PubMed]
8. Coombs, M.; Long-Sutehall, T.; Shannon, S. International Dialogue on End of Life: Challenges in the UK and USA. *Nurs. Crit. Care* **2010**, *15*, 234–240. [CrossRef] [PubMed]
9. Cohen, M.J.; McCannon, J.B.; Edgman-Levitan, S.; Kormos, W.A. Exploring Attitudes toward Advance Care Directives in Two Diverse Settings. *J. Palliat. Med.* **2010**, *13*, 1427–1432. [CrossRef] [PubMed]
10. Vig, E.K.; Taylor, J.S.; Starks, H.; Hopley, E.K.; Fryer-Edwards, K. Beyond Substituted Judgment: How Surrogates Navigate End-of-Life Decision-Making. *J. Am. Geriatr. Soc.* **2006**, *54*, 1688–1693. [CrossRef] [PubMed]
11. Winzelburg, G.S.; Hansen, L.C.; Tulsky, J.A. Beyond Autonomy: Diversifying End-of-Life Decision-Making Approaches to Serve Patients and Families. *J. Am. Geriatr. Soc.* **2005**, *53*, 1046–1050. [CrossRef] [PubMed]
12. Bauer-Wu, S.; Yeager, K.; Norris, R.L.; Liu, Q.; Habin, K.R.; Hayes, C.; Jurchak, M. Communication and Planning at the End-of-Life: A Survey of Women with Advanced Stage Breast Cancer. *J. Commun. Healthc.* **2009**, *2*, 371–386. [CrossRef]
13. California Health Care Foundation. Final Chapter: Californians' Attitudes and Experiences with Death and Dying. 2012. Available online: http://www.chcf.org/~/media/MEDIA%20LIBRARY%20Files/PDF/PDF%20F/PDF%20FinalChapterDeathDying.pdf (accessed on 23 April 2017).
14. The Conversation Project. 2013. Available online: http://theconversationproject.org/wp-content/uploads/2013/09/TCP-Survey-Release_FINAL-9-18-13.pdf (accessed on 23 April 2017).
15. Carr, D.; Khodyakov, D. Health Care Proxies: Whom Do Young Adults Choose and Why? *J. Health Soc. Behav.* **2007**, *48*, 180–194. [CrossRef] [PubMed]
16. Silveira, M.J.; Kim, S.Y.H.; Langa, K.M. Advance Directives and Outcomes of Surrogate Decision Making Before Death. *N. Engl. J. Med.* **2010**, *362*, 1211–1218. [CrossRef] [PubMed]
17. High, D.M. Families' Roles in Advance Directives. *Hastings Cent. Rep.* **1994**, *24*, S15–S18. [CrossRef]
18. Kwak, J.; Haley, W.E. Current Research Findings on End-of-life Decision Making among Racially or Ethnically Diverse Groups. *Gerontologist* **2005**, *45*, 634–641. [CrossRef] [PubMed]
19. Meeker, M.A. Family Surrogate Decision Making at the End of Life: Seeing Them Through with Care and Respect. *Qual. Health Res.* **2004**, *14*, 204–225. [CrossRef] [PubMed]
20. Meeker, M.A.; Jezewski, M.A. Family Decision Making at the End of Life. *Palliat. Support. Care* **2005**, *3*, 131–142. [CrossRef] [PubMed]
21. Bute, J.J.; Petronio, S.; Torke, A.M. Surrogate Decision Makers and Proxy Ownership: Challenges of Privacy Management in Health Care Decision Making. *Health Commun.* **2015**, *30*, 799–809. [CrossRef] [PubMed]
22. Radwany, S.; Albanese, T.; Clough, L.; Sims, L.; Mason, H.; Jahangiri, S. End-of-Life Decision Making and Family Burden: Placing Family Meetings in Context. *Am. J. Hosp. Palliat. Care* **2009**, *26*, 376–383. [CrossRef] [PubMed]
23. Kossman, D. Prevalence, Views, and Impact of Advance Directives among Older Adults. *J. Gerontol. Nurs.* **2014**, *40*, 44–50. [CrossRef] [PubMed]
24. Hsieh, H.; Shannon, S.E.; Curtis, J.R. Contradictions and Communication Strategies during End-of-Life Decision Making in the Intensive Care Unit. *J. Crit. Care* **2006**, *21*, 294–304. [CrossRef] [PubMed]
25. Ohs, J.E.; Trees, A.R.; Gibson, C. Holding On and Letting Go: Making Sense of End-of-Life Care Decisions in Families. *South. Commun. J.* **2015**, *80*, 353–364. [CrossRef]
26. Kramer, B.J.; Kavanaugh, M.; Trentham-Dietz, A.; Walsh, M.; Yonker, J.A. Predictors of Family Conflict at the End of Life: The Experience of Spouses and Adult Children of Persons with Lung Cancer. *Gerontologist* **2009**, *50*, 215–225. [CrossRef] [PubMed]
27. Winter, L.; Parks, S.M. Family Discord and Proxy Decision Makers End-of-Life Treatment Decisions. *J. Palliat. Med.* **2008**, *11*, 1109–1114. [CrossRef] [PubMed]

28. Parks, S.M.; Winter, L.; Santana, A.J.; Parker, B.; Diamond, J.J.; Rose, M.; Myers, R.E. Family Factors in End-of-Life Decision-Making: Family Conflict and Proxy Relationship. *J. Palliat. Med.* **2011**, *14*, 179–184. [CrossRef] [PubMed]
29. Khodyov, D.; Carr, D. The Impact of Late-Life Parental Death on Adult Sibling Relationships: Do Parent's Advance Directives Help or Hurt? *Res. Aging* **2009**, *31*, 495–519. [CrossRef] [PubMed]
30. Rodgers, R.H.; White, J.M. Family Development Theory. In *Sourcebook of Family Theories and Methods: A Contextual Approach*; Boss, P.G., Doherty, W.J., LaRossa, R., Schumm, W.R., Steinmetz, S.K., Eds.; Plenum Press: New York, NY, USA, 1993; pp. 225–257.
31. Salazar, A. An Analysis of the Development and Evolution of Roles in the Small Group. *Small Group Res.* **1996**, *27*, 485–503. [CrossRef]
32. Stamp, G.H. The Appropriation of the Parental Role through Communication During the Transition to Parenthood. *Commun. Monogr.* **1994**, *61*, 89–112. [CrossRef]
33. Deaux, K.; Major, B. Putting Gender into Context: An Interactive Model of Gender-Related Behavior. *Psychol. Rev.* **1987**, *94*, 369–389. [CrossRef]
34. Lincoln, Y.S.; Guba, E.G. *Naturalistic Inquiry*; Sage Publications: Newbury Park, CA, USA, 1985.
35. Glaser, B.G.; Strauss, A.L. *The Discovery of Grounded Theory: Strategies for Qualitative Research*; Aldine: Chicago, IL, USA, 1967.
36. Braun, U.K.; Beyth, R.J.; Ford, M.E.; McCullough, L.B. Voices of African American, Caucasian, and Hispanic Surrogates on the Burdens of End-of-life Decision Making. *J. Gen. Intern. Med.* **2007**, *23*, 267–274. [CrossRef] [PubMed]
37. Chatfield, D.A.; Lee, S.; Cowley, J.; Kitzinger, C.; Kitzinger, J.; Menon, D.K. Is There a Broader Role for Independent Mental Capacity Advocates in Critical Care? An Exploratory Study. *Nurs. Crit. Care* **2017**. [CrossRef] [PubMed]
38. Levine, C.; Zuckerman, C. The Trouble with Families: Toward an Ethic of Accommodation. *Ann. Int. Med.* **1999**, *130*, 148–152. [CrossRef] [PubMed]
39. Breslin, J.M. Autonomy and the Role of the Family in Making Decisions at the End of Life. *J. Clin Ethics* **2005**, *11*, 15–18.
40. Abbott, K.H.; Sago, J.G.; Breen, C.M.; Abernethy, A.P.; Tulsky, J.A. Families Looking Back: One Year After Discussion of Withdrawal or Withholding of Life-sustaining Support. *Crit. Care Med.* **2001**, *29*, 197–201. [CrossRef] [PubMed]
41. Ketrow, S.M.; DiCioccio, R.L. Family Interaction in Consequential or Crisis Decisions. *China Media Res.* **2009**, *5*, 81–86.
42. Blank, R.H. End-of-Life Decision Making Across Cultures. *J. Law Med. Ethics* **2011**, *39*, 201–214. [CrossRef] [PubMed]

behavioral sciences

MDPI

Article

How Older Adults and Their Families Perceive Family Talk about Aging-Related EOL Issues: A Dialectical Analysis

Nichole Egbert *, Jeffrey T. Child, Mei-Chen Lin, Carol Savery and Tammy Bosley

School of Communication Studies, Kent State University, Kent, OH 44242-001, USA; jchild@kent.edu (J.T.C.); mlin@kent.edu (M-C.L.); csavery@kent.edu (C.S.); tbosley5@kent.edu (T.B.)
* Correspondence: negbert@kent.edu; Tel.: +1-330-672-3314

Academic Editor: Maureen P. Keeley
Received: 13 February 2017; Accepted: 14 April 2017; Published: 17 April 2017

Abstract: For older adults, approaching end-of-life (EOL) brings unique transitions related to family relationships. Unfortunately, most families greatly underestimate the need to discuss these difficult issues. For example, parents approaching EOL issues often struggle with receiving assistance from others, avoiding family conflict, and maintaining their sense of personhood. In addition, discussions of EOL issues force family members to face their parents' mortality, which can be particularly difficult for adult children to process emotionally. This study explored aging issues identified by aging parents and their families as they traverse these impending EOL changes. Ten focus groups of seniors ($n = 65$) were conducted. Focus groups were organized according to race (African-American/European-American), gender, and whether the older adult was living independently or in an assisted care facility. When asked open-ended questions about discussing aging and EOL issues with family members, participants revealed tensions that led us to consider Relational Dialectics Theory as a framework for analysis. The predominant tension highlighted in this report was certainty versus uncertainty, with the two sub-themes of sustained life versus sustained personhood and confronting versus avoiding EOL issues. For these data, there were more similarities than differences as a result of gender, race, or living situation than one might expect, although culture and financial status were found to be influential in the avoidance of EOL discussions. The results of this study help to provide additional insight into relational dialectics related to aging, EOL, and the importance of communication in facilitating family coping.

Keywords: end-of-life (EOL); relational dialectics theory (RDT); older adults (OA); aging; families

1. Introduction

In 2014, the number of Americans 65 years and older was 45.2 million. By 2060, this group will number 98.2 million, nearly one in four U.S. residents [1]. Based on these numbers, one would think that aging and end-of-life (EOL) issues would inhabit a prominent place in American discourse. However, older individuals and their families still greatly underestimate the need to discuss end-of-life (EOL) issues, even when family members approach old age. Fewer than 50% of adult children discuss EOL issues with their aging parents [2,3]. There are various explanations for why families avoid these discussions. Hummert and Morgan [4] suggest that discussions of aging-related issues may force family members to face unavoidable issues related to mortality, which can be particularly difficult for adult children to process emotionally. Old age also creates uncertainty for parents as they struggle between receiving assistance from others, maintaining personal independence, and providing continuous nurturance and support to other family members [5]. To investigate this issue further, this study explores the tensions felt by older adults and their families and how the tensions constrain and shape conversations about EOL issues.

Aging-related EOL negotiations and decisions are clearly communicative in nature and thus are best understood through the lens of communication theory. Relational Dialectics Theory (RDT) is well-suited for investigating the interplay of opposing forces such as those experienced by older adults and their families regarding the discussion of EOL issues [6]. "Dialectical tensions are the conflicts felt between two or more opposing forces, frames, or themes" [6] (p. 548). Although RDT conceptualizes dialectical tensions as opposites, other factors can also play important roles. For example, the interdependent nature of the opposing forces is equally critical. In other words, there cannot be tension or interplay without interdependence. In essence, the elements are unified at the same time they are opposites.

Thus, RDT helps us to understand how we construct meaning for our relational experiences through the interplay of competing discourses [7]. Relationships, themselves, are created through conversation [8]. Furthermore, Baxter and Norwood [7] emphasize that conversation includes an utterance chain, which means that all dialogue is connected to the past and the future. The utterance chain demonstrates that RDT is not linear. The conversational aspect highlights both the history and the ongoing nature of the relationship. Additionally, we see instances of power and struggle within discourse. However, Baxter and Norwood [7] do not see these two components as negative. Power and struggle are important because they lead relationships into what Baxter and Norwood describe as turning points.

A turning point is some sort of change in the relationship brought on by a transformative event, such as an illness or relocation due to aging [6,9]. Turning points, arguably, provide a better explanation than stage models in terms of understanding how relationships progress over time [10]. Turning points can be positive or negative, or a combination of both. For example, a tragedy might prompt relational partners to be grateful for their relationship. Interestingly, relational partners do not necessarily identify the same turning points.

RDT is an elegantly simple theory [7]. The core components of the theory (e.g., dialectical tensions and turning points) provide the appropriate foundation to investigate what happens to relationships as we age and face major turning points in life, such as confronting EOL decisions. To that end, we offer the following research questions:

RQ$_1$: What are the inherent tensions embedded in the discourse of older adults with their families about end-of-life (EOL) issues?

Although it is informative to investigate this discourse broadly, as researchers, we also understand the heterogeneity of human experience, especially as it exists in the experiences of different cultural groups. To this end, Morycz [11] argues that "each ethnic and minority group retains its own individual meaning of family structure and family caregiving" (p. 68). One's cultural understanding of old age or EOL affects how family members approach these topics in conversation. For example, although younger family members from Eastern cultures such as China and Japan report more respect for their elders than younger adults from Western cultures, they also find intergenerational communication more problematic [12]. Latinos living in the U.S. are incredibly family-centric, but avoid EOL discussions to a much greater extent than white, non-Latinos in the U.S. [13].

Along the same lines, cultural understandings of both "family" and "gender" are always changing, however, there is still recent evidence that family caregivers tend to be female and that women do more domestic labor and are more likely to seek medical care than men [14]. Thus, in keeping with previous research that has found differences between ethnic and gender groups with regard to aging issues [15,16], we explore:

RQ$_2$: How do these inherent tensions differ based on the gender, ethnicity (African American/ European-American), and living situation (living independently/living in a residential care facility) of older adults?

Behav. Sci. **2017**, *7*, 21

2. Materials and Methods

2.1. Participants

Participants were purposely selected and placed into one of eight distinct focus groups using a theoretical sampling technique. Because the two original focus groups of the independent-living African American (A-A) participants were much smaller than the other groups, we added two more groups—one additional group for A-A independent-living women, and one additional group for A-A independent-living men. In addition, the experiences of individuals who live on their own were expected to differ markedly from those of individuals who require daily assistance in their activities. Thus, four focus groups were planned with independent-living seniors, and four with assisted-living seniors living in a long-term care facility. Separate focus groups were arranged according to race, and male and female focus groups were also held independently. In the end, the eight focus groups were as follows: independent-living A-A men (2 groups), independent-living European-American (E-A) men, independent-living A-A women (2 groups), independent-living E-A women, assisted-living A-A men, assisted-living E-A men, assisted-living A-A women, and assisted-living E-A women. These eight groups, along with two doubled groups, yielded a total of ten focus groups.

To recruit focus group participants, we contacted area senior centers, churches, nursing homes, and assisted living homes. A member of each participating organization then advertised the study to members. In total, participants were recruited from one senior center ($n = 37$), one church group ($n = 11$), and two nursing home/long-term care facilities ($n = 17$). In all, 65 seniors participated in the ten focus groups, averaging approximately six to seven individuals per group. The study included 33 female participants (50.8% of the sample) and 32 male participants (49.2%). The average focus group participant age was 75 years old ($M = 74.95$; $SD = 9.98$). Regarding marital status, the majority of participants was still married (34 participants, 52.3%), with 17 seniors widowed (26.2%), nine seniors single (13.8%), and five seniors divorced (7.7%). The average senior had three children ($M = 3.28$; $SD = 2.27$). Educational attainment was varied, with 14 seniors (22%) having some high school, 20 (31.7%) with a high school diploma, 13 (22.2%) having some college, and 15 (23.8%) with a graduate degree or some post-graduate education. Focus group members received a $25 gift card for their participation in the study.

2.2. Procedures

To increase comfort and self-disclosure in focus groups, the researchers used gender and ethnicity to determine focus group membership [17]. In each case, the focus group moderator was over 50 years old and matched to the focus group participants according to ethnicity, gender, or both ethnicity and gender. The focus group moderators were experienced interviewers who were well-versed in the goals and dynamics of qualitative focus group interviews.

2.3. Data Analysis

The researchers used a semi-structured interview protocol to guide the focus group discussion. Open-ended questions sparked conversation among participants and enabled them to build on one another's responses, thus yielding more natural data. Probes were used when necessary to clarify participants' responses. The focus groups each lasted approximately 60–90 min, and were audiotaped and transcribed verbatim for further analysis. In the end, the transcripts comprised 159 single-spaced pages of text.

The researchers used open, axial, and selective coding to analyze the data [18]. During the first phase of open coding, the researchers individually read through the transcripts and identified emergent categories of dialectics. The researchers then compared their codes by applying them to the first focus group transcript and developing a codebook, which was subsequently used to analyze and interpret the remaining transcripts. After discussing the fit of these codes and making revisions where necessary, the codebook was finalized.

Once the codebook was finalized, the researchers coded the transcripts using axial coding, a strategy in which a set of defined codes are applied to the data. The unit of analysis was a turn of talk, and more than one code could be applied to each turn of talk. However, no matter how many times a participant discussed a particular code in a turn of talk, each code was only counted once per unit of analysis. Two researchers independently coded each transcript. Any disagreements on the fit of codes were discussed among all researchers until consensus was reached.

3. Results

The focus of this current study was on EOL issues (specifically wills and distribution of property, living wills, funerals, etc.). Older adults discussed how they communicated (or did not communicate) with family members about these topics. The prominent dialectic that colored these focus group narratives was that of certainty versus uncertainty. This theme depicts the opposing desires of knowing exactly what is happening or going to happen versus not worrying about the unknown. (1) *Sustained life* versus *sustained personhood* and (2) *avoiding aging and end-of-life issues* versus *confronting them* were prominent sub-themes for this dialectic. Previous research suggests that individuals differ in their demands for certainty and uncertainty, and that managing uncertainty is vital for relational well-being [19].

Often, participants' communication with family members was viewed as an important tool for dealing with the uncertainty of EOL. An independent-living, A-A woman shared, "I saw how quickly changes come about. How unpredictable life is, you know, and that everybody needs to be prepared in the family, you know, and that, and I constantly talk to my family." Sometimes older adults' uncertainty can make it difficult for family members to provide support. For example, an independent-living, E-A female shared how uncomfortable this uncertainty is for both her and her daughter, "Our daughter wants to know if she's doing what Mom would be happiest with and Mom doesn't know what she'd be happiest with."

On the other hand, seniors without strong family bonds may turn to others to help cope with uncertainty about EOL. For instance, there were voices that expressed gratitude for the certainty of life in a care facility, as described by one assisted-living A-A woman, "We don't know how we [are] gonna be treated at home. But you know when you come in here and be here a couple of weeks, somethin' like, you know how you gonna be treated." Thus, the dialectic of certainty versus uncertainty was often expressed as a relative concept, with participants weighing their current set of circumstances against another perceived situation, either one that they witnessed in the lives of other people or one that they, themselves, had previously experienced.

3.1. Sustained Life Versus Sustained Personhood

This sub-category was described as the struggle for older adults to choose between factors that may sustain their physical lives or their overall personhood by either allowing or not allowing extensive medical interventions at the EOL stage. For example, one independent-living E-A male was cognizant of making decisions about quality of life, "And uh, I made up my mind I went to see my wife's uncle in Medina, and he was on the iron lung that was keeping him alive … Don't you ever do that to me. I said that's not living … " The importance of communicating quality of life desires to the family was reiterated by an independent-living A-A female, "I've talked with my children and siblings … I wouldn't want to be on life support unless it was something that would make a positive difference." The word "unless" in the second excerpt clearly suggests the dialectic tension as her responses switched back and forth between sustaining life and sustaining personhood.

The sustained life versus sustained personhood tensions were also linked to the uncertainty/certainty of respecting religious beliefs. An independent-living A-A female discussed the sanctity of her beliefs even though her husband did not share them,

"My children, three of my children are Jehovah's Witnesses and three of my immediate family members are Witnesses, so you know, I know they will be there … My husband is very much aware of my wishes that I want, only be on the machine if the neurologist says, well there's some brain waves, she may come through. But longer than a week, I think that a punishment. Don't keep me on that machine ... I know they will all be there and do what I asked them to do, simply because they are of the same faith."

In this case, it is not only the woman's personhood that was at stake, but her ability to do what she saw as consonant with God's will.

3.2. Avoiding Aging and EOL Issues Versus Confronting Them

This tension was described as evading thoughts or conversations about aging and death versus dealing with them directly within the family unit. The E-A focus group members (regardless of living situation) typically spoke of ways in which their EOL plans were in order. One independent-living E-A woman shared, "I talk with my daughter, my son too, but my daughter especially, with anything. They got all my papers, double my insurance. They got everything in the safety deposit box." On the other hand, an independent-living A-A female discussed her mixed feelings in confronting EOL issues, "I'm with the group that, uh, contemplates it and has not just gotten around to it yet. Looked at it, talked about it, read the entire booklet, and looked at it but just didn't act on it." Avoidance of EOL issues was shared by an independent-living A-A male who discussed preparing a living will, "I haven't done any of this. I mean, I've done a lot of talkin' but in terms of puttin' things down on paper, I think I'm too young to be. But it looks like I better start."

Other older adults shared stories of reluctance to communicate about EOL issues, either from the family or within themselves. An independent-living A-A female recounted, "Basically, they don't want to hear it because it is like, I'm planning my demise or something, you know? And I'm saying, really I'm just trying to prepare you guys in case I do leave this world early." One of the A-A women in the assisted-living home spoke of not wanting to communicate at all about EOL issues, "I didn't even talk about it. I haven't talked about it. Whatever they want to do after I'm gone, do it ... If you gonna burn me, burn me, if you gonna put me in the ground, put me in the ground. I don't know anything about it anyway."

When comparing the transcripts of the A-A focus groups with the E-A focus groups, there were more similarities than differences. Recent research shows that both E-A and A-A elders prefer to remain at home until the demands of their care exceed personal and family resources [20]. That being said, the independent-living African Americans in our focus groups spoke vehemently against the idea of nursing homes. One independent-living A-A woman said she was open to the idea but her family would not hear of it, "To me it would be sound to put me in one place and then you come and visit and see to me. Oh no, oh no, no you're not goin' there." Another woman from the same group concurred, "There's no way. [My daughter] would die first before she put me in a nursing home." This aspect of African-American culture was brought to the forefront in the independent-living A-A male focus groups, regarding avoidance of EOL planning. One independent-living A-A man explained that, "Basically and this is what happens to a lot of us in the Black community and the Black culture, is that we never prepare ourselves for the day we go into the ground."

4. Discussion

The findings of this study easily merge with the larger corpus of relational dialectic research dealing with families. Talk about relationships is a vital part of the coping process for families during relationship turning points [21]. Toller [22] provided some more specific advice for families in transition, such as teaching others how to communicate with you, taking initiative in conversations, communicating needs clearly, and being open and willing to talk about important issues even when you are not comfortable. Conflict is another important aspect of relationship change, so when it arises between family members, it is important to recognize opposing needs and manage them through discourse, conflict resolution, or mediation [23]. In the case of these families of older adults, both parties frequently reported avoiding conversations about EOL because they did not want to think about the death of their loved one. Many people fear that bringing up taboo topics would damage relationships or bring about some other negative outcome [22,24]. Alternatively, Zhang and Siminoff [25] suggest that silence serves to protect the other person (or oneself) from psychological stress and emphasizes positive thinking. Unfortunately, avoiding discussions of EOL only delays the confusion and conflict until another day, which may be precipitated by a destabilizing life event such as a major illness or accident. Although one may never be fully prepared for the changing family dynamics of older adulthood, direct communication about relationships and EOL can allow family members to negotiate some of the more pressing relational tensions before a crisis occurs.

Relational Dialectics Theory provided a helpful lens for considerations of the multiple competing goals that exist in all family relationships, but especially in situations involving older adults. Other helpful theoretical perspectives have also been used to lend insight to EOL family issues, such as Politeness Theory [26], Communication Privacy Management Theory [27], and the Theory of Motivated Information Management [28]. These studies and others that focus on family communication at EOL all grapple with when and how to initiate difficult conversations related to aging and EOL. Although these various theories differ somewhat in their strategies, they share an emphasis on the importance of collaboration and mutual respect in these family discussions.

Any distinctions based on gender, living status or race/culture in this study are only exploratory, as the study included only a small sample of individuals from one geographic region in northeast Ohio. African-American reticence may have roots in cultural distrust of local residential care agencies. However, research shows that A-A residents are more likely to report experiences and fears of discrimination occurring in long-term care facilities [20]. Culture, poverty, as well as historical discrimination and mistreatment on the basis of race may partially explain why only 27% of A-A nursing home residents have a living will as compared with 63% of E-A older adults residing in nursing homes [29]. Thus, culture and financial status may still play an important role in how older adults communicate about EOL issues with family members. Based on our findings, we did not determine that gender played a significant role in perceptions of family conversations related to EOL.

5. Limitations

Based on these transcripts and the subsequent analysis, conversations about EOL need to be understood in the broader context of family communication. The conclusions derived from these ten focus groups are not intended to be generalizable, but rather illustrative of the complex and multi-layered tensions experienced by older adults and their families. For example, although we sought to acknowledge the roles of ethnicity and culture in aging by including both African American and European American seniors in our study, other geographical, cultural, and/or situated groups of seniors may experience tensions not named here. In addition, the arrangement of focus groups that isolated participants based on gender, race/culture, and living status may have de-emphasized the similarities that are shared amongst these groups. However, family research on families of color in later life is scant at best and in need of further exploration [30].

Author Contributions: N.E., J.C., and M.-C.L. conceived the study and analyzed the data, C.S. served as moderator and prepared all data for analysis, N.E. and T.B. wrote the paper.

Conflicts of Interest: The authors declare no conflict of interest.

References

1. U.S. Census Bureau. Available online: http://www.census.gov/newsroom/facts-for-features/2016/cb16-ff08.html (accessed on 27 January 2017).
2. Bromley, M.C.; Blieszner, R. Planning for Long-Term Care: Filial Behavior and Relationship Quality of Adult Children with Independent Parents. *Fam. Relat.* **1997**, *46*, 155–162. [CrossRef]
3. Pecchioni, L.L. Implicit Decision-Making in Family Caregiving. *J. Soc. Pers. Relationsh.* **2001**, *18*, 219–237. [CrossRef]

4. Hummert, M.L.; Morgan, M. Personal and Familial Identity in Later Life: Decision-Making About Lifestyle Changes. Presented at the Annual Meeting of the International Communication Association, San Francisco, CA, USA, 25 May 1997.

5. Pinquart, M.; Sörensen, S. Ethnic Differences in Stressors, Resources, and Psychological Outcomes of Family Caregiving: A Meta-Analysis. *Gerontologist* **2005**, *45*, 90–106. [CrossRef] [PubMed]

6. Baxter, L.A.; Erbert, L.A. Perceptions of Dialectical Contradictions in Turning Points of Development in Heterosexual Romantic Relationships. *J. Soc. Pers. Relationsh.* **1999**, *16*, 547–569. [CrossRef]

7. Baxter, L.A.; Norwood, K.M. Relational Dialectics Theory. In *The International Encyclopedia of Interpersonal Communication*; Roloff, M., Berger, C., Eds.; Wiley-Blackwell: New York, NY, USA, 2015; pp. 1–9.

8. Baxter, L.A. A tale of two voices: Relational dialectics theory. *J. Fam. Commun.* **2004**, *4*, 181–192. [CrossRef]

9. Baxter, L.A.; Bullis, C. Turning points in developing romantic relationships. *Hum. Commun. Res.* **1986**, *12*, 469–493. [CrossRef]

10. Baxter, L.A.; Braithwaite, D.O.; Nicholson, J.H. Turning points in the development of blended families. *J. Soc. Pers. Relationsh.* **1999**, *16*, 291–314. [CrossRef]

11. Morycz, R. Caregiving families and cross-cultural perspectives. In *Caregiving Systems: Informal and Formal Helpers*; Zarit, S.H., Pearlin, L.I., Schaie, K.W., Eds.; Erlbaum: Hillsdale, NJ, USA, 1993; pp. 67–73.

12. Pecchionio, L.L.; Otta, H.; Sparks, L. Cultural Issues in Communication and Aging. In *Handbook of Communication and Aging Research*; Nussbaum, J.F., Coupland, J., Eds.; Lawrence Erlbaum: Mahwah, NJ, USA, 2004; pp. 167–207.

13. Kreling, B.; Selesky, C.; Perret-Gentil, M.; Huerta, E.E.; Mandelblatt, J.S. "The Worst Thing about Hospice is That They Talk About Death": Contrasting Hospice Decisions and Experience amount Immigrant Central and South American Latinos with U.S. Born White, non-Latino Cancer Caregivers. *Palliat. Med.* **2010**, *24*, 427–434. [CrossRef] [PubMed]

14. Raley, S.; Bianchi, S. Sons, Daughters, and Family Processes: Does Gender of Children Matter? *Annu. Rev. Sociol.* **2006**, *32*, 401–421. [CrossRef]

15. Depaola, S.J.; Griffin, M.; Young, J.R.; Neimeyer, R.A. Death Anxiety and Attitudes toward the Elderly among Older Adults: The Role of Gender and Ethnicity. *Death Stud.* **2003**, *27*, 335–354. [CrossRef] [PubMed]

16. Phipps, E.; True, G.; Harris, D.; Chong, U.; Tester, W.; Chavin, S.I.; Braitman, L.E. Approaching the End of Life: Attitudes, Preferences, and Behaviors of African-American and White Patients and Their Family Caregivers. *J. Clin. Oncol.* **2003**, *21*, 549–554. [CrossRef] [PubMed]

17. Krueger, R.A.; Casey, M.A. *Focus Groups: A Practical Guide for Applied Research*, 3rd ed.; Sage Publications: Thousand Oaks, CA, USA, 2000.

18. Strauss, A.; Corbin, J. *Basics of Qualitative Research: Grounded theory Procedures and Techniques*, 2nd ed.; Sage: Newbury Park, CA, USA, 1990; pp. 1–13.

19. Baxter, L.A.; Montgomery, B.M. *Relating: Dialogues and Dialectics*; The Guilford Press: New York, NY, USA, 1996.

20. Hutchinson, S.; Hersch, G.; Davidson, H.A.; Chu, A.; Mastel-Smith, B. Voices of Elders: Culture and Person Factors of Residents Admitted to Long-Term Care Facilities. *J. Transcult. Nurs.* **2011**, *22*, 397–404. [CrossRef] [PubMed]

21. Cissna, K.N.; Bochner, A.P.; Cox, D.E. The Dialectic of Marital and Parental Relationships within the Stepfamily. *Commun. Monogr.* **1990**, *57*, 44–61. [CrossRef]

22. Toller, P.W. Negotiation of Dialectical Contradictions by Parents Who Have Experienced the Death of a Child. *J. Appl. Commun. Res.* **2005**, *33*, 46–66. [CrossRef]

23. Erbert, L.A. Conflict and Dialectics: Perceptions of Dialectical Contradictions in Marital Conflict. *J. Soc. Pers. Relationsh.* **2000**, *17*, 638–659. [CrossRef]

24. Baxter, L.A.; Wilmot, W.W. Taboo Topics in Close Relationships. *J. Soc. Pers. Relationsh.* **1985**, *2*, 253–269. [CrossRef]

25. Zhang, A.Y.; Siminoff, L.A. Silence and Cancer: Why do Families and Patients Fail to Communicate? *Health Commun.* **2003**, *15*, 415–429. [CrossRef] [PubMed]

26. Pitts, M.J.; Fowler, C.; Fisher, C.L.; Smith, S. Politeness Strategies in Imagined Conversations Openers about Eldercare. *J. Lang. Soc. Psychol.* **2014**, *33*, 29–48. [CrossRef]

27. Petronio, S. Communication Privacy Management Theory: What do we Know About Family Privacy Regulation? *J. Fam. Theory Rev.* **2010**, *2*, 175–196. [CrossRef]

Behav. Sci. **2017**, *7*, 21

28. Fowler, C.; Afifi, W.A. Applying the Theory of Motivated Information Management to Adult Children's Discussions of Caregiving with Aging Parents. *J. Soc. Pers. Relationsh.* **2011**, *28*, 507–535. [CrossRef]
29. Troyer, J.L.; McAuley, W.J. Environmental Contexts of Ultimate Decisions: Why White Nursing Home Residents Are Twice as Likely as African American Residents to Have an Advance Directive. *J. Gerontol. Psychol. Sci.* **2006**, *61*, S194–S202. [CrossRef]
30. Silverstein, M; Giarrusso, R. Aging and Family Life: A Decade Review. *J. Marriage Fam.* **2010**, *72*, 1039–1058. [CrossRef] [PubMed]

behavioral sciences

MDPI

Article

Dementia at the End of Life and Family Partners: A Symbolic Interactionist Perspective on Communication

Christopher Johnson [1,*], Jordan Kelch [1] and Roxanna Johnson [2]

[1]   Department of Sociology, 601 University Drive, Texas State University, San Marcos, TX 78666-4684, USA; j_k92@txstate.edu

[2]   Gerontologist and Dementia Specialist, Aging Consultants, Austin, TX 78733, USA; agingconsultants@gmail.com

*   Correspondence: cjj38@txstate.edu; Tel.: +1-512-245-5693

Academic Editor: Maureen P. Keeley

Received: 19 June 2017; Accepted: 4 July 2017; Published: 9 July 2017

Abstract: People with dementia are not dying; they are experiencing changes in the brain. This paper utilizes a symbolic interaction theoretical perspective to outline communicative alternatives to polypharmacy. There is a growing interest in sociological interventions to untangle the "disordered discourses" associated with dementia. Such practices challenge common stigmas attached to dementia as an "ongoing funeral" or "death certificate." Changing the expectations, attitudes and communication patterns of family care partners can positively impact them and the person living with dementia at the end of life. This paper delineates multiple non-verbal communication interventions (e.g., the trip back in time, dementia citizenship and sensory engagement modalities) to explore techniques to engage persons with advanced dementia.

Keywords: communication; symbolic interaction; end of life; family care partners; persons living with dementia

1. Introduction

This article uses a symbolic interactionist perspective to view the salience of developing ways to communicate with end of life persons living with dementia. This paper is about radical social change in care partnering with the "persons living with dementia" (PLWD). Elements of symbolic interactionist theory provide an explanation of experiences and communication patterns of PLWD and their significant others at the end of life [1,2]. The phrase "end of life" is used as a relative term because the dying process begins at birth. PLWD are not dying from their diseases, they are living with them. Moreover, they are aging like all of us; some are aging more rapidly than others. This paper disrupts the commonly held assumptions about end of life dementia care. The authors further inspect partnerships and offer new therapeutic symbols to surround such relationships. When you enter the social world of a PLWD at the end of life, there are already well formed negative public perceptions driven by sociological forces of stigma and ageism [3]. This paper focuses on social exclusion and loss of dementia citizenship and offers strategies to alter family interactions and communication styles to more effectively connect with PLWD at the end of life. The symbolic interactions suggested are non-normative and offer methods of making social connections at the end of life with PLWD with aphasia. All PLWD have disabilities with unexplored abilities and it is those unexplored strengths that we seek to identify for families. The medical definition of dementia views dementia as loss. The Alzheimer's Association website defines dementia as a general term for the loss of memory and other mental abilities severe enough to interfere with daily life [4]. However, this paper follows the experiential school of thought which defines dementia as a "shift in the way we experience the world" [5].

2. Family Perceptions of End of Life Dementia as Tragedy and Loss

Sociologist W.I. Thomas developed a theory of sociology which maintains, "If men define situations as real, they are real in their consequences" [6] (p. 62). In the context of the disease model of dementia, the subjective interpretation of being diagnosed with the label of dementia influences actions on both the part of the "patient" and the family. In partnerships, all participants negotiate shared meanings. Family behaviors are affected by negative views of dementia that already exist in American culture. Drawing on the work of W.I. Thomas, Sociologist Robert Merton maintains that any definition of a situation influences the present [7]. The negative expectations and behaviors of loved ones do adversely affect PLWD. Societal views which associate aging with memory loss are common and such stigmas affect the perceptions of family members [3]. It is possible for negative stigmas to be projected onto the PLWD by significant others [8].

Dementia as a tragedy motif has a long history in American medicine. Gerontologists today attack traditional symbolic representations of dementia as loss [9]. Some scholars point out that symbolic meanings attached to the label dementia are interpreted, embodied, or resisted by families in their social contexts [10]. These processes are shaped according to their social location (ethnicity, gender, and social class) and each PLWD's social history. The PLWD's "death certificate" is not signed with the label dementia. The tragedy lies in the social consequences of stigmas attached to diagnostic labels, described in the United Kingdom mainstream press as a "panic blame discourse" producing views of dementia as inevitable loss and decline while simultaneously telling stories about ways of staving off the disease [10]. This reframes dementia as something within the realm of individual choices and suggests a potential judgment of PLWD as not having aged successfully. Gerontological literature over the years has been full of negative labels for dementia associating it with dying. Decades ago, social workers described the grieving process of families who live with a PLWD as experiencing an "ongoing funeral" [11]. As a result, finding a positive or hopeful view of the disability of dementia amidst such "malignant" metaphors are virtually impossible [12].

A physician study discusses the lack of reciprocity in family members caring for PLWD in end of life conditions [13]. Physicians can offer more positive views of dementia as a disability with abilities. Doctors are in a position to dispel myths, stereotypes and stigmas of dementia with family members. The emphasis is on the potential that medical professionals have to educate care partners of PLWD by providing information on better non-verbal communication techniques at the end of life [13]. Implementing these skills would enhance PLWD's ability to reciprocate. For example, "Such changes have implications for improved care and quality of life through the continued maintenance of social inclusion and perceptions of personhood" [13] (p. 1). Doctors can take the lead in destigmatizing PLWD as persons with disabilities rather than persons who are dying or dead. Studies focusing on dementia as a tragedy theme are prolific and point out different ways in which dementia is experienced negatively. They also suggest that the cultural meanings attached to dementia vary by society [14]. Sociological research in India delineates cultural representations of dementia as being mixed with other symbolic meanings such as the social expectations of aging [15]. By understanding the different symbols attached to dementia that are culturally-based, families can identify how particular meanings associated with dementia govern others' behaviors and are sociologically significant [16]. This perspective allows families to see the implications of cultural representations for those living with dementia, and how these implications may differ according to a person's socio-cultural background.

Industrialized societies offer a proliferation of scary dementia stories and labels that are reflected in mainstream media, fictional books and literature. Accounts of dementia present this condition as a kind of living death for its sufferers and to their family members [17]. Some have argued that both the bio-medicalization of dementia and the social construction of PLWD as "zombies" create fear of the disease [18]. Likewise, this fear marginalizes and disempowers a person given the label of dementia [16]. Public fear translates into "dehumanization based on disgust and terror and influences perceptions of family members, including children" [18] (p. 70). Such symbolic representations create public reactions of revulsion and fear of losing your mind that people associate with aging. The language of loss and determinism pervades these cultural symbols of ageism and stigma. For example, the rising tide of dementia has been described as a "tsunami", suggesting an unstoppable wave [19]. As a result, these stigmas lay the ground work for negative perceptions for families of persons with dementia [18]. Kitwood [12] referred to a "malignant social psychology" of dementia, where families experience unfair discrimination, disempowerment and prejudices (stigma, stereotyping etc.) directed toward their loved one with dementia [12]. Others have used such examples as the foundation for his theory of "malignant social positioning" [20]. Labels of PLWD as "dying" or being in a "vegetative state" serve as triggers for the frequent social disengagement of family members, especially at the end of life.

3. End of Life and the 'Trip Back in Time'

Johnson and Johnson's concept of the 'trip back in time' offers a paradigm which explains how persons experience time travel through the cognitive, emotional, social, physical and functional domains with Alzheimer's disease (AD) [9]. The 'trip back in time' utilizes a downward spiral diagram with connecting loops (see Figure 1) to demonstrate the fluctuating, non-linear, but progressive course of the disability. The 'trip back in time' from age of onset back to early childhood is both fluid and fluctuating for the AD person. The 'trip back in time' model can account for the person's ability to fluctuate in both memory and recognition of family members as they travel back through time. The capabilities of the AD persons vary throughout, beginning with the changes in short term memory followed by long term memory. The AD person's physical time travel traverses from normal to super human strength, to reduced ambulation, and finally to the fetal position (i.e., bedridden) similar to a baby in the womb. The connecting loops progressing downward also account for adult development in reverse as identified by previous research [21]. Additionally, the 'trip back in time' model allows for the non-linear variances on a daily basis through time travel in all domains. The connected loops demonstrate how an AD person can make small or quantum leaps springing up from the past to the present for brief periods of time. Past studies have suggested theoretical time travel although it had not been identified as a 'trip back in time' to infancy or what is referred to here as end of life care [9]. Ironically, both the bedridden AD person who has time traveled back to infancy and the infant are more in touch with their emotions than any other time in their life. This is a time when emotions are raw with no pretenses. It is healthy to be in touch with emotions although it can make families uncomfortable, especially when PLWD express sadness, loneliness or pain by crying.

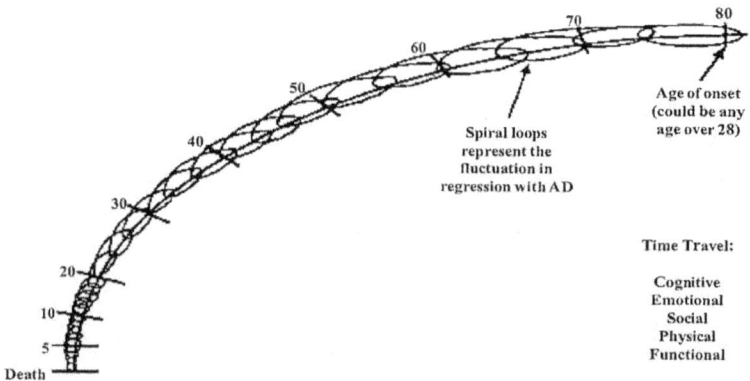

Figure 1. Alzheimer's disease (AD) as a "trip back in time".

Case Study, Susan and Dan: An 80-year-old woman named Susan diagnosed with AD experiences a downward spiral back and forth through time, traveling and revisiting persons, pleasant and traumatic events that occurred throughout her life. She travels in her mind back to age 20 and no longer recognizes significant others who are currently in her life but does recognize pictures of her parents and siblings. Imagine that Susan is visited by her nuclear family and grandchildren but she mislabels or mixes up the generations calling her son by her husband's name. The family is frustrated by these actions and assumes Susan is confused or "crazy."

Again, Susan has traveled back to age 20 in her mind and upon looking in the mirror sees an 80-year-old face and asks "What are you doing in my bathroom?" All along it was the same person, Susan, with cognitive fluctuations. Later, Susan's 84-year-old husband Dan enters her room and identifies himself as her husband, although in her mind she is 20 years old. When Dan identified himself as her husband he imposed his "reality" (time frame and definition of the self) upon Susan. This is extremely confusing for Susan and can trigger aggression and fear of Dan. Validation of the AD person's experiences is empowering for them because to them the experiences are real [22]. Therefore, care partners are trained on how to roughly identify where their loved one with AD is in the time travel experience [22]. Then, they validate the AD person's definition of the situation and self. Validations are accomplished through various forms of non-verbal communication such as sharing old pictures of family and friends from yesteryear in photo albums, listening to music from the person's distant past and other special interests. Instead of labeling the person as having delusions, care partners are trained to recognize the 'trip back in time' process, no longer invalidating their reality [22]. Understanding the 'trip back in time' model and how to join one on their time travel journey with appropriate communication can help avoid the frustration and heartache from an unnecessary reality orientation. Families who understand this model refrain or resist identifying current grandchildren and nuclear family members. These care partners will instead join the person on the trip back in time to connect in their time frame.

4. Symbolic Interactions with End of Life PLWD

For family care partners who are in daily interaction with PLWD, the symbolic label "dementia" triggers grief due to many social factors. Such disease labels cause a great deal of frustration and pain for families as they attempt to deconstruct their view of the self of the PLWD. Families grieve the person (self) they once knew and then try to reconstruct a new "dementia as tragedy" view of the PLWD in what symbolic interactionists call the "sick role." Family usually see the loved one as a "victim of a disease" rather than a person with a disability. This can be the case when there is lack family dementia education in understanding time travel and a more holistic view of the disability through the disease process.

There is a great deal of ambiguity around how social expectations drive care partners' behaviors. Loved ones wonder what kind of roles should be enacted, what to say and what to do around PLWD in the new status of being bedridden. Significant others either adjust their behaviors to accommodate PLWD or they choose to disengage, usually with justifications for doing so. Communications and interactions between PLWD, professionals and family care partners construct a perceptual framework for what needs to be done. Culture and society play a role in this construction as well. Some of this framework is based upon the preconceived views of significant others (family and friends) about PLWD's bedridden status and her inability to verbally communicate. This perception of "an ongoing funeral" for PLWD is socially negotiated and constructed, aided by stereotypes and the media. The meanings constructed of the life of the bedridden persons are created by symbolic interactions that are shared between the PLWD, staff and significant others within the culture in which they live. It is through dementia education that care partners can learn how to effectively join the end of life PLWD on their 'trip back in time.'

Behav. Sci. **2017**, *7*, 42

5. Medicalized Care and End of Life Dementia Care

Bedridden PLWD who are in distress in institutions are often sedated with medications. However, family care partners who understand the role of medications at the end of life dementia care can be advocates for sociological interventions when appropriate. An astounding statistic is that 13% of the population comprises elders over 65 years of age, yet they consume 34% of prescription drugs [23]. According to some, the pharmaceutical industry is driven by profit and most other concerns are usually secondary [24]. Elders are the largest consumers of prescription medications [25]. End of life dementia care has been increasingly medicalized over the course of the past few decades. Some medications are necessary when caring for PLWD due to frequent comorbid health conditions [26]. Polypharmacy or over use of medications can be excessive and it does impact social engagement between the family care partners and the PLWD. There is a plethora of new research on sociological interventions for end of life PLWD. The sociological (non-pharmaceutical) interventions for end of life care can be overlooked by an emphasis on medical solutions to distress in PLWD [27]. Recent literature suggests that quality of life for PLWD can be significantly improved when the pharmacological treatment is sufficient but not excessive [27]. Anti-psychotic medications are often utilized as both treatment and chemical restraint when the care plan does not expressly limit their use [28,29].

Pain or discomfort is frequently difficult for PLWD to communicate, especially if they are deemed non-communicative [30]. As a result, family care partners in long- term care environments may stop making efforts that directly affect medications and dosages. Research suggests that under and overmedication as a result of poor communication can increase cognitive impairments in PLWD [31]. A recent study interviewed doctors and disclosed that anti-psychotic medications were frequently prescribed based on the PLWD's exhibition of aggression or anger [32]. For the bedridden PLWD, behavioral symptoms can accompany chronic boredom or loneliness due to sociological factors or lack of social engagement and meaningful activities [33].

6. Sensory Engagement Modalities for End of Life Person Centered Care

A critical concept in the school of symbolic interactionism is that there is no social life without communication and shared symbols [1]. There is, in effect, no self. However, by maintaining positive social engagement experiences for end of life PLWD, we avoid many medication interventions through expanded two-way communication opportunities. Families are challenged to learn and identify symbolic and non-verbal communication interactions or representations (such as pictures, touching, hugs, pointing, smiles, gestures and facial expressions etc.). A smile is a smile in any language. Here, family care partners are encouraged to learn to identify the PLWD's facial expressions as ways of understanding and communicating with them. During end of life care for PLWD, the borders between the self and environment merge so that care partners are challenged to communicate with persons with advanced dementia through the senses. For example, interventions such as arts-based embodiment engagements like the use of elder clowns has been shown to encourage reciprocal communication between PLWD and their care partners [34]. The efficacy of interventions similar to this within the medical model may be limited, but from a sociological perspective they are meaningful.

Person centered care (PCC) seeks to maintain the self throughout the disability [35]. PCC promotes communication in self-determination and empowerment for PLWD, and has been shown to generate better communication outcomes in some situations as opposed to the biomedical approach [36]. At the early stages, PCC can relieve some of the intense stress that accompanies diagnosis for both PLWD and care partners [37]. PCC is a way to connect family care partners to PLWD in highly idiosyncratic ways, drawing from the PLWD's person centered life history that relates to sensory stimulation. In order to establish PCC with PLWD, care partners can learn how to frame interactions in a manner that generates new meanings within the realm of competencies that PLWD maintain at any given point in their disability [38]. PCC is an alternative to the predominately medical approach to clinical care for PLWD as it attempts to link the person's lifelong habits and behaviors with their 'trip back in time.'

Activating the five senses (taste, touch, smell, hearing and sight) of the end of life PLWD is a way for family care partners to connect. For example, family care partners have access to the relevant information on the PLWD's 'trip back in time.' Creating photo albums using enlarged photos from the past offers better opportunities for recognition, visual stimulation and non-verbal communication. Family care partners are in a difficult situation because the photos often do not include them but instead the PLWD's family of origin, parents and siblings. This is an example of how ego can inhibit positive communication. Opportunities abound for family care partners who see the possible benefits of these interventions and aim to help PLWD.

Verbal communication is difficult when PLWD are bedridden. Namaste is an end of life or late stage dementia care program that utilizes the five senses to cultivate communication with PLWD [39]. The Namaste program is provided 7 days a week and staffed by specially trained persons who provide activities of daily living in a calm manner, with a "loving touch" approach to care [40]. The program takes place in a room with lowered lighting, soft music playing, and the scent of lavender nurturing PLWD to feel comforted, cared for, and cared about in a unique loving environment. Such programs are viewed as vehicles to emotionally connect with bedridden PLWD. By stimulating multiple senses, one can increase the chances of propagating positive interactions and communication. Accessing taste and smell can be achieved through cooking at the bedside using ingredients that produce odors, flavors and sounds from the past. Essential oils that emanate familiar smells and touch using massage, or simply holding hands to convey love and affection, are all legitimate forms of communication. Hearing music from one's past can evoke positive responses and connections. Other non-verbal forms of communication that are currently used include visual stimuli through Snoezelen (a multi-sensory stimulation therapy in a room created for delivering high levels of stimuli to PLWD), pet therapy, doll therapy, robotics, reminiscence therapy with objects and pictures, and other modifications to the milieu which are impactful [27,39].

7. Dementia Citizenship for End of Life Care

Citizenship is a human right that is bestowed on all persons. However, when people are diagnosed with dementia their citizenship is often stripped, similar to that of a prisoner, although they did not choose to have dementia. The concept of dementia citizenship is used in dementia studies to promote the status of discriminated groups of cognitively disabled persons. Dementia citizenship recognizes the self-cognizance of PLWD to exercise rights and responsibilities [41]. PLWD are entitled to live life fully until death. Although the notion of citizenship may not appear to be appropriate for persons with severe dementia in their limited decision-making abilities, it still assumes they want and deserve a full social engagement until death. The citizenship approach is a narrative framework in which a person is included in a community and granted the presumption of autonomy [42]. Research indicates that as a concept it is strongly linked to resilience, an important attribute in end of life care both for PLWD and care partners [30]. Optimizing the social integration and identity of PLWD can have a wide range of positive effects on their course of treatment and quality of life [16]. These outcomes provide incentives for family care partners to stay connected to PLWD.

During the course of time travel for PLWD, it becomes difficult to maintain integration and identity with their present and former self. Identity, in this sense, is inextricably tied to agency that is so important to dementia citizenship. Autonomy, in this sense, is the ability for a person to determine their own life course and agency, and can be defined as a person's capacity to propel one's self along that life course. Dementia citizenship is the recognition of those capabilities. It is the treatment that a person receives when they are perceived and interacted with as unique individuals capable of making their own decisions.

The adaptive response to losses associated to those "living with" life-threatening illnesses change as circumstances change. The key is having compassion and genuinely caring for the person. Being with the person living with dementia has the potential to be a spiritual experience where nothing has to be said but hearts connect. The communication occurs on a number of levels. One of the authors found this to be true with his mother (who had dementia) just sitting with her and holding her hand [42]. PLWD go through daily adjustments to their disability. Among the tasks in coping with life-threatening illness the chronic phase is characterized by "living with the disease" [43]. Unlike compressed morbidity, with chronic morbidity the grief process is prolonged.

Dying is taboo in modernity but even worse is prolonged bedridden experiences. In industrialized countries like the U.S., Japan, or Europe, life-threatening illnesses put everything on pause. In such cultures, the care partner can create difficulties in communication and thwart family support of the PLWD. For example, lack of communication is a common issue among family members of bedridden PLWD [20]. Symbolic interaction and psychological constructivist theories have provided useful understandings of how families create and reconstruct meaning and identity in the midst of loss [44]. These understandings of living with a chronic illness are applicable to dementia [45]. Similar approaches may focus on the ways that meanings frame the process of dying. For example, it is helpful to postulate how individuals and families identify the self or another as "dying" and how these expectations affect subsequent interactions. Such work builds upon early theoretical work in the field [46].

8. Discussion

Family members are challenged to eliminate personal egos in dementia care. It is human nature to want to be recognized by PLWD, and to be disappointed when one is no longer known. Yet, with the framework of time travel, there will be a day when we cannot and should not continue reality orientation with PLWD. Social models of care outlined in this paper include the trip back in time; dementia citizenship and sensory engagement modalities for person centered end of life care. In such instances, family care partners play an important role in providing salient symbolic interactions for PLWD and this can add to the quality of life.

In the medical models, elders living at the end of life with dementia can become objectified. Medications are often used to stop PLWD from calling out for help, although such efforts are clear forms of communication to the staff. These residents are lonely and benefit from human contact and social engagement. Family care partners often feel powerless in the absence of training and education to understand how to communicate with their loved one. As change agents, clinical sociologists are interested in empowering families to learn new non-verbal ways to communicate at the end of life. For PLWD end of life care should be tailored to their life history, hobbies, and interests. In the book, *The Veneration of Life*, Diamond writes:

> "Alzheimer's is distinguished from most other diseases in that the ego becomes progressively smaller, allowing more and more of the innate Spirit to become apparent. In contrast, nearly all diseases are characterized by an increased self-concern. In fact, this may very well be at the root cause of the particular disease. As the patient surrenders to the disease, he becomes increasingly more ego-oriented, radiating ever less of his Spirit". [42] (p. 4)

The self, or ego, and environment of the bedridden PLWD become one [41]. End of life PLWD have withdrawn into their own social worlds and their vocabularies have shrunk. The environment which surrounds the PLWD becomes their world and their reality. This has immense implications for professional and family care partners who are challenged to use the five senses to effectively communicate with PLWD. End of life therapies have expanded considerably beyond the medical model in the past few years to symbolically link the milieu with PLWD in a powerful dialectic. Treatments that minimize or distract from the depersonalizing experiences that accompany institutionalization include Namaste, Snoezelen and various therapeutic modalities [39,47]. The end of life is full of opportunities to engage in meaningful social connections. The interventions discussed in this paper offer new paradigms for social engagement that can enhance communication.

9. Conclusions

The sociological interventions that deconstruct excessively medicalized dementia care include meaningful social connections for end of life persons with dementia. When family members are empowered by learning how to interact on symbolic levels with PLWD and join them in their time travel, powerful connections can be made. Family dementia education can result in change, while bringing joy to the life of bedridden persons living with dementia.

Author Contributions: Christopher Johnson provided the conceptual and theoretical idea for this paper, as well as the bulk of the writing. Jordan Kelch provided an annotated review of the current literature and research support. Roxanna Johnson contributed emphasis on persons living with dementia and human rights implications for dementia citizenship. Christopher Johnson and Roxanna Johnson formulated the concept of dementia as a 'trip back in time' and applied it to a new body of literature. All three authors edited the manuscript once complete.

Conflicts of Interest: The authors declare no conflict of interest.

References

1. Blumer, H. *Symbolic Interactionism: Perspective and Method*; Prentice-Hall: Englewood Cliffs, NJ, USA, 1969.
2. Mead, G.H. *Mind, Self and Society*; University of Chicago Press: Chicago, IL, USA, 1934; Volume 111.
3. Dobbs, D.; Eckert, J.K.; Rubinstein, B.; Keimig, L.; Clark, L.; Frankowski, A.C.; Zimmerman, S. An ethnographic study of stigma and ageism in residential care or assisted living. *Gerontologist* **2008**, *48*, 517–526. [CrossRef]
4. Alzheimer's Association. 2017. Available online: http://www.alz.org/dementia/types-of-dementia.asp (accessed on 28 May 2017).
5. Power, G.A. *Dementia Beyond Drugs: Changing the Culture of Care*; Health Professions Press: Baltimore, MD, USA, 2010.
6. Smith, R.S. Contested memory: Notes on Robert K. Merton's "The Thomas Theorem and the Matthew Effect". *Am. Sociol.* **1999**, *30*, 62–77. [CrossRef]
7. Merton, R.K. The Thomas theorem and the Matthew effect. *Soc. Forces* **1995**, *74*, 379–422. [CrossRef]
8. Zimmerman, S.; Dobbs, D.; Roth, E.G.; Goldman, S.; Peeples, A.D.; Wallace, B. Promoting and protecting against stigma in assisted living and nursing homes. *Gerontologist* **2016**, *56*, 535–547. [CrossRef] [PubMed]
9. Johnson, C.J.; Johnson, R.H. Alzheimer's disease as a "trip back in time". *Am. J. Alzheimer's Dis. Other Demen.* **2000**, *15*, 87–93. [CrossRef]
10. Peel, E.; Harding, R. 'It's a huge maze, the system, it's a terrible maze': Dementia carers' constructions of navigating health and social care services. *Dementia* **2014**, *13*, 642–661. [CrossRef] [PubMed]
11. Kapust, L.R. Living with dementia: The ongoing funeral. *Soc. Work Health Care* **1982**, *7*, 79–91. [CrossRef] [PubMed]
12. Kitwood, T. The dialectics of dementia: With particular reference to Alzheimer's disease. *Ageing Soc.* **1990**, *10*, 177–196. [CrossRef]
13. Gove, D.; Small, N.; Downs, M.; Vernooij-Dassen, M. General practitioners' perceptions of the stigma of dementia and the role of reciprocity. *Dementia* **2016**. [CrossRef] [PubMed]
14. Faure-Delage, A.; Mouanga, A.; M'belesso, P.; Tabo, A.; Bandzouzi, B.; Dubreuil, C.; Preux, P.; Clément, J.; Nubukpo, P. Socio-cultural perceptions and representations of dementia in Brazzaville, Republic of Congo, the EDAC survey. *Dement. Geriatr. Cogn. Disord. Extra* **2012**, *2*, 84–96. [CrossRef] [PubMed]
15. Cohen, L. *No Aging in India Berkley*; University of California Press: Berkeley, CA, USA, 1998.
16. Sabat, S.; Harrét, R. The Construction and Deconstruction of Self in Alzheimer's Disease. *Ageing Soc.* **1992**, *12*, 443–461. [CrossRef]
17. Dening, K.H.; King, M.; Jones, L.; Sampson, E.L. Healthcare decision-making: Past present and future, in light of a diagnosis of dementia. *Int. J. Palliat. Nurs.* **2017**, *23*, 4–11. [CrossRef] [PubMed]
18. Behuniak, S.M. The living dead? The construction of people with Alzheimer's disease as zombies. *Ageing Soc.* **2011**, *31*, 70–92. [CrossRef]
19. MacKinlay, E.; Trevitt, C. *Facilitating Spiritual Reminiscence for People with Dementia: A Learning Guide*; Jessica Kingsley Publishers: London, UK, 2015.

20. Sabat, S.R. Malignant positioning and the predicament of people with Alzheimer's disease. In *The Self and Others: Positioning Individuals and Groups in Personal, Political, and Cultural Contexts*; Haeer, R., Moghaddam, F.M., Eds.; Praeger: Westport, CT, USA, 2003; pp. 85–98.
21. Reisberg, B.; Ferris, S.H.; de Leon, M.J.; Crook, T. The Global Deterioration Scale for assessment of primary degenerative dementia. *Am. J. Psychiatry* **1982**, *139*, 1136. [PubMed]
22. Feil, N. *The Validation Breakthrough: Simple Techniques for Communicating with People with Alzheimer's-Type Dementia*; Health Professions Press: Baltimore, MD, USA, 1993.
23. Cruikshank, M. *Learning to Be Old: Gender, Culture and Aging*; Rowman & Littlefield Publishers: Lanham, MD, USA, 2003.
24. Smith, T.; Maidment, I.; Hebding, J.; Madzima, T.; Cheater, F.; Cross, J.; Poland, F.; White, J.; Young, J.; Fox, C. Systematic Review Investigating the Reporting of Comorbidities and Medication in Randomized Controlled Trials of People with Dementia. *Age Ageing* **2014**, *43*, 868–872. [CrossRef] [PubMed]
25. Deeks, L.S.; Cooper, G.M.; Draper, B.; Kurrle, S.; Gibson, D.M. Dementia, Medication and Transitions of Care. *Res. Soc. Adm. Pharm.* **2016**, *12*, 450–460. [CrossRef] [PubMed]
26. Wucherer, D.; Eichler, T.; Hertel, J.; Kilimann, I.; Richter, S.; Michalowsky, B.; Thyrian, J.R.; Teipel, S.; Hoffmann, W. Potentially Inappropriate Medication in Community-Dwelling Primary Care PLWDs Who Were Screened Positive for Dementia. *J. Alzheim. Dis.* **2016**, *55*, 691–701. [CrossRef] [PubMed]
27. Brooker, D.J.; Latham, I.; Evans, S.C.; Jacobson, N.; Perry, W.; Bray, J.; Ballard, C.; Fossey, J.; Pickett, J. FITS into Practice: Translating Research into Practice in Reducing the Use of Anti-psychotic Medication for People with Dementia Living in Care Homes. *Aging Ment. Health* **2015**, *20*, 709–718. [CrossRef] [PubMed]
28. Foebel, A.D.; Onder, G.; Finne-Soveri, H.; Lukas, A.; Denkinger, M.D.; Carfi, A.; Vetrano, D.L.; Brandi, V.; Bernabei, R.; Liperoti, R. Physical Restraint and Antipsychotic Medication Use Among Nursing Home Residents With Dementia. *J. Am. Med. Dir. Assoc.* **2016**, *17*, 184.e9–184.e14. [CrossRef] [PubMed]
29. Molist, B.N.; Sevilla-Sanchez, D.; Novellas, J.A.; Jana, C.C.; Gamez-Batiste, X.; Mcintosh, J.; Panicot, J.E. Optimizing Drug Therapy in PLWDs with Advanced Dementia: A PLWD-centered Approach. *Eur. Geriatr. Med.* **2014**, *5*, 66–71. [CrossRef]
30. Clarke, C.L.; Bailey, C. Narrative citizenship, resilience and inclusion with dementia: On the inside or on the outside of physical and social places. *Dementia* **2016**, *15*, 434–452. [CrossRef] [PubMed]
31. Monroe, T.B.; Misra, S.K.; Habermann, R.C.; Dietrich, M.S.; Cowan, R.L.; Simmons, S.F. Pain Reports and Pain Medication Treatment in Nursing Home Residents with and without Dementia. *Geriatr. Gerontol. Int.* **2013**, *14*, 541–548. [CrossRef] [PubMed]
32. Bonner, A.F.; Field, T.S.; Lemay, C.A.; Mazor, K.M.; Andersen, D.A.; Compher, C.J.; Tjia, J.; Gurwitz, J.H. Rationales That Providers and Family Members Cited for the Use of Antipsychotic Medications in Nursing Home Residents with Dementia. *J. Am. Geriatr. Soc.* **2015**, *63*, 302–308. [CrossRef] [PubMed]
33. Thomas, W.H. *Life Worth Living: How Someone You Love Can Still Enjoy Life in a Nursing Home: The Eden Alternative in Action*; Vander Wyk & Burnham: St. Louis, MO, USA, 1996.
34. Kontos, P.; Miller, K.L.; Colobong, R.; Lazgare, P.; Luis, I.; Binns, M.; Naglie, G. Elder-clowning in long-term dementia care: Results of a pilot study. *J. Am. Geriatr. Soc.* **2016**, *64*, 347–353. [CrossRef] [PubMed]
35. Doyle, P.J.; Rubinstein, R.L. Person-Centered Dementia Care and the Cultural Matrix of Othering. *Gerontologist* **2013**, *54*, 952–963. [CrossRef] [PubMed]
36. Molony, S.L.; Bouma, R. The Care Manager Role in Person-Centered Care for People with Dementia. *Generations* **2013**, *37*, 79–82.
37. Whitlatch, C.J. Centered-Person Care in the Early Stages of Dementia: Honoring Individuals and Their Choices. *Generations* **2013**, *37*, 30–36.
38. Livingston, G.; Lewis-Holmes, E.; Pitfield, C.; Manela, M.; Chan, D.; Constant, E.; Morris, J. Improving the end-of-life for people with dementia living in a care home: An intervention study. *Int. Psy.* **2013**, *25*, 1849–1858. [CrossRef] [PubMed]
39. Simard, J. *The End-Of-Life Namaste Care Program for People with Dementia*; Health Professions Press: Baltimore, MD, USA, 2007.
40. Simard, J.; Volicer, L. Effects of Namaste Care on residents who do not benefit from usual activities. *Am. J. Alzheimers. Dis. Other Demen.* **2010**, *25*, 46–50. [CrossRef] [PubMed]
41. Bartlett, R.; O'Connor, D. From personhood to citizenship: Broadening the lens for dementia practice and research. *J. Aging Stud.* **2007**, *21*, 107–118. [CrossRef]

42. Diamond, J. *The Veneration of Life: Through the Disease to the Soul*; Enhancement Books: Bloomingdale, IL, USA, 2000.
43. Doka, K.J. *Living with Life-Threatening Illness*; Lexington Books: Lexington, MA, USA, 1993.
44. Nadeau, J.W. *Families Making Sense of Death*; Sage: Thousand Oaks, CA, USA, 1998; Volume 10.
45. Neimeyer, R.A. Death anxiety research: The state of the art. *Omega-J. Death Dying* **1998**, *36*, 97–120. [CrossRef]
46. Glaser, B.G.; Strauss, A.L. Discovery of substantive theory: A basic strategy underlying qualitative research. *Am. Behav. Sci.* **1965**, *8*, 5–12. [CrossRef]
47. Volicer, L.; Simard, J.; Pupa, J.H.; Medrek, R.; Riordan, M.E. Effects of continuous activity programming on behavioral symptoms of dementia. *J. Am. Med. Dir. Assoc.* **2006**, *7*, 426–431. [CrossRef] [PubMed]

behavioral sciences

MDPI

Article

Cancer Communication and Family Caregiver Quality of Life

Elaine Wittenberg *, Tami Borneman, Marianna Koczywas, Catherine Del Ferraro and Betty Ferrell

City of Hope Comprehensive Cancer Center, 1500 E. Duarte Road, Duarte, CA 91010, USA; tborneman@coh.org (T.B.); mkoczywas@coh.org (M.K.); cdelferraro@coh.org (C.D.F.); bferrell@coh.org (B.F.)
* Correspondence: ewittenberg@coh.org; Tel.: +1-626-256-4673

Academic Editor: Maureen P. Keeley
Received: 10 January 2017; Accepted: 28 February 2017; Published: 2 March 2017

Abstract: Family caregivers have enormous communication responsibilities tied to caregiving, such as sharing the patient's medical history with providers, relaying diagnosis and prognosis to other family members, and making decisions about care with the patient. While caregiver stress and burden has been widely documented in the caregiving literature, little is known about how communication burden, real or perceived communication challenges, impacts caregiver quality of life. In family caregiving, the City of Hope (COH) Quality of Life model proposes that the caregiving experience is reciprocal to the patient experience, impacting physical, social, psychological, and spiritual quality of life. We used data from a pilot study testing a communication coaching call intervention with family caregivers of lung cancer patients to analyze caregiver reported communication burden and quality of life. We found variances in each quality of life domain, suggesting that caregiver interventions should range from self-care skill building for physical care to psycho-educational interventions that support caregiver coping and communication skill building. These findings demonstrate the importance of caregiver assessment and attention to communication burden in quality cancer care.

Keywords: cancer; communication; oncology; family caregiving; caregiver; quality of life

1. Introduction

Family caregivers of lung cancer patients have challenging communication roles related to caregiving responsibilities [1]. Caregivers are often tasked with sharing news of the diagnosis, a complex role that involves making decisions about what information should be shared, when to share it, whether they or the patient should give the news, and how the news should be shared [2]. During treatment, disagreements between patient and caregiver can occur about treatment side effects and benefits as well as what to report to physicians [3]. Lung cancer caregivers may be further challenged with patient discussions about continued tobacco use [1]. Communication dilemmas occur between patient, family, and healthcare providers when the family caregiver struggles to meet the collective interests of others by keeping them informed yet maintain individual interests by withholding information about the patient or themselves [4]. These dilemmas arise when a caregiver reluctantly serves as a family caregiver to the patient (either because there are no other family members present or others are unwilling), when caregivers must make patient care decisions but are uninformed about the patient's wishes, or when collaboration with other family members is necessary yet family members do not have a history of collaboration. Difficult communication circumstances create communication burden [5,6], a concept we define as real or perceived communication challenges, and may impact caregiver quality of life.

Quality of life concerns of both patient and caregiver should be addressed throughout the cancer trajectory. The City of Hope Quality of Life (QOL) model [7] depicts four domains: physical, psychological, social, and spiritual as priorities for assessment to ensure comprehensive, holistic quality care. In a large, randomized controlled trial that included a tailored education intervention [8], caregivers identified patient fatigue, worry, fear, anger, cognitive changes, communication, advance directive planning, purpose and meaning, hope, and inner strength as the most common topics. While many of these topics are dependent on the caregiver's ability to convey these needs in order to receive support, there is little understanding of the impact of these quality of life domains and communication. Understanding communication burden in the caregiving experience could inform the design of communication interventions, potentially enhancing caregiver quality of life and decreasing stress. The goal of this study was to use the Quality of Life model to examine the four quality of life domains so as to aid in the future development of customized communication interventions.

2. Materials and Methods

The qualitative findings from a pilot study testing the acceptability and feasibility of a nurse-delivered communication coaching call intervention are presented here. The intervention was designed to improve caregiver confidence in communication with the patient, family members, and healthcare providers. During the call, the research nurse asked the caregiver the following: Who is the most challenging to talk to about cancer (the patient, family members, or healthcare providers)? What is the most challenging for you to talk about? When you think about having to talk about cancer, and you know it will be challenging, how does this impact you physically? Psychologically? Socially? Spiritually?

The intervention protocol was based on the City of Hope Quality of Life (QOL) model and was intended to explore how communication dilemmas impact family caregivers. The intervention protocol did not change over the course of data collection and was delivered by the same nurse to all caregivers. Data were collected from consenting caregivers of lung cancer patients in an outpatient setting of a comprehensive cancer center and was approved by the hospital's institutional review board.

2.1. Participants

Eligibility criteria included age 18 years of age or older, English-speaking, and primary family caregiver as identified by the lung cancer patient.

2.2. Procedure

Caregivers were approached by the research nurse during a routine clinic visit, an explanation of the study provided and written consent was obtained. After completing baseline questionnaires measuring psychological distress and confidence in communication, a date and time were set for the research nurse to call the following week to conduct the coaching call. Caregivers were given a copy of *A Communication Guide for Caregivers* © (2016, COMFORT Communication Project) [9] and asked to read the guide before the following week's call. Calls were digitally recorded and served as the corpus of data for this study.

2.3. Data Analysis

Transcripts from the digitally recorded discussions were analyzed by two coders over two research team meetings. Caregiver responses to each quality of life domain were grouped according to a direct qualitative approach [10], and grouped data was inductively analyzed using an iterative process of theme analysis [11]. Open coding was first used to identify chunks of text suggesting a theme, themes were collapsed or associated, and interpretive claims about each domain were identified through discussion within the research team. Through this process, we discerned themes within each quality of life domain. Demographic data were summarized using SPSS.

Behav. Sci. **2017**, *7*, 12

3. Results

Transcripts from communication coaching calls for 20 lung cancer caregivers were used for this analysis. The mean age of caregivers was 56.1 years. Most caregivers were Caucasian (80%), female (70%), and college-level educated (75%). The majority of caregivers were spouse/partner (65%). Table 1 shows a summary of caregiver characteristics. In the following section, we detail the thematic analysis of physical, psychological, social, and spiritual quality of life as it relates to caregiver communication burden. Figure 1 illustrates the QOL model with these themes.

Table 1. Caregiver characteristics.

Characteristic	$n = 20$ (%)
Age, mean (range)	56.1 (35–76)
Gender	
Female	14 (70%)
Male	6 (30%)
Relationship to Patient	
Spouse/Partner	13 (65%)
Adult child	6 (30%)
Other	1 (5%)
Education	
Secondary School	5 (25%)
College	15 (75%)
Hispanic Ethnicity	
Yes	4 (20%)
No	16 (80%)
Race	
African-American	1 (5%)
Asian	3 (15%)
Caucasian	16 (80%)
Employment Status	
At least 32 h	11 (55%)
Retired	7 (35%)
Self-employed	2 (10%)
Household Income	
$10,000 or less	1 (5%)
$20,001 to $30,000	2 (10%)
Greater than $50,000	14 (70%)
Prefer not to answer	3 (15%)

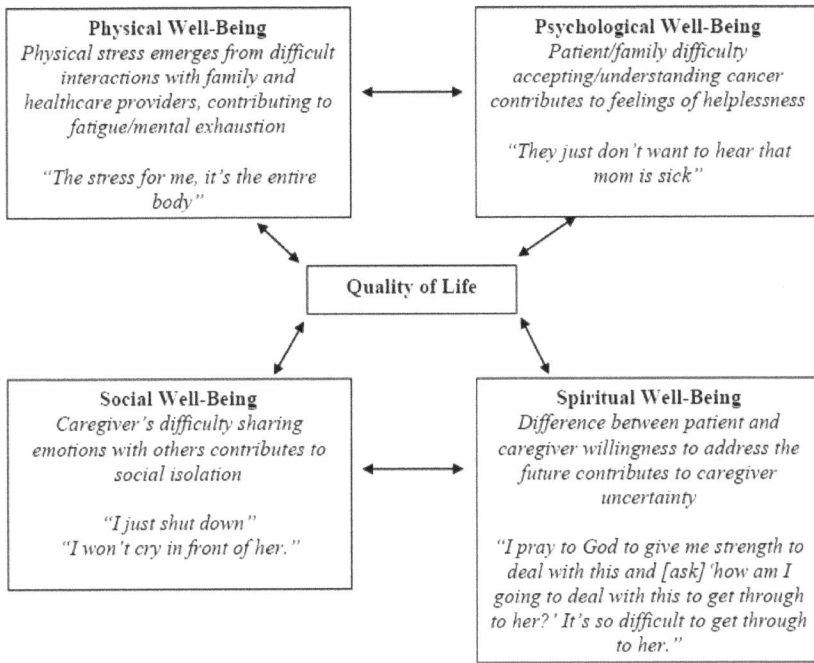

Figure 1. City of Hope Quality of Life model applied to caregiver communication burden.

3.1. Physical Well-Being

Physical well-being includes fatigue, sleep disruption, nausea, appetite (increase or decrease), and aches and pains from providing physical patient care. While the majority of caregivers described their own personal physical limitations due to illness or disability, they also described how communication burden was created by stress from difficult interactions. Stressful interactions contributed to feelings of fatigue and mental exhaustion. One caregiver described communication about her husband's cancer with her daughter: "It's mentally exhausting. She just stresses me out ... When we get into it, it's physically ... I start shaking and I can feel my blood pressure go up. I have headaches." Another caregiver shared that her blood pressure increases: "I lose my breath. When you take a deep breath and you kind of forget to take another breath ... the stress for me, it's the entire body."

Talking with healthcare providers was acknowledged as a physically stressful event. Reflecting on prior experiences with a particular physician, one caregiver explained: "It was horrible for me because I get choked up and I couldn't speak and I had heart palpitations." Other caregivers shared that they were anxious about sitting down to talk about the diagnosis or prognosis ("I feel nervous, especially if the news is not as good as had hoped") and doubted their "ability to communicate properly."

3.2. Psychological Well-Being

Psychological well-being includes feelings of anxiety, depression, helplessness, difficulty coping, and fear. Feelings of helplessness surfaced for caregivers when the patient or a family member had difficulty accepting or understanding the severity of the cancer diagnosis and treatment side effects. In one instance, a caregiver described how her husband's avoidance of cancer was problematic given her role as both a caregiver and mother: "We have a problem ... he doesn't want me to talk, to tell the kids. We haven't told our children because he doesn't want me to tell them ... Do I just go ahead and do it and go behind his back and tell them, or do I let him have this wish?" A lack of opportunity to discuss cancer with others left caregivers feeling helpless. There was an acute awareness among caregivers that others were unable to engage in conversations about cancer. Caregivers recognized clear attempts by others to block, ignore, or avoid discussions about cancer. One caregiver explained his daughter's unwillingness to talk about her mother's illness:

> "She just brushes it off and when you try to talk to her about it, she gets very frustrated about it because she doesn't want to accept that her mother might possibly pass on due to cancer ... So you really can't talk ... She just won't hear it ... She gets in this mood, so it's something you don't want to have to bring up."

In response to his daughter's reluctance to discuss the topic, this caregiver described reciprocally avoiding the topic in order to circumvent stress.

Communicating with children was identified as another form of communication burden as caregivers worried that talking about cancer would impact their child's psychological well-being. One caregiver described wanting to achieve a delicate balance of addressing the topic and keeping the child informed, yet not causing alarm: "I have to be very accurate, but at the same time cushion it and not cause induced stress." Another caregiver explained that she worried about the impact on her son: "Anything I say has immediate ramifications as to his mental well-being and this mood ... and lasting ramifications." The decision over whether or not to talk with children impacted psychological well-being for caregivers who often struggled with how to talk with kids about cancer:

> "We don't know what approach we should talk to them or even if we should not talk to them ... If we were to talk to them, how are we going to approach how they are going to understand."

Anxiety about communication caused caregivers to be mindful of how communication about cancer occurs with others, as one caregiver described: "It just took me awhile to think or how to approach what words I'm going to use to describe [her being sick] ... my wife doesn't even mention cancer ... we always say illness." Anxiety also triggered reflective thinking about the caregiver's own communication performance and strategies for communication:

> "It was just this continuous dialogue in my head after I've spoken with them ... you know, I probably should have said or that I didn't convey things properly ... I have increasing anxiety afterwards ... after the conversation that I didn't convey my message properly."

> "They refuse to hear, see above my mom's illness or they don't bother to ask. I have to take the initiative and make the conversation and try to see how I could talk about it with them."

3.3. Social Well-Being

Role adjustment, changes to relationships, leisure activities, and employment impact social-well being, sometimes leading to isolation. Difficulty sharing emotions and feelings about cancer added to communication burden and caregivers described withdrawing from others to avoid communication. One caregiver shared that he wanted to protect his wife by hiding his emotions: "I try to pretend I'm being tough (laughs) so I don't cry in front of her ... I just swallow it ... my emotions." Another caregiver summarized his family's indirect nature about his wife's cancer: "We really don't discuss that [cancer] much unless she has an episode or something while we are all together, but basically we don't bring it up as to how serious it is."

Emotional distancing was also illustrated as a way of avoiding communication and sharing feelings. Separating from others to avoid communication about cancer was shared by one caregiver: "I just shut down and change the subject and find a reason to leave the conversation or leave completely." A caregiver recalled learning about the initial cancer diagnosis from a radiologist and being asked to relay the news to her mother. In thinking about sharing this news with her mother, she described: "I wanted to disappear and go into a black hole and not think about it ... because my mom was still in the wheel chair and my dad with her ... I didn't even want to see my mom. I was completely shut down." Another woman explained: "Actually right now we are avoiding. We don't talk to most family ... a lot of my further family, I can't talk about him [patient]. I can't discuss it." Engaging in social isolation was a way of navigating communication burden.

3.4. Spiritual Well-Being

Feelings of uncertainty, a search for hope and meaning, and religiosity all comprise spiritual well-being. Communication burden was created when there was a difference between patient and caregiver willingness to address feelings of uncertainty and explore the meaning of illness. One caregiver shared that "talking about the cancer outcome as far as the quality of life or what's to come ... that's what makes it more challenging ... talking about the cancer and what's the future." Caregivers felt nervous communicating with the patient about the disease and "not wanting to go in certain directions with the conversations." Fear of upsetting the patient was a concern for one caregiver: "I know he will get disappointed. He will get upset. I don't want him to go through that. Emotionally, for me, it would be hard for ... to let him know about those [sic] stuff." When asked to describe the biggest barrier to communicating better, another caregiver replied, "Not knowing, the unknown, not knowing what's going to happen ... because right now it's arrested somewhat but it has not disappeared." "It's hard for me to talk to him (patient)." Another caregiver articulated the same for his family: "I have a level of acceptance that is relatively high, and they have a level of acceptance that is relatively low, and it makes it difficult to talk."

On the other hand, there was an absence of communication burden described by caregivers with spiritual beliefs. Caregivers described that a sense of spirituality gave them strength to have conversations about cancer with others: "I have to work myself up to it (talking with family) and talk with my higher power about how I am going to approach this next conversation." Praying together was also identified as a way of engaging in conversations about cancer and the future. Notably, a patient's deep religious beliefs were characterized as enabling open conversation about illness: "I think the strongest support has been our whole family's strong spiritual belief."

4. Discussion

The QOL model is a theoretical framework that offers a way to understand the impact of cancer caregiving. The model outlines four domains as the components for caregiver assessment. Our aim in this study was to describe how communication burden impacts caregiver quality of life in each domain. An extensive meta-analyses has shown that interventions with family caregivers of cancer caregivers result in improved quality of life [12], and the analyses presented here extends the use of the QOL model to understand how communication negatively impacts caregiver quality of life, thus informing the need for future interventions to include caregiver assessment and communication skills training content.

Findings from this study confirm that caregiver quality of life is impacted by stress about communication across all domains. Future intervention content should address the caregiver's unique communication role by (a) including a baseline assessment of caregiver communication skills; (b) providing intervention materials and content that teach new communication skills, especially for sharing difficult news with others; and (c) measures of communication that assess the efficacy of teaching communication to family caregivers. For example, a caregiver communication skills training program may be organized by the quality of life domains and include ways to take practice self-care (physical well-being), suggestions for how to share concerns or feelings (psychological well-being), ways to ask for help from other family members and healthcare providers (social well-being), and example questions to ask to explore life meaning and purpose (spiritual well-being).

Initiating conversations was identified in this study as a critical role for caregivers that caused stress and burden, impacting their quality of life. Among cancer caregivers, relationship quality between patient and caregiver is an important contextual factor that aids caregiver coping and impacts the caregivers' stress process [13]. In the present study, caregivers reported a clear understanding of the need to bring up topics in order to carry out caregiving duties and how this would evoke stress. When conversations about caregiving and patient care were blocked by the patient or family members, this created communication-related burden that impacted caregiver quality of life. Future intervention research should include attention to the caregiver's role in sharing information with other family members and friends about the patient's cancer. Caregiver interventions that include communication skills building have the potential to decrease caregiving burden related to role changes and improve caregiver quality of life [14].

Prior research has documented that the lung cancer experience has a profound impact on the well-being of both patient and family caregiver and is largely influenced by communication within the family environment [15,16]. Lung cancer caregivers attempt to protect the patient and maintain hope by avoiding discussions about the diagnosis and illness trajectory [17]. The desire to protect each other results in topic avoidance between caregiver and patient, impacting communication with other family members and healthcare providers. Communication avoidance from patient and family members was reported by caregivers in this study, impacting caregiver psychological and spiritual quality of life. Communicating with children about cancer was also identified as a challenging caregiving task characterizing communication burden, and future research should address the need for caregivers to learn new skills for relaying and sharing news to children within the family structure.

Research on adult children caring for a parent with lung cancer found that emotional overload was common and that negative emotions resulted in communication avoidance [5]. Patient anxiety is associated with family's avoidance of cancer communication [18,19] and can be triggered by conflict with family members [20]. Disagreements between patient and caregiver are also associated with depression [3] and can impact the caregiver's ability to provide care [15]. Findings from this study demonstrate that caregivers need skill training in how to navigate topic avoidance, geographic distance of key family members, and changing family relationships [5].

Limitations

During the communication coaching call, not all caregivers commented on all QOL domains. Thus, this analysis may not have identified the proportion of caregivers who experienced a particular QOL domain communication issue. Among caregivers in this study, psychological well-being was impacted most by communication burden. However, this study is limited by a small sample size and a predominant sample of college-educated, Caucasian caregivers.

5. Conclusions

The findings of this study indicate that communication-related burden, as perceived by lung cancer caregivers, impacts all four QOL domains. When communication avoidance is apparent, it is important to address caregiver communication burden. Content for cancer caregiving interventions should include communication skill building, including strategies for self-care.

Acknowledgments: This pilot study was funded by the City of Hope Cancer Center Support Grant (P30CA33572; Rosen).

Author Contributions: Elaine Wittenberg and Betty Ferrell conceived and designed the study; Catherine Del Ferraro collected data; Elaine Wittenberg and Tami Borneman analyzed the data, with input from Betty Ferrell and Marianna Koczywas; Elaine Wittenberg and Tami Borneman wrote the paper.

Conflicts of Interest: The authors declare no conflict of interest.

References

1. Mosher, C.E.; Jaynes, H.A.; Hanna, N.; Ostroff, J.S. Distressed family caregivers of lung cancer patients: An examination of psychosocial and practical challenges. *Support Care Cancer* **2013**, *21*, 431–437. [CrossRef] [PubMed]

2. Ewing, G.; Ngwenya, N.; Benson, J.; Gilligan, D.; Bailey, S.; Seymour, J.; Farquhar, M. Sharing news of a lung cancer diagnosis with adult family members and friends: A qualitative study to inform a supportive intervention. *Patient Educ. Couns.* **2016**, *99*, 378–385. [CrossRef] [PubMed]

3. Zhang, A.Y.; Zyzanski, S.J.; Siminoff, L.A. Differential patient-caregiver opinions of treatment and care for advanced lung cancer patients. *Soc. Sci. Med.* **2010**, *70*, 1155–1158. [CrossRef] [PubMed]

4. Bonacichi, P. Communication dilemmas in social networks: An experimental study. *Am. Sociol. Rev.* **1990**, *55*, 448–459. [CrossRef]

5. Stone, A.M.; Mikucki-Enyart, S.; Middleton, A.; Caughlin, J.P.; Brown, L.E. Caring for a parent with lung cancer: Caregivers' perspectives on the role of communication. *Qual. Health Res.* **2012**, *22*, 957–970. [CrossRef] [PubMed]

6. Shaunfield, S. *"It's a Very Tricky Communication Situation": A Comprehensive Investigation of End-of-Life Family Caregiver Communication Burden*; University of Kentucky: Lexington, KY, USA, 2015.

7. Ferrell, B.R.; Dow, K.H.; Grant, M. Measurement of the quality of life in cancer survivors. *Qual. Life Res.* **1995**, *4*, 523–531. [CrossRef] [PubMed]

8. Eames, S.; Hoffmann, T.; Worrall, L.; Read, S. Delivery styles and formats for different stroke information topics: Patient and carer preferences. *Patient Educ. Couns.* **2011**, *84*, e18–e23. [CrossRef] [PubMed]

9. The Comfort Communication Project. A Communication Guide for Caregivers. Available online: www.communicatecomfort.com/resources (accessed on 1 March 2017).

10. Hsieh, H.F.; Shannon, S.E. Three approaches to qualitative content analysis. *Qual. Health Res.* **2005**, *15*, 1277–1288. [CrossRef] [PubMed]

11. Creswell, J.W. *Qualitative Inquiry and Research Design: Choosing among Five Traditions*; Sage: Thousand Oaks, CA, USA, 1998.

12. Northouse, L.L.; Katapodi, M.C.; Song, L.; Zhang, L.; Mood, D.W. Interventions with family caregivers of cancer patients: Meta-analysis of randomized trials. *CA Cancer J. Clin.* **2010**, *60*, 317–339. [CrossRef] [PubMed]

13. Fletcher, B.S.; Miaskowski, C.; Given, B.; Schumacher, K. The cancer family caregiving experience: An updated and expanded conceptual model. *Eur. J. Oncol. Nurs.* **2012**, *16*, 387–398. [CrossRef] [PubMed]

14. Waldron, E.A.; Janke, E.A.; Bechtel, C.F.; Ramirez, M.; Cohen, A. A systematic review of psychosocial interventions to improve cancer caregiver quality of life. *Psychooncology* **2013**, *22*, 1200–1207. [CrossRef] [PubMed]

15. Fujinami, R.; Otis-Green, S.; Klein, L.; Sidhu, R.; Ferrell, B. Quality of life of family caregivers and challenges faced in caring for patients with lung cancer. *Clin. J. Oncol. Nurs.* **2012**, *16*, E210–E220. [CrossRef] [PubMed]

16. Siminoff, L.A.; Wilson-Genderson, M.; Baker, S., Jr. Depressive symptoms in lung cancer patients and their family caregivers and the influence of family environment. *Psychooncology* **2010**, *19*, 1285–1293. [CrossRef] [PubMed]

17. Caughlin, J.P.; Mikucki-Enyart, S.; Middelton, A.; Stone, A.; Brown, L. Being open without talking about it: A rhetorical/normative approach to understanding topic avoidance in families after a lung cancer diagnosis. *Commun. Monogr.* **2011**, *78*, 409–436. [CrossRef]

18. Jeong, A.; Shin, D.W.; Kim, S.Y.; Yang, H.K.; Park, J.H. Avoidance of cancer communication, perceived social support, and anxiety and depression among patients with cancer. *Psychooncology* **2016**, *25*, 1301–1307. [CrossRef] [PubMed]

19. Chen, S.C.; Chiou, S.C.; Yu, C.J.; Lee, Y.H.; Liao, W.Y.; Hsieh, P.Y.; Jhang, S.Y.; Lai, Y.H. The unmet supportive care needs-what advanced lung cancer patients' caregivers need and related factors. *Support Care Cancer* **2016**, *24*, 2999–3009. [CrossRef] [PubMed]

20. Hendriksen, E.; Williams, E.; Sporn, N.; Greer, J.; DeGrange, A.; Koopman, C. Worried together: A qualitative study of shared anxiety in patients with metastatic non-small cell lung cancer and their family caregivers. *Support Care Cancer* **2015**, *23*, 1035–1041. [CrossRef] [PubMed]

behavioral sciences

MDPI

Article

Communication Matters: Exploring the Intersection of Family and Practitioner End of Life Communication

Leah M. Omilion-Hodges * and Nathan M. Swords

School of Communication, Western Michigan University, 1903 W Michigan Ave, Kalamazoo,
MI 49007-5318, USA; Nathan.M.Swords@wmich.edu
* Correspondence: Leah.Omilion-Hodges@wmich.edu; Tel.: +1-269-387-3149

Academic Editor: Maureen P. Keeley
Received: 31 January 2017; Accepted: 15 March 2017; Published: 19 March 2017

Abstract: After establishing a baseline understanding of some of the factors that influence and shape family end of life communication, empirical research centered on the communication tendencies of nationally-recognized palliative care clinicians is presented. Because death is no longer confined to the bedroom and individuals are increasingly turning to hospitals and health care institutes to assist with end of life, the role of palliative care practitioners is vital. To that end, common communication-rooted issues that may transpire among various medical personnel are explored. Focus on a shared underlying tension—care vs. cure—links the findings between family and palliative care clinician communication regarding end of life. Practical communication solutions and suggestions are offered to facilitate productive and mindful end of life communication between and among family members and health care practitioners.

Keywords: end of life communication; palliative care; contemporary approaches to end of life; dialectic tensions

1. Introduction

Oftentimes family communication about end of life (EOL) does not occur until circumstances force loved ones to have these conversations. Moreover, because families are not always preemptive in talking about the death and dying process coupled with the shift of where dying is occurring, these conversations are often taking place within hospitals and health care institutes. As such, health care professionals—commonly palliative care practitioners—become active participants and even leaders in facilitating family communication regarding EOL. Palliative care is patient-centered care, comfort, and support for individuals with chronic and terminal illness and is available to people at any age and at any state of illness unlike hospice.

The current research explores the intersection of palliative care practitioners' interpersonal and interprofessional communication and the impact practitioners' communication tendencies may have on families' EOL communication. More specifically, we focus on how contemporary end of life practices, such as the transition from death at home to death in the organizational setting, is prompting changes such as communal coping where patients, family members, and healthcare personnel collaborate to make EOL decisions.

Through previous work with nationally-recognized palliative care practitioners [1,2] and more current work with use of metaphors and euphemistic language to bridge the topic of death, we have found a common tension. The stress coiled between cure and care continues to complicate family end of life conversations much in the same way it can hinder the interprofessional relationships between medical professionals. The former, cure, aligns with the traditional biomedical approach to medicine that focuses on diagnosing and treating and largely advocates for prolonging life at all costs. This approach has been criticized for treating diseases rather than patients, where a lower quality of life or abatement of one's wishes may accompany the continued extension of life. Care, the latter, aligns with the more contemporary biosocial model that promotes a patient-centered approach inclusive of a patient's physical, emotional, spiritual, and psychological needs.

In this essay, we draw from two original data sets to trace the evolution of society's perceptions of death and how this transition impacts patients, their family members, and health care professionals. In this sense, communication becomes the vehicle through which we make sense of end of life, express or withhold our desires, and influence others whether we are a patient, a family member, or a clinician. Ultimately we leave readers with concrete, communication-rooted suggestions for initiating EOL conversations and for reducing the stigma often part and parcel with the subject. However, we begin by teasing out differences between traditional and contemporary approaches to death and dying and by showing how current practices impact family and practitioner conversations about EOL.

2. Contemporary Approaches to Death and Dying

Although death is a natural process, Western cultures have come to understand the end of life process as something we should avoid and privatize, particularly in the United States. Roughly 63% of Americans die while in hospitals, while an additional 17% die in other institutional settings such as hospice or palliative care [3]. The sustained shift from death at home to death in institutional settings has prompted changes within health care organizations. One transformation is the continued upsurge in palliative care (PC) programs.

PC delivers holistic care addressing patient physical, psychological, emotional, practical and spiritual needs at end of life or in concert with curative treatment. This progressive medical specialty employs individualized communication to provide relief and help alleviate the stress or confusion that may be associated with medical procedures in addition to helping mitigate family dynamics when necessary. Similarly, PC practitioners embrace patients' families as part of their charge and therefore, often become integral components of family EOL communication. When we consider the change of where dying occurs, it begs the question of how the location change influences EOL communication. Thus in many ways, the conversations that once occurred in a private residence among family are now more collaborative or communal in nature because of the desire to integrate health care facilities and personnel into the end of life process.

We now turn our attention to EOL communication, where we discuss the importance of these conversations from a family standpoint and from the perspective of PC practitioners. We then explore the intersection to illustrate how focusing on a tension common to patients, families, and practitioners privileges a powerful and productive starting point for making sense of and engaging in these pivotal discussions.

3. End of Life Conversations

Though often deflected, conversations about end of life can provide a buffer against emotional isolation, ensure that one's wishes are honored, and reduce possible miscommunication between medial teams, patients, and their families. Although beneficial, these conversations and even the word "death" is often evaded in communication surrounding end of life processes by both health care practitioners and lay people alike [4]. In its place, euphemistic expressions are favored as softer means to explain the harsh reality of death and dying [5]. The pervasiveness of avoiding talk about death and dying or using indirect or euphemistic language in U.S. American culture indicates a societal fear regarding end of life. In fact, death and the associated grieving process are often seen as a taboo topic and equated with a "disease" and something that one needs to quickly "get over" [6]. However, Western society's avoidance or fear of talking openly about death does more harm than good for individuals actively dying and for the bereaved.

Although in many ways death is an individualized experience, a multitude of interpersonal others are affected by one's EOL experience. Among other things, those we have relationships with provide us social support, inform the decisions we make regarding treatment, and ultimately survive us when we pass. A particularly salient group during EOL communication is our family.

3.1. Family End of Life Conversations

Paramount to family scholarship is the recognition that family communication involves a set of interrelated and interdependent parts and in order to be fully understood families should be viewed as a system. Structure, organization, and transactional patterns within the family system influence individual behavior and communication [7]. To fully understand EOL within the family, researchers must examine the interplay of individual, relationship specific (e.g., brother-sister, father-daughter) and overall family-level influences that emerge in communication.

One promising approach to family EOL conversations would be to recognize the communication patterns within the family. Family Communication Patterns (FCP) theorizing has a longstanding history in family scholarship, and has provided researchers and practitioners a means of predicting and measuring the ways in which families communicate with one another [8]. FCP measures families in terms of conformity—the degree of homogeneity in attitudes, values, and beliefs amongst family members, and conversation—the degree of participation amongst family members in unrestrained interaction that covers a wide range of topics. Based on these two orientations, families can be categorized as either (a) *consensual*—those high in conversation and conformity; (b) *pluralistic*—those high in conversation but low in conformity; (c) *protective*—those low in conversation but high in conformity; or (d) *laissez-faire*—those low in conversation and low in conformity. More recent scholarship has moved away from a trait-like approach to FCP to investigate how the theory may be used to conceptualize family communication as state-like and that patterns vary depending on topic [9]. This research argues that patterns of family communication reorient depending on the topic being discussed, and that families do not necessarily possess static communicative orientations that encapsulate all potential topics that emerge during interaction. Regardless if viewing family communication orientations as static patterns or contingent upon topic, EOL conversations represent a complex communication context for families due to the variation in individual, relational, and family-level degrees of conformity and conversation. Considering family communication patterns toward end-of-life communication enables practitioners to gauge desired content and the degree or amount of communication desired by families.

Similar to how families orient around EOL conversations based on degrees of conformity and conversation, families also employ patterned privacy rules that shape their orientations to privacy choices [10]. EOL conversations in the family are ripe with dialectical tensions of privacy-disclosure as family members must negotiate what information is beneficial or detrimental to share and with whom to share it with. In order to manage information dissemination and ownership, families must construct and socialize its members to boundary rules.

Boundary rules provide guidelines to family members about sharing jointly owned information internally, as well as sharing information to those external of the family system. Successful boundary management requires families to recognize who is fastened into the privacy boundary, to what degree each individual has ownership rights to information, and what information can or cannot be leaked to parties outside of the family. Others [10] have identified three orientations to information boundaries exercised by families: (a) highly permeable—families that are prone to disclose information to one another and those outside of the family; (b) moderately permeable—families that are more judicious in their choices about who knows family information both internally and externally; and (c) lowly permeable—families where private information is highly restricted and where thick boundary lines reside around information. When managed successfully, privacy boundaries give families the ability to govern private information. However, and as is likely the case in EOL conversation, boundary turbulence often occurs in four specific ways.

First, family members disclose unexpected private information to certain individuals and ask those they tell to keep it confidential. An example of this would be in EOL conversations where a father tells his oldest child about his terminal illness, but requests the son keeps the information from his younger siblings. Second, family members may stumble across information they feel should be shared, but find themselves in situation where either disclosing or concealing the information would result in hurting another family member. For example, if the son in the previous example were to find documentation about his father's diagnosis, the son may be at odds with addressing his father and concealing the information from his mother. Third, family members sometimes snoop and dig up information, but cannot act upon that information without admitting they've snooped. In this situation, the son may have shuffled through his dad's dresser drawer and found documentation, but doesn't want to admit he was rummaging through his dad's private information. Finally, family members must make choices about what is best for them compared to the family as a whole or a specific family member. In this case, the father may be a struggling with sharing the information about his diagnosis to his family, or concealing it for fear of hurting his family.

Examining family communication orientations to conversation and conformity, as well as the ways in which families control and share information, augments how challenging EOL communication may be for families. In order to best understand EOL communication within the family, it is necessary to recognize the interdependent nature of families and the transactional patterns that construct family life. Given the complications of EOL conversations, families often turn to practitioners in championing their decisions during end of life. However, practitioners often find themselves navigating their own unique set of complications and tensions during EOL communication.

3.2. Practitioner End of Life Conversations

Just as patients and their family members experience challenges in their EOL communication, practitioners too have to navigate various tensions. Palliative care clinicians, in particular, may find themselves in a precarious position. As medical professionals who frequently work with end of life patients and their families, they have been dubbed enforcers of death [11] because an initial purpose of the specialty was to predict the progression of an illness. Unfortunately, recent research [2] has revealed that this trend remains. That is, between the rise of the specialty and the incorporation of the communicatively oriented, patient-centered biosocial model of medicine, PC practitioners may be misunderstood and incur resistance from other medical professionals, while also shouldering the emotional weight of caring for patients with chronic and terminal illnesses.

Interprofessional communication among health care personnel of various disciplines is part of the challenge associated with practitioner EOL conversations. While collaboration among disparate medical areas, such as cardiology and palliative care, has been commonplace for decades and there is a hearty reliance on interdisciplinary healthcare teams, research continues to reveal misunderstandings, medical errors, and power struggles. Moreover, medical professionals tend to underestimate the importance of peers' roles and or value in the process and therefore, then tend to discount their opinions or suggestions [12,13]. Researchers have long suggested that a core challenge associated with interprofessional communication is the fact that each medical specialty anchors its focus only on areas "which the profession has selected for observation and concern" [14] (p. 1799). This then suggests that medical professionals largely reject assumptions or points that are contrary to their conceptual framework. Put simply, it is not necessarily the inability to communicate clearly across medical disciplines that hinders interdisciplinary collaboration and promotes medical mistakes, but rather the fact that individual specialties may subscribe to different and competing goals.

Omilion-Hodges and Swords [2] found that PC practitioners frequently navigate two primary communication challenges: living-dying and practicing-advocating. These dialectics—tension between two opposing forces—present clear complications for practitioners as they work to administer holistic care inclusive of end of life conversations with patients and their important others. For instance, unlike other medical specialties, such as orthopedics or obstetrics and gynecology, PC practitioners often have to explain their purpose, persuade others of their value, and answer the question of "why do I need a doctor to help me die?" As such, PC practitioners have indicated feeling as though they have to serve as spokespeople for the profession so that they continue to secure resources ranging from marketing communication materials to easily accessible physical space and additional hires. In this sense, PC physicians are not only medical practitioners who are actively working to minimize the pain, fear and stress commonly associated with death and dying, but are also cheerleaders for the profession [2].

Another, and more cumbersome, communication challenge PC practitioners face is the perceived conflict between the focus of palliative care and that of the larger medical community: Living-dying. While palliative care is frequently administered in tandem with curative treatment, practitioners care for many near end of life and view death as natural. However, a steadfast commitment to prolonging life is embraced by virtually all other medical specialties. Considering that these foci can be interpreted as divergent, it is not surprising that many practitioners experience tension, confusion, or discomfort in EOL conversations. Moreover, research [2] has found that when attending physicians realize that extension of life is unlikely and recommend palliative care, they often forgo end of life conversations all together. PC professionals report that this likely stems from attending physicians who are in denial about a patient's health status or are otherwise experiencing challenges in accepting that at patient is no longer a candidate for curative treatment. Avoidance of these sensitive conversations, therefore, is not confined within the dynamics of the family unit, but is also interwoven into the structure of the health system. The circumvention of the topic of death and dying by other medical professionals means that PC practitioners often find themselves in the position of having to explain to patients that they are not there to "build strength", but rather because they are no longer responding to curative treatment. PC practitioners then serve as active and collaborative communicators for patients and their families in terms of discussing end of life concerns and wishes. Owing to this change and the raise of deaths that are occurring in organizational settings, it is important to consider how professionals and families communicate and cope during this decisive life experience. In this sense, neither practitioners nor patients and their families cope or communicate independently, but rather contemporary approaches to end of life have transformed this into an interdependent, relational, communicative process.

4. The Intersection of Family and Practitioner End of Life Communication

We have demonstrated how practitioners and families experience unique tensions surrounding conversations regarding EOL. However, we now narrow our focus to examine the communication challenges and foci common among patients, families, and health care practitioners. In particular, we will discuss the impact of communal coping and how commitment to quality of life, discussion of care vs. cure, and a resolute focus on communication is transforming EOL conversations.

Unlike individual coping and differentiated from social support, communal coping is largely defined by two criteria: appraisal and action [15]. In communal coping, appraisal and action suggest that members within a group co-own a specific stressor and experience it together. Put simply, "our problem, our responsibility" [15]. Applied to EOL communication, communal coping privileges a lens to explore how a patient, their family, and their PC team each assume a role and work together to assist in managing stressors. One particular stressor that is relevant across each of these groups is the tension between cure and care.

This tension can be a particularly challenging one to navigate for patients, families, and practitioners alike. While PC affirms death as a natural process, it does the same for life—so long as the patient indicates that he/she is satisfied with their quality of life. That is, for some curative treatment may mean severe sacrifices to daily life. In an editorial [16] a palliative care nurse shared the story of a young mother whose aggressive curative chemotherapy treatment came with feelings of impaired decision making, fogginess, pain and fatigue—and no noticeable change to the size of the growth. Therefore, after lengthy discussions with her family and PC team, the decision was made to reorient focus on care, rather than cure. This shift allowed the patient to spend her time as she wished, feeling like herself, and free from the painful side effects of the earlier intrusive curative treatment plan. Certainly, the decision made by the patient, her family, and her PC team is not a one size fits all solution. Moreover, it is likely that at times, the young mother, her spouse and their daughters, and perhaps even members of her PC team, did not necessarily want to accept care over cure. However, by taking a communal approach where each individual assumed responsibility for the illness and dedicated energy to actively considering how to address the disease, no one was left to navigate the EOL process unaided. Therefore, while the patient and her family may have been hesitant to support the cure to care shift, collectively with the woman's PC team, they were able to discuss the probable progression of the disease, quality of life markers, and EOL fears. In this sense, even though the decision may not have been readily or immediately accepted by all, shared responsibility and concern for the patient's wellbeing meant that pain control, fatigue management, and counseling would better support her needs.

This example helps to show how tightly coiled the tension between cure and care can be. Certainly the illustration above is one that tugs at the heart strings as the patient in question is youthful and has three young children. However, regardless of station in life, the natural inclination at a serious or terminal diagnosis is a focus on cure. In this traditional approach, typically the expert clinician orders a series of diagnostic tests, provides an opinion, prescribes a course of treatment, and uses an analysis pathway to compute the best possible outcome [17]. While often described as or perceived as in competition with one another, others [18] have argued that the two models—cure and care—are actually better considered as end points on one continuum. This conceptualization places more focus on the individual needs of the patient, where practitioners and the patient's family collaborate for all members' mutual benefit. This perspective intrinsically emphasizes the pivotal role that communication plays at end of life. In this sense, communication allows patients, families, and practitioners to engage in thoughtful conversations about goals and fears and to give and receive support. Since research indicates that initiating EOL discussions can be challenging for lay people and medical personnel alike, we offer two tangible communication suggestions for facilitating these conversations. Moreover, we provide ideas for how the suggestions may be utilized by a patient, his or her family, and or healthcare employees.

5. Takeaways: How to Initiate EOL Conversations

While we have demonstrated some of the challenges of EOL communication, such as family dynamics or the tension between living-dying for PC practitioners, we have also begun to demonstrate how thoughtful communication can create opportunities for discussion. We now provide additional concrete communicative suggestions that may assist patients, family members, and practitioners in initiating and maintaining EOL dialogue. A constant commitment to thoughtful communication is key because patients expect compassion in others' words and actions due to the emotional nature of end of life [19]. We now provide specific recommendations for the use of metaphors and key mindful communication practices to facilitate these complex conversations.

5.1. Metaphors

Though EOL conversations are often avoided, talking about death is important for myriad reasons. While individuals may be hesitant to discuss death in direct terms, use of metaphors may ease the uncertainty surrounding these important conversations. That is, if we consider the abstract ways that individuals perceive death, such as a savior or thief, it can help us to make sense of how they ascribe meaning to death. Subsequently, this provides cues as how to initiate and maintain a conversation on the topic. Metaphors are powerful because they are central to how we reason and understand the world around us, particularly abstract, difficult subjects like death [20]. In this sense, metaphors can be interpreted as an opportunity to initiate a conversation about death, rather than an abstraction to be evaluated as either good or bad. Below we discuss common metaphors used to describe and make sense of death [21].

Individuals who may be more hesitant to discuss death and dying may consider death as inevitable or as the elephant in the room. Use of these metaphors accentuate the importance of the communication context in that some consider death as a complex and private topic and therefore are much more selective in terms of when or with whom they discuss it with. Moreover, because individuals who consider death in terms of an elephant in the room or inevitable often experience uncomfortable feelings that accompany these conversations and they see death as a boundary for communication. This reluctance may also stem from not knowing how to engage EOL conversations if we're not certain of the beliefs of our conversational partner. In this sense, individuals who see death in this manner may wish to discuss EOL, but may be tentative because they don't know how to broach the topic nor do they want to cause others' discomfort.

If conceptualized as a mystery or a thief, it is a strong inclination that someone perceives EOL conversations as anxiety-ridden or personally painful and therefore, perceives them as something that should be avoided. When considered as a mystery, individuals expressly indicate a fear of the unknown or have challenges accepting the finality of death. Some who perceive death as a mystery may not necessarily view it as personally painful, but remain fixated on the unknown nature of what happens after death and what, if it exists, the afterlife might consist of. Others in this sample have suggested, particularly those without a particular spiritual or religious bend that fear of the afterlife prevents them from engaging in these conversations. Whereas the metaphor of death as a mystery is related to the unknown aspect of what happens after one dies, the use of a thief metaphor may show that the person in question has lost a number of loved ones or perceives death as stealing our time on earth. In this case, research [21] has indicated that individuals fostering these metaphors of death may avoid conversations because they serve as a painful reminder of feelings associated with the loss of a loved one.

While there are a number of metaphors linked with a reluctance to engage in EOL conversations, there are also several that may suggest a willingness or importance to discussing death. In an ongoing research project, Omilion-Hodges, Manning, and Swords [21] found that the largest proportion of participants viewed death in fairly positive terms, indicating an inclination to broach the subject. Within this camp, participants conceptualized death as natural, a savior, a motivator, and the unifier. The specific perspectives on death vary among these four metaphors, but they are all commonly linked by the notion that positive outcomes can be reached through open communication. Similar to the metaphor of death as inevitable, participants who frame death as natural see dying as a part of life. The distinction lies in the way that the individuals understand this perspective and their openness in communication as a result of their understanding. Relatedly, death as a savior, a motivator, and a unifier all rest of positive connotations of end of life suggesting that death may provide relief to loved ones who are in pain, can serve as a reminder of how precious and short life is, and that due to the rawness of death, boundaries are often broken down. An additional underlying theme is the idea that patients, families, and practitioners become co-owners of information about EOL processes including grieving and therefore, relationships may flourish because of the communal coping that occurs.

Death is not an easy topic for many, however, research indicates a growing willingness to engage in conversations about EOL. One way to learn another's (or your own) perceptions of death, may be to ask them how they consider death. In learning how one refers to death, you may have a baseline understanding of how to initiate a conversation. Moreover, learning one's metaphor may facilitate an opportunity to probe the metaphor to garner a deeper understanding of their perceptions of death. However, it is important to remember not to use the metaphor as a tool for binary evaluation—good or bad—but rather as a means to talk about EOL. Upon assessing someone's conceptualization of death, use of mindful communication may then assist in maintaining a conversation.

5.2. Mindful Communication

In addition to employing common metaphors for death, use of mindful communication is also likely to increase the ease of EOL conversations. Mindful communication is an active process where communicators remaining attentive and engage in constant sensemaking of the content and context of the conversation. This allows individuals to employ reflective, authentic, and adaptive communication in any given situation. Considering this, mindful communication has been studied extensively within interpersonal and health communication settings and is linked with decreases in stress and professional isolation among physicians [22] and also with delegation of tasks and patient safety increases among nurses [23]. This practice has also been linked with success in communicating across cultures [24]. Most applicably, perhaps, mindful communication has been recommended as a vehicle for having EOL conversations and as a buffer against the emotional work of palliative care [1].

Omilion-Hodges and Swords [1] studied nationally-recognized palliative care practitioners to learn how industry leaders employed mindful communication to stave off burnout and deliver exemplary, patient-focused care. Ultimately, four key communication practices emerged that benefit patients, their family members, and the practitioners. The first key practice is to consider your audience. Knowing one's audience means fundamentally rejecting a cookie-cutter approach to end of life communication. Bill, a hospice and palliative care physician and medical director, suggested that employing an authentic and individually-tailored approach to communication acted like a "relational slingshot" [1] (p. 331). To this effect, Bill found that use of mindful communication and a series of innocuous getting to know you questions, spurred the development of trusting, two-way relationships. Therefore, we stress, especially to practitioners, the importance of developing rapport with a patient and their loved ones before fixing focus on one's medical history or care goals.

Relatedly, the second key practice resolved around asking questions, listening, and repeating the process. This mindful communication practice reminds practitioners and family members that the patient may need them to be a "person" before a "medical practitioner" or a "loved one" before a "patient advocate". Therefore, during especially challenging communication encounters such as the delivery of a terminal diagnosis or offering an opinion in support of full-time or hospice care, practitioners and family members are encouraged to care for the patient holistically by affording them opportunities to ask questions, express disappointment, or emote sadness, anger, or fear. Further, by asking questions and listening, practitioners can gain insight into family desires regarding conversation initiation (i.e., practitioner or family) and the amount of communication they wish to engage in. The use of questions and engaged attention may help to facilitate this individual specific process. Similarly, palliative care leaders have found that mindful communication implicitly requires one to discard their scripts. As the third key practice, while scripts can be a helpful tool to spark ideas of how to breach EOL conversations, especially for new physicians or those in training, ultimately adherence to a pre-written narrative does not convey the authentic, adaptive communication required at EOL. This key practice ties in with the first in the sense that considering your audience often means that practitioner or family discomfort is relegated beneath patient needs. Certainly we do not recommend practitioners and family members to abandon self-care or individual needs, but rather remember to prioritize patient comfort at EOL which may include displaying genuine emotions such as disappointment or sadness.

The final key practice, and perhaps the most crucial, is to recognize your role. In this sense, PC practitioners emphasized the importance of remembering that a typical day in the office for them is a transformative event for patients and family members. To that end, the final key practice blends each of the previous to remind patients, families and practitioners that each is serving a crucial role. The patient, for example, may need to share or recant favorite memories in order to preserve them and promote generativity. Family members may need to ask questions or simply listen to their loved one's stories, fears, or concerns. Finally, while practitioners are navigating organizational dynamics and stressors, it is essential that when they are communicating with patients and their important others, that they remain mindful and recognize that they a "main character" in each of their stories.

6. Discussion

In this essay, we have focused on how contemporary approaches to death and dying have prompted changes in the conversations that are occurring at EOL. While once confined to private residences, there has been a steep increase in demand for death to occur within organizational settings aligning patients, their important others, and medical professional as collaborators in the decision making and discussions that are part and parcel with EOL. Therefore, instead of the patient, family, or practitioner having to cope alone, current medical options—such as PC—meet society's desire to utilize institutions at end of life and provide additional resources to help patients and their families to cope with this critical life experience.

Coping at end of life has also changed. While there is still a healthy level of stigma attached to discussing death and dying, at least in the Western context, interventions like Death over Dinner and the Conversation Project are helping people to talk about their wishes for EOL care. Sources such as these are empowering individuals to broach a once taboo topic and take the reins in terms of EOL planning. This same phenomenon is allowing families and practitioners to assume a "our problem, our responsibility" stance and work collaboratively to explore options, maintain quality of life, and when necessary, grieve [15]. Thus these transitions have prompted a healthier and more communicative approach to EOL where patients, families, and practitioners are active participants in designing and delivering a good death.

7. Conclusions

In conclusion, we have demonstrated how various tensions, especially the stress coiled within cure vs. care, are experienced by all members. While cure aligns more readily with the traditional biomedical model of care and cure with the more modern biosocial model, they both offer benefits to patients. Moreover, scholars [2] have continued to point out that there is room for the traditional cure model and the more nuanced care model in postmodern medicine. Considering this, communication becomes the key to determining specific, patient-tailored approaches to healthcare. Some tensions, such as care—cure, will likely never disappear, but communication can be the vehicle to spark and negotiate essential conversations and a means to cope.

Author Contributions: Both authors contributed substantially to the present manuscript in terms of idea generation, review of literature, and writing. Moreover, the present essay advances earlier work conducted by the publishing team.

Conflicts of Interest: The authors declare no conflict of interest.

References

1. Omilion-Hodges, L.M.; Swords, N.M. Communication that heals: Mindful communication practices from palliative care leaders. *Health Commun.* **2016**, *31*, 328–335. [CrossRef] [PubMed]
2. Omilion-Hodges, L.M.; Swords, N.M. The grim reaper, hounds of hell, and Dr. Death: The role of storytelling for palliative care leaders in competing medical meaning systems. *Health Commun.* **2016**. [CrossRef]
3. World Palliative Care Alliance. Available online: http://thewhpca.org (accessed on 28 January 2017).
4. Berry, S.R. Just say die. *J. Clin. Oncol.* **2008**, *26*, 157–159. [CrossRef] [PubMed]
5. Kreps, G.L. Communicating about death. *J. Commun. Ther.* **1998**, *4*, 95–106.
6. Sleeman, K.E. End-of-life communication: Let's talk about death. *J. R. Coll. Phys. Edinb.* **2013**, *43*, 197–199. [CrossRef] [PubMed]
7. Miller, I.W.; Ryan, C.E.; Keitner, G.I.; Bishop, D.S.; Epstein, N.B. The McMaster approach to families: Theory, assessment, treatment and research. *J. Fam. Ther.* **2000**, *22*, 168–189. [CrossRef]
8. Koerner, A.F.; Fitzpatrick, M.A. Toward a theory of family communication. *Commun. Theory* **2002**, *12*, 70–91. [CrossRef]
9. Baxter, L.A.; Akkoor, C. Topic expansiveness and family communication patterns. *J. Fam. Commun.* **2011**, *11*, 1–20. [CrossRef]
10. Petronio, S.; Caughlin, J.P. Communication privacy management theory: Understanding families. In *Engaging Theories in Family Communication: Multiple Perspectives*; Braithwaite, D.O., Baxter, L.A., Eds.; Sage Publications: Thousand Oaks, CA, USA, 2006; pp. 35–49.
11. Rokach, A. Caring for those who care for the dying: Coping with the demands on palliative care workers. *Palliat. Support. Care* **2005**, *3*, 325–332. [CrossRef] [PubMed]

12. Lingard, L.; Reznick, R.; Espin, S.; Regehr, G.; DeVito, I. Team communications in the operating room: Talk patterns, sites of tension, and implications for novices. *Acad. Med.* **2002**, *77*, 232–237. [CrossRef] [PubMed]

13. Lingard, L.; Whyte, S.; Regehr, G. Counting silence: Complexities in the evaluation of team communication. In *Safer Surgery: Analysing Behaviour in the Operating Theatre*; Flin, R., Mitchell, L., Eds.; Ashgate: Farnham, UK, 2009; pp. 283–300.

14. Frank, L.K. Interprofessional communication. *Am. J. Public Health Nat. Health* **1961**, *51*, 1798–1804. [CrossRef]

15. Lyons, R.F.; Mickelson, K.; Sullivan, J.L.; Coyne, J.C. Coping as a communal process. *J. Soc. Pers. Relatsh.* **1998**, *15*, 579–607. [CrossRef]

16. Miller, E.T. Care vs. Cure? *Rehabil. Nurs.* **2012**, *37*, 161–162. [CrossRef] [PubMed]

17. Lawler, F.H. Clinical use of decision analysis. *Prim. Care* **1992**, *22*, 281–293.

18. Baumann, A.O.; Deber, R.B.; Silverman, B.E.; Mallette, C.M. Who cares? Who cures? The ongoing debate in the provision of health care. *J. Adv. Nurs.* **1998**, *28*, 1040–1045. [CrossRef] [PubMed]

19. Slocum-Gori, S.; Hemsworth, D.; Chan, W.W.Y.; Carson, A.; Kazanjian, A. Understanding compassion satisfaction, compassion fatigue and burnout: A survey of the hospice palliative care workforce. *Palliat. Med.* **2013**, *27*, 172–178. [CrossRef] [PubMed]

20. Johnson, M.; Lakoff, G. Why cognitive linguistics requires embodied realism. *Cogn. Linguist.* **2002**, *13*, 245–263. [CrossRef]

21. Omilion-Hodges, L.M.; Manning, B.L.; Swords, N.M. Metaphors for Death: Exploring the Elephant in the Room and the Great Unifer. In Proceedings of the 103rd Annual National Communication Association, Dallas, TX, USA, November 2017.

22. Beckman, H.B.; Wendland, M.; Mooney, C.; Krasner, M.S.; Quill, T.E.; Suchman, A.L.; Epstein, R.M. The impact of a program in mindful communication on primary care physicians. *Acad. Med.* **2012**, *87*, 815–819. [CrossRef] [PubMed]

23. Anthony, M.K.; Vidal, K. Mindful Communication: A novel approach to improving delegation and increasing patient safety. *Online J. Issues Nurs.* **2010**, *15*. [CrossRef]

24. Ting-Toomey, S. *Communicating across Cultures*; Guilford Press: New York, NY, USA, 2012.

behavioral sciences

MDPI

Article

Physicians' Religious Topic Avoidance during Clinical Interactions

Melinda M. Villagran [1,*], Brenda L. MacArthur [2], Lauren E. Lee [1], Christy J. W. Ledford [3] and Mollie R. Canzona [4,5]

[1] Department of Communication Studies, Texas State University, San Marcos, TX 78666, USA; lauren_lee@txstate.edu
[2] Department of Communication, George Mason University, Fairfax, VA 22207, USA; bmacarth@gmu.edu
[3] Department of Family Medicine, Uniformed Services University of the Health Sciences, Bethesda, MD 20814, USA; christian.ledford@usuhs.edu
[4] Department of Communication, Wake Forest University, Winston-Salem, NC 27109, USA; canzonmr@wfu.edu
[5] Department of Social Sciences & Health Policy, Wake Forest University School of Medicine, Winston-Salem, NC 27109, USA
* Correspondence: mvilla@txstate.edu; Tel.: +1-512-245-4026

Academic Editor: Maureen P. Keeley
Received: 10 March 2017; Accepted: 30 April 2017; Published: 8 May 2017

Abstract: Religious and spiritual (R/S) conversations at the end-of-life function to help patients and their families find comfort in difficult circumstances. Physicians who feel uncertain about how to discuss topics related to religious beliefs may seek to avoid R/S conversations with their patients. This study utilized a two-group objective structured clinical examination with a standardized patient to explore differences in physicians' use of R/S topic avoidance tactics during a clinical interaction. Results indicated that physicians used more topic avoidance tactics in response to patients' R/S inquiries than patients' R/S disclosures; however, the use of topic avoidance tactics did not eliminate the need to engage in patient-initiated R/S interactions.

Keywords: communication; religion; clinical interactions

---

1. Introduction

Family communication at the end of life often includes discussions with physicians about the physical, emotional, and spiritual needs of a dying loved one [1]. Conversations about religious and spiritual (R/S) issues related to death can reduce uncertainty for patients and their families by framing health issues in the context of shared religious belief systems and personal philosophies [2], and by integrating scientific medical information with R/S beliefs about hope and healing [3]. Unfortunately, physicians who are not receptive to R/S discussions at the end of life use verbal and nonverbal tactics to avoid these discussions, even though addressing R/S topics could meet communicative needs of their patients [4,5].

Topic avoidance tactics can limit the amount and content of information and disclosure between two parties based on personal and professional boundaries and goals [6]. In the case of R/S conversations at the end of life, physicians may employ topic avoidance tactics to limit challenging R/S discussions or avoid disclosing personal R/S beliefs due to a lack of perceived religious concordance with patients and their families. Although shared R/S beliefs can bring confidence to the interaction, a perceived lack of R/S concordance may ultimately limit a physician's ability to address patients' R/S questions directly [7].

This study extends research on R/S conversations in healthcare [8,9] to explore religious topic avoidance tactics used by physicians during clinical interactions. Specifically, we examined differences in physicians' topic avoidance tactics in response to patient's R/S inquiries and disclosures in a structured clinical setting. Information uncertainty management is proposed as a framework for understanding how these crucial conversations shape the end of life experience for patients and families.

1.1. Uncertainty Management in Healthcare

Information uncertainty management theory suggests people judge the meaning of an event based on how it will affect them [10]. Uncertainty results from a perceived lack of relevancy, and congruency of a topic, and the response to uncertainty often hinges on the need for self-protection in dealing with sensitive or difficult topics [11]. As a form of uncertainty management, topic avoidance may occur when individuals seek to strategically divert conversations away from a particular topic to meet their goals for an interaction [12]. To avoid discussing R/S with a patient or family member and limit self-disclosure or discomfort with the R/S topic, physicians may seek to refocus the conversation on the medical goals of the interaction [7,8].

Patient care requires physicians to manage uncertainty about various patient disclosures [13], concurrently with uncertainty about disclosing their personal information and or beliefs. Although many physicians believe it is preferable for a patient to initiate R/S conversations [14], physicians may also feel uncertain about discussing R/S topics with patients and families, especially when the patient is at the end of life. When patients and families seek to avoid scientific information about an adverse prognosis, they often focus instead on R/S beliefs such as hope, faith, or life after death based on their religious or spiritual affiliations [14].

Recent self-report data from physicians found those who often or always encourage patients' to express their R/S beliefs and practices do so to better understand the role of faith in the patient's medical decisions [14]. Despite a desire to understand the patients' R/S beliefs, a meta-analysis of the literature found between 62% and 66% of physicians reported actively seeking to avoid the topic by changing the subject when the patient introduced R/S topics during clinical interactions [15]. Some physicians even refused to discuss R/S when the patient directly asked them to do so. Efforts to avoid R/S conversations may be a result of little formal training on how to discuss R/S with patients [16] or the result of a desire to protect the physician–patient relationship [17]. When physicians sought to avoid conversations about religion with patients, more than half indicated they did so because they lacked experience with the topic. Other reasons for avoiding the topic of religion included physicians' inability to identify whether it was appropriate to discuss religion with a particular patient, and uncertainty about whether discussing religious beliefs was part of their professional role [18]. Research suggests physicians are more likely to tolerate discussions of R/S beliefs if they are perceived to be beneficial to the patient's overall health [19]. Potentially due to the way R/S topics were introduced in clinical interactions, most physicians reported some level of uncertainty about when, whether, and how to respond [20].

1.2. Religion in the Physician–Patient Interaction

Sensitive topics such as religion may or may not be relevant or appropriate in professional settings, and it is often left to the individual to decide whether such topics are inside or outside of their professional jurisdictions [19]. Physicians respond to R/S questions or disclosures from patients based on issues including a lack of communication skills training and preparation to address difficult patient-initiated topics, an unwillingness to disclose personal beliefs in patient interactions, or a desire to manage the length of a clinical visit to stay on schedule with other patients.

Despite research and educational practices that encourage physicians to communicate during frequent and regular interactions with patients and families using open-ended questions, active listening, and empathic responses, many medical schools still lack focused instruction on communication skills training for patient interactions at the end of life [21]. Except in cases when patients cite R/S as the reason for refusal of care, a lack of relevant communication skills training can lead physicians to feel uncertain and unprepared to manage R/S issues in a competent manner [16]. Even when general communication skills are taught in medical schools, few programs focus specifically on how to respond to a patient's religious questions, and some programs even characterize R/S conversations as outside of the physician's role [17]. Training that stresses a direct focus on disease and illness during clinical visits may limit the ability to competently address R/S topics, even though R/S conversations could provide comfort to patients and families during end-of-life healthcare.

Physicians' who are unwilling to disclose personal beliefs about R/S in healthcare settings often avoid R/S topics as a way limit or redirect the conversation away from the subject of R/S. When physicians perceive an R/S topic to be too personal, or if the physician perceives a lack of concordance between their own R/S beliefs and those of the patient, they may use topic avoidance to maintain a favorable relationship with the patient [22]. Some physicians also express a sense of uncertainty about whether and how to disclose their personal feelings and R/S beliefs in combination with more fact-based medical knowledge, judgments, and decisions about end-of-life care [14]. Topic avoidance tactics such as mirroring the patient's views may also serve as a buffer for physicians who seek to maintain a professional boundary between their personal and professional beliefs.

Physicians' willingness to engage in R/S conversations in the clinic may depend on how much time is needed to discuss uncertain, complex, and emotional R/S health issues during end-of-life processes. As a form of uncertainty management, a physician may avoid R/S/conversations to maintain control over the conversation and limit the amount of time spent in each clinical interaction by using controlling messages, or messages that demonstrate a lack of supportive talk in response to patient inquiries about R/S [8]. Questions from a patient that are unexpected or seem unrelated to the medical goal of the clinical visit could elicit R/S topic avoidance when the physicians seek to redirect the conversation back to the medical issue or goal of the visit. Control messages used by physicians can help demonstrate a lack of support for a patient-initiated topic in a physician-driven process of interaction [23]. Research on R/S conversations in clinical interactions found physicians expressed significantly more controlling messages in response to questions about R/S than when patients shared their own beliefs about R/S issues with their doctor [8]. Direct questions about R/S may be more threatening to physicians who seek to avoid R/S topics because of the implied time need to respond to a patient or family member who raises the R/S issue.

Despite uncertainty about how and whether to talk with patients about R/S issue at the end of life, research suggests medical decisions are often influenced by health care providers' personal R/S beliefs, regardless of whether or not the beliefs are disclosed to the patient. Curlin found, for instance, that 63% of Catholic physicians and 70% of protestant physicians agreed that, "my religious beliefs influence my practice of medicine," but only 14% of atheists or agnostics said their beliefs played a role in patient care [23].

In summary, this study examines use of topic avoidance as a way to limit conversation about R/S topics in clinical interactions. End-of-life communication about R/S can be especially challenging for physicians seeking to manage a variety of personal and professional sources of uncertainty during clinical interactions. Topic avoidance tactics may be employed by physicians to manage their uncertainty about R/S discussions, and to limit self-disclosure and time needed to engage with patients and their families about R/S topics. Based on previous research on topic avoidance and research on R/S conversations in clinical interactions, it is hypothesized that direct R/S inquiries from a patient will result in more topic avoidance by physicians than responses to patients' R/S disclosures. Furthermore, it is hypothesized that physicians who employ topic avoidance tactics will talk less about R/S during a clinical visit than those who do not employ topic avoidance tactics during the interaction.

2. Methods

Participants

Faculty and resident physicians at a mid-Atlantic community hospital family medicine department participated in this study. Participants were 27 (10 female, 17 male) staff and resident physicians, with an average age of 31.11 years (SD = 5.71). Participants reported an average of 3.42 years (SD = 5.45) service as a physician. The majority of the sample was white (n = 25). The two other participants listed their ethnicity as black (n = 1), and Asian (n = 1). Participants represented a variety of religious backgrounds. The majority identified as Protestant (n = 10) and Catholic (n = 8). Other participants reported their religious affiliation as Agnostic (n = 3), Atheist (n = 3), and Jewish (n = 1). (See [8]).

3. Procedure

The use of trained standardized patients during objective standard clinical examinations (OSCEs) allows clinicians to be evaluated on the same clinical or communicative tasks without variation in the patient portion of the conversation. This strategy prevents also the distress or fatigue of actual patients [24]. Following approval of the Hospital Institutional Review Board, participants were invited to participate in an OSCE activity regarding personal topics.

The study employed a two-group comparison design with random assignments to one of two experimental conditions. As physicians volunteered to participate in the study, they were scheduled for an OSCE appointment, asked to complete informed consent documents, and assigned to one of two experimental conditions. In the first condition, at some point during a clinical interaction about the patients' life-threatening hypertension, the patient revealed that her mother had hypertension and died in her 60s. The patient then either asked the physician about the potential for her R/S beliefs to heal her disease or told the physician that she believed R/S could help improve her condition. The point at which the topic of R/S was introduced varied by the individual encounter, to allow for a natural conversation flow in the OSCE. In the other condition, at some point in the conversation, the standardized patient expressed personal views about the importance of R/S beliefs in making healthcare decisions such as the one being discussed. Prior to a videotaped encounter, participants received the patients' case notes to prepare for the semi-structured OSCE. In the clinic room, the standardized patient followed the OSCE guide for one of the two conditions, patient's disclosure of his or her own R/S beliefs, or patients' inquiry about the physicians' R/S beliefs (see Table 1). Physician participants were blinded to the R/S topic and to the respective condition.

Table 1. Religious and Spiritual (R/S) Inquiry and Disclosure Conditions.

Sample Standardized Patient Religion/Spirituality Prompts Form Clinical Interaction
Inquiry: "I'm just wondering, do you think God could heal me?" "Do you think that my getting sick is part of God's plan for me?"
Disclosure: "I guess I'm sort of frightened, but then I tell myself you know I'm a woman of faith." "As you've been working here at the hospital, and you see so many patients, you must see some divine comfort in prayer here."

4. Measures

To assess the extent to which the physicians avoided engaging in patient-initiated conversations about religious issues, the first and second authors coded the OSCE transcripts to count the number of physician and patient utterances (conversation turns) about religious or spiritual topics in each interaction. Topic avoidance tactics in the transcripts were coded based on Dailey and Palomares' taxonomy and definitions of topic avoidance tactics (see Table 2). The tactics identified mirrored tactics found in existing topic avoidance research, which identified at least 47 tactics used as part of a larger strategy to avoid a topic or discussion. Individual utterances were coded based on the manifest content (occurrences of words or phrases identified in previous research as topic avoidance tactics), and based on the context of how the words and phrases were used during the OSCE scenario. After the OSCE interactions, participants completed a short debriefing interview and questionnaire, which informed them of the topic of the study and asked for demographic information including age, sex, ethnicity, and years of medical practice. In addition, a single Likert-type item was collected following the encounter to measure physician-perceived concordance with the patients' R/S beliefs to control for differences in perceived religious concordance between the patient and physician. This item asked, "How much do you think the patient's beliefs were like your own?"

Table 2. Topic Avoidance Tactics Identified in Transcripts.

Topic Avoidance Tactic	Definition	# Used
Related Question	Ask a question somewhat related to the current topic to avoid a topic	12
Summary Assessment	Say a brief summary or general conclusion of the previous topic to avoid a topic; e.g., "That was interesting"; "You have really strong feelings about this".	8
Emotion Talk	Talk about either person's emotions to avoid a topic	3
Pause, Silence, or Hesitation	Say nothing; remain silent; and/or be hesitant in what you say to avoid a topic	6
Response Words	"Anyway"; "Oh"; "Yeah"; "So"; "Well" "Umm"	11
Don't Let Other Person Talk	Control the conversation so that the other person cannot get a word in	6
Delay Topic	Say/ask to talk about it later to avoid a topic; put it off	1
Side Statement	Say a side statement about something else to avoid a topic; "By the way ... "; "Not to change the subject but ... "; "This is a little off topic ... "	1
Unrelated Question	Ask question unrelated to the current topic to avoid a topic	3
Past Topic	Bring up or reintroduce a previous topic in the same conversation to avoid a topic; "Like I said earlier ... "; "Like we talked about before ..."	1
Using Idioms	Use a saying or idiom to avoid a topic e.g., "That's the way the ball bounces"; "Take it with a gram of salt"	1
Historical Life Event Talk	Talk about a previous event or story from your life	4
Current Setting Talk	Talk about the current situation or present environment to avoid a topic, e.g., talk about thin or people nearby	3

5. Results

A total of 57 topic avoidance tactics were employed by physicians in 28 OSCE clinical interactions (see Table 2). The majority of the interactions included combinations of summary assessments or related question topic avoidance tactics, uttered just before or just after pauses, hesitations, or response words such as "uh", or "well".

To examine differences in physicians' responses to R/S disclosures and inquiries during clinical interactions, analysis of covariance (ANCOVA) were performed on the two experimental message conditions, controlling for physicians' perceived religious concordance with the patient. Power analysis confirmed sufficient power to detect significance in the outcome variables.

The first hypothesis predicted physicians in the R/S inquiry condition would use significantly more topic avoidance tactics than physicians in the R/S disclosure condition. This hypothesis was supported (F (1, 54) = 19.15, p = 0.00). During the OSCE clinical interaction, the physicians in the R/S inquiry condition used significantly more topic avoidance tactics (M = 1.71, SD = 0.83) in response to patients questions about R/S issues, compared to physicians using topic avoidance tactics in response to R/S disclosures ($M = 0.64$, $SD = 0.63$). All of the physicians in the R/S inquiry condition used at least one topic avoidance tactic, but only half of the physicians in the R/S disclosure condition responded using a topic avoidance tactic. No physician used more than three topic avoidance tactics in one interaction. The three most commonly used tactics were the use of response words ($n = 12$), related questions ($n = 11$), and summary assessments ($n = 8$).

Many of the related questions and summary assessment involved topic shifts ($n = 18$) that diverted the attention away from their need to respond to the patient's R/S inquiry or disclosure, and when the topic was not shifted away from R/S, topic avoidance tactics such as bringing up past topics, or controlling the conversation without responding were employed.

The second hypothesis posited that physicians who employ topic avoidance tactics will talk less about R/S in OSCE conversations with patients than those who do not employ topic avoidance tactics. In other words, active topic avoidance in response to a patient initiated R/S inquiries and disclosures will result in proportionally less interaction focused on R/S versus other health-related issues. This hypothesis was not supported. Specifically, an analysis of covariance (ANCOVA) controlling for perceived R/S concordance revealed although physicians who sought to avoid an R/S conversation by using topic avoidance tactics did talk significantly less overall during OSCE interactions ($M = 19.82$, $SD = 1.5$) compared to those who did not employ topic avoidance tactics ($M = 14.66$, $SD = 0.84$); $F (1, 24) = 4.510$, $p = 0.044$, partial $\eta^2 = 0.16$, there was no significant difference in the amount of talk focused specifically on R/S during the OSCEs. There was also no significant difference in the length of the OSCEs based on whether or not a single topic avoidance tactic was employed by the physician. In other words, physicians did not reduce the total time spent talking about R/S during the OSCE, but the nature of R/S conversation was either focused on avoiding or addressing the topic of R/S. However, one pattern was uncovered regarding significant differences in the length of clinical interactions based on specific combinations of R/S topic avoidance tactics. Physicians who used short response words to immediately buffer the introduction of R/S topics, and followed by using response words with summary assessments of the previous conversation to switch back to the previous topic ($r = 0.58$, $p = 0.00$), had significantly shorter clinical interactions than those not using this combination. In other words, when physicians used a response word, they quickly adapted by following up with a summary of the patient's remarks as a way to respond without disclosing their own views on the topic, they controlled the conversation in a way that shortened the overall visit.

Finally, to further explore the nature of clinical interactions involving R/S topic avoidance, an analysis of covariance (ANCOVA) controlling for perceived R/S concordance examined differences in R/S talk among physicians who employed topic avoidance tactics in response to patient R/S questions and disclosures. The results revealed physicians responding to questions talked significantly more about R/S ($M = 12.74$, $SD = 1.17$) than those responding to R/S disclosures ($M = 7.63$, $SD = 0.84$); $F (1, 24) = 7.4$, $p = 0.014$, partial $\eta^2 = 0.28$.

6. Discussion

The purpose of this study was to investigate physicians' use of religious topic avoidance tactics in clinical interactions. The role of R/S in end-of-life communication is essential for patients and families coping with end-of-life issues, but little is known about how physicians encourage or avoid R/S discussions [8]. Results from the two group experimental study supported the first hypothesis, which predicted physicians in the R/S inquiry condition would use significantly more topic avoidance tactics than physicians in the R/S disclosure condition. Avoiding an R/S conversation in response to a direct question was assumed to require more direct verbal tactics than a response to a patient disclosure, and the data supported this assumption. Interestingly, physicians spent about the same amount of time responding to patient-initiated R/S topics regardless of whether or not they used topic avoidance tactics. Although the amount of talk was approximately the same, the goal of the

R/S conversation was different based on whether the physician was addressing or avoiding the R/S topic. This finding implies physicians discussed R/S regardless of whether or not they used topic avoidance tactics. However, those who did not use topic avoidance tactics focused the conversation on addressing the patients' R/S concerns, while those who did use topic avoidance tactics spent a comparable amount of time avoiding the issue. In other words, use of topic avoidance tactics did not result in less R/S conversation between patients and physicians.

Although the use of topic avoidance tactics did not reduce the total amount of R/S talk in the OSCEs overall, they did lead to significantly less R/S talk in the patient disclosure condition. The nature of a direct R/S inquiry by a patient led physicians to talk significantly more about R/S, perhaps to avoid personal disclosures about R/S or to control the conversation. Many physicians believe it is important to allow patients to decide how much they wish to incorporate religion into their healthcare [16], but physicians also have the right to make decisions about personal R/S disclosures. Perhaps physicians who sought to limit self-disclosure about their own R/S beliefs ultimately spent more time elaborating on R/S issues as a way to avoid directly answering the patient's question.

When physicians engaged in R/S talk, they most typically included the use of response words to avoid the topic. Perhaps when physicians mention religion, they experience the dissonance between that communication and what they were formally taught about religious communication. Response words such as "Anyway", "So", and "Umm" may, in turn, reflect physicians' thought processes related to their sudden awareness of the tension. Physicians generally believe that religion is a topic for personal discussion, which is outside of their professional role [9,16]. So, it makes sense that they would try to compensate for instances where they accidentally engage in religious dialogue, resulting in utterances such as "anyway", "so", or "umm" that reflect their thinking process. Because talk about religion may reveal more private information about the individual [12], physicians may elect to not reveal such information to patients, to keep their relationship professional and effective.

The directness of patients' inquiries about religion seems to play a role in the topic avoidance process for physicians in this study [12]. While topic avoidance can either employ positive or negative messages, the directness of inquiries about such topics also seems to have the power to impact the use of topic avoidance strategies, at least for the physicians in this study. Physicians in the inquiry condition used more topic avoidance tactics than physicians in the disclosure condition, perhaps due to the direct nature of inquiry and the need to provide some form of response. If the patient asked a direct question, there would be less opportunity to gloss over the topic than if the R/S disclosure was made in the context of a larger statement that did not warrant a response. Direct inquiries seemed to garner more responses in general, and more use of topic avoidance specifically, thus indicating that patients who engage in direct forms of R/S dialogue are more likely to have subsequent R/S discussions with their physician. The nature of the inquiry could be a factor worthy of future consideration. This did not however, impact the success of topic avoidance tactics in limiting the amount of R/S talk during the interaction. Because physicians are likely caught off guard when they are asked about their religious beliefs, it makes sense that they would attempt to avoid discussing the sensitive topic, and try to quickly adapt with "thinking" words such as "well" or "um". These attempts did not, however, limit their amount of R/S talk, so topic avoidance did not always occur after the use of topic avoidance tactics.

Because more than half of physicians lack experience discussing religion in clinical interactions [7] it would make sense that they may feel uncomfortable engaging in conversations about religion with patients. Because physicians must redirect patients' focus on the spot, it makes sense that they would ask the patient a question related to the previous topic or make a summary statement to redirect or control the direction of the conversation. When physicians used response words to avoid the topic of religion, they also combined that strategy with a summary assessment of what the patient said previously. Despite these efforts to avoid the topic of R/S, the physicians did not significantly reduce their own R/S talk during the interaction. Perhaps physicians do not want to appear rude and figure that redirecting the focus of the conversation back to the patient would be positively received by the patients.

7. Conclusions

The results of this study provide important insights for physicians who engage in R/S conversations with patients and families, but the study had some limitations. First, the study employed a standardized patient, so the realistic emotion of the conversation was limited. It is also possible physicians could be more emotional and uncertain in a non-experimental setting while interacting with a patient at the end of life. Although families are often involved in R/S interactions at the end of life, this study focused only on the patient to control potential error in the experiment caused by introducing more people into the interaction. Future research should examine religious conversations among physicians, families, and patients at the end of life in more realistic settings to examine the affective and cognitive processes of topic avoidance and R/S conversations.

Although this study held constant the structure of the R/S inquiries and disclosures in the two conditions, end-of-life conversations involving patients and family members would likely vary greatly regarding the structure of the interaction, and in the form of the R/S disclosure itself. Future research should further explore the content of R/S disclosures at the end of life, and focus greater attention on the source of the disclosure when it comes from the patient or family member. Variance in the source of the R/S disclosure could shape the physician's response, especially if topic avoidance tactics are used to maintain control in the clinical interaction.

It is also possible that patients might prefer to initiate more religious conversations with nurses than physicians since nurses typically spend more time in conversations with patients and their families, and may have more relational history with the patient during their treatment over time. Future research should investigate patient preferences for engaging in religious conversations in the clinical setting. Along those lines, the nature and severity of a patient's illness undoubtedly impact whether and how physicians engage in religious conversations, and the standardized patient did not appear to be significantly ill for a patient at the end of life. The standardized patient OSCE did not account for variance in the severity of patients' conditions. On the other hand, the OSCE did allow the researchers to control for patient characteristics in the study. Future studies should vary patients based on demographic and medical conditions and should examine the alternative types of R/S talk when topics are approached versus avoided in clinical interactions.

Finally, the severity of patient's condition leading to an end-of-life conversation could impact physicians' willingness to engage in R/S conversation, and this study did not include patients with differing medical conditions. Families who seek R/S information might be looking for ways to maintain hope in light of a negative prognosis, but they also might be seeking to gain a sense of agency their family members' health. Patients and family members who engage in prayer or other actions as an outcome of R/S conversations could use these behaviors as a way to cope with the patient's impending death.

Author Contributions: Melinda Villagran conceived of the study in consultation with Christy Ledford and Mollie Canzona, who also collected data for the experiment. Brenda MacArthur led the analysis of data presented in this study, and worked with Melinda Villagran to code the transcript data for topic avoidance tactics. Lauren Lee drafted the first version of this paper, and worked in consultation with the first and second author on revisions.

Conflicts of Interest: The authors declare no conflicts of interest.

References

1. Keeley, M.P. Final conversations: Survivors' memorable messages concerning religious faith and spirituality. *Health Commun.* **2004**, *16*, 87–104. [CrossRef] [PubMed]
2. Marrone, R. Dying, Mourning, and Spirituality: A Psychological Perspective. *Death Stud.* **1999**, *23*, 495–500. [CrossRef] [PubMed]

3. Fieweger, M.; Smilowitz, M. Relational conclusion through interaction with the dying. *Omega* **1985**, *15*, 161–172. [CrossRef]
4. Sloan, R.P.; Bagiella, E. Should physicians prescribe religious activities? *N. Engl. J. Med.* **2000**, *342*, 1913–1916. [CrossRef] [PubMed]
5. Naghi, J.; Philip, K.; Phan, A.; Cleenewerck, L.; Schwarz, E. The effects of spirituality and religion on outcomes in patients with chronic heart failure. *J. Relig. Health* **2012**, *51*, 1124–1136. [CrossRef] [PubMed]
6. Afifi, W.A.; Guerrero, L.K. Motivations underlying topic avoidance in close relationships. In *Balancing the Secrets of Private Disclosures*; Petronio, S., Ed.; Erlbaum: Mahwah, NJ, USA, 2000; pp. 165–179.
7. Ellis, M.R.; Campbell, J.D. Concordant spiritual orientations as a factor in physician-patient spiritual discussions: A qualitative study. *J. Relig. Health* **2005**, *44*, 39–53. [CrossRef] [PubMed]
8. Ledford, C.J.; Canzona, M.R.; Seehusen, D.A.; Cafferty, L.A.; Schmidt, M.E.; Huang, J.C.; Villagran, M.M. Differences in Physician Communication When Patients Ask Versus Tell About Religion/Spirituality: A Pilot Study. *Fam. Med.* **2015**, *47*, 134–137.
9. Canzona, M.; Peterson, E.; Villagran, M.; Seehusen, D. Constructing and communicating privacy boundaries: How family medicine physicians manage patient requests for religious disclosure. *Health Commun.* **2015**, *30*, 1001–1012. [CrossRef] [PubMed]
10. Brashers, D.E. Communication and uncertainty management. *J. Commun.* **2001**, *51*, 477–497. [CrossRef]
11. Larzarus, R.S.; Folkman, S. *Stress, Appraisal, and Coping*; Springer: New York, NY, USA, 1984.
12. Dailey, R.M.; Palomares, N.A. Strategic topic avoidance: An investigation of topic avoidance frequency, strategies used, and relational correlates. *Commun. Monogr.* **2004**, *71*, 471–496. [CrossRef]
13. Lewis, C.; Matheson, D.H.; Brimacombe, E. Factors influencing patient disclosure to physicians in birth control clinics: An application of the communication privacy management theory. *Health Commun.* **2011**, *26*, 502–511. [CrossRef] [PubMed]
14. Best, M.; Butow, P.; Oliver, I. Doctors discussing religion and spirituality: A systematic literature review. *Palliat. Med.* **2016**, *30*, 327–337. [CrossRef] [PubMed]
15. Faber, N.J.; Novack, D.H.; Silverstein, J.; Davis, E.B.; Weiner, J.; Boyer, E.G. Physicians' experiences with patients who transgress boundaries. *J. Gen. Intern. Med.* **2000**, *15*, 770–775. [CrossRef]
16. Cadge, W.; Ecklund, E.; Short, N. Religion and spirituality: A barrier and a bridge in the everyday professional work of pediatric physicians. *Soc. Probl.* **2009**, *56*, 702–721. [CrossRef]
17. Koenig, H. Religion, spirituality, and medicine: Research findings and implications for clinical practice. *South. Med. J.* **2004**, *97*, 1194–1200. [CrossRef] [PubMed]
18. Ellis, M.R.; Vinson, D.C.; Ewigman, B. Addressing spiritual concerns of patients: Family physicians' attitudes and practices. *J. Fam. Pract.* **1999**, *48*, 105–109. [PubMed]
19. Abbott, A. *The System of Professions: An Essay on the Division of Expert Labor*; University of Chicago Press: Chicago, IL, USA, 1988.
20. Ellis, M.; Thomlinson, P.; Gemmill, C.; Harris, W. The spiritual needs and resources of hospitalized primary care patients. *J. Relig. Health* **2013**, *52*, 1306–1318. [CrossRef] [PubMed]
21. Street, R.L.; Krupat, E.; Bell, R.A.; Kravitz, R.L.; Haidet, P. Beliefs about Control in the Physician-patient Relationship. *J. Gen. Intern. Med.* **2003**, *18*, 609–616. [CrossRef]
22. Donovan-Kicken, E.; Caughlin, J.P. A multiple goals perspective on topic avoidance and relationship satisfaction in the context of breast cancer. *Commun. Monogr.* **2010**, *77*, 231–236. [CrossRef]
23. Curlin, F.A.; Lantos, J.D.; Roach, C.J.; Sellergren, S.A.; Chin, M.H. Religious Characteristics of U.S. Physicians. *J. Gen. Intern. Med.* **2005**, *20*, 629–634. [CrossRef] [PubMed]
24. Yudkowsky, R.; Alseidi, A.; Cintron, J. Beyond fulfilling the core competencies: An objective structured clinical examination to assess communication and interpersonal skills in a surgical residency. *Curr. Surg.* **2004**, *61*, 499–503. [CrossRef] [PubMed]

behavioral sciences

MDPI

Concept Paper

Palliative Care and the Family Caregiver: Trading Mutual Pretense (Empathy) for a Sustained Gaze (Compassion)

Joy Goldsmith [1],* and Sandra L. Ragan [2]

[1] Department of Communication, University of Memphis, 235 Art and Communication Building, Memphis, TN 38152-3150, USA
[2] Department of Communication, University of Oklahoma, Norman, OK 73019, USA; sragan@gvtc.com
* Correspondence: jvgldsmt@memphis.edu

Academic Editor: Maureen P. Keeley
Received: 27 February 2017; Accepted: 7 April 2017; Published: 13 April 2017

Abstract: In this conceptual piece, we survey the progress of palliative care communication and reflect back on a chapter we wrote a decade ago, which featured the communication concept of mutual pretense, first described by Glaser and Strauss (1965). This work will include an update on family caregivers and their role in cancer caregiving as well as a review of current palliative care communication curriculum available for providers. And finally, we will spotlight the conversation and research going forward on the subject of health literacy for all stakeholders; patients, families, providers, and systems. We feature one family's story of incurable cancer and end of life to revisit the needs we identified ten years ago, which are still present. Goals for going forward in chronic and terminal illness are suggested in a health care context still too void of palliative care communication resources for providers, patients, and especially family caregivers.

Keywords: palliative care; family caregiver; health literacy; communication training; compassion

---

It had been nearly a month since I had seen her. When she opened the front door, I felt sure that she was dying. Sheila had moved into a house at the end of my street with her 24-year old daughter, Cass, and her daughter's two young children, aged 1 and 8. The 8 year old was my daughter's age and they had become fast friends and playmates. Sheila had raised her grandchildren while her daughter came and went as a very young single parent. Their arrival to the neighborhood had happened six months before, and upon my first meeting with Sheila, she shared about her ovarian cancer and how this had precipitated her move to our neighborhood—to be near another daughter who also lived a few houses away. In her seventh year with the disease, and still receiving treatment, it seemed clear that she had advanced terminal cancer. She mentioned things that told the story of her disease status: the recent discovery of a 'new' breast cancer, the language of hope confused by descriptions of ongoing aggressive treatments, and the notion of cure being mentioned as a possibility with her new doctors. Though I tried to share my thoughts about palliative care, this was never a topic we found a way to engage.

As I stood at her front door, the day I thought she looked like she was dying, she looked very thin. But her belly was enormous. Her eyes had a far off look and she described having bloating from diverticulitis, and that she was going to a GI doctor the next week to get it "taken care of". I knew she was full of cancer and dying; I felt pretty sure that she might know this; and I was positive that no one in her world was talking with her about it.

1. Palliative Care and Mutual Pretense

When we wrote a piece for Kevin Wright's and Scott Moore's *Applied Health Communication* in 2008 [1], we were novices in the scholarly investigation of palliative care. Differing significantly in our academic pathways, and one a mentor and one an advisee, we each had recently watched and endured the loss of a sister from terminal cancer. These losses coupled with our own academic experience and turn toward health communication ignited a call toward a newer kind of medicine called palliative care. Palliative care is unique in that it attends especially to relief from biomedical and psychosocial pain that accompanies serious illness [2]. This kind of care includes a team-based approach that attends not only to the patient, but also to the family caregivers by helping determine a patient's goals of care through communication, attending to distressing symptoms, and coordinating care. Unlike the United States' basic approach to hospice care, palliative care can be provided at the same time as curative treatments; it is appropriate at any age and at any stage of a serious illness [3]. In our first joint writing venture exploring this topic, we examined and found confusing, harmful, social scripts performed by physicians and patients/families at end of life, highly compelling. Looking back into the text we created ten years ago, we are reminded that our chapter was built around these ideas:

- Americans are death-avoidant; thus we often die in hospitals, tethered to invasive medical machinery, and without benefit of having acknowledged death's imminence and life's remaining opportunities.
- As a result, we frequently live the end of our lives without the comfort of having addressed our emotional, psychic, spiritual, and existential pain—and without our family's solace. Family members and patient alike are denied the relational closeness that living fully in the knowledge of an illness can bring.
- As patients and family members—we collude with our care providers to live in aggressive treatments as though we actually can avoid death, that our providers can solve the medical Riddle [4] of our illness. All parties to life-threatening or life-ending illness collaborate to produce a script boosted by the talk of treatment: we subscribe to Frank's (1995) "restitution narrative" in that we believe that life, with appropriate (curative) medical treatment, can return to normal—to what it was before the anomaly of illness intervened, no matter the physical and emotional costs incurred [5].
- What Glaser & Straus describe is the ritual drama of mutual pretense, and it is enacted to manifest consensus that we are not dying [6]. It is an agreement between healthcare providers and patient/family, rarely spoken yet intricately coordinated, that all will behave as if advancing disease and loss of what was—is not an option [1].

In discussing this phenomenon of "mutual pretense" as described in these bullet points, we pointed up many of the problematic, undergirding props in current healthcare practice that augment its likelihood in the context of serious illness and dying:

- The sender-based patient/physician model rather than the preferred collaborative model.
- The lack of patient-centered and family-centered care, such that the Voice of Medicine overtakes the patient's Voice of the Lifeworld [7].
- The limited provider training in communicating with serious and terminal patients and their families.
- The ignorance about palliative care and hospice among providers, patients, family, community, and healthcare systems.
- The unavailability of palliative care in most U.S. hospitals.
- The belief by both medical caregivers and patients/families that hope inherently is cancelled if sustained and worsening illness is acknowledged.

We concluded the chapter by seeking antidotes for these concerns in patient-centered medicine, in narrative medicine (privileging the patient's voice rather than trying to solve the Riddle), and in routinely incorporating palliative care into the care of patients with serious illness.

Now, ten years later, we wonder whether "mutual pretense" and this list of undergirding props are outdated notions, whether futile (allegedly curative) care is still prominent, whether palliative care is widely utilized, and whether our culture has become a bit more realistic about the inescapability of dying. This decade has been filled with research, initiatives, and training programs to better teach providers, systems, and caregiver/patient teams about the provisions of palliative care. We take this opportunity to pause and reflect on the productivity and labor of these years, and see what is ahead for palliative care and the family caregiver.

2. The Family Caregiver and Palliative Care Growth

The dimensions of burden, distress, and health of a family caregiver for a chronically or terminally ill loved one have moved into the cross-hairs of interest for researchers, hospital systems, providers, and health agencies. Health systems rely on the family caregiver to provide 80% of care that chronically and acutely-ill patients with cancer receive, and in managing adverse effects from disease and treatment in chronically and acutely-ill cancer patients [8]. Despite the demand for these high-level caregiving skills, family members often are unprepared and unable to navigate progressing disease and the decisions that accompany treatment processes [9]. Caregiver burden and distress are highest among those whose family member is living with increased symptom burden [10], underscoring the particular necessity for caregiver preparation and knowledge of symptom and pain management at home. As caregiver demands increase, caregivers who are unprepared may face greater adverse outcomes, including depression and mortality [11,12]. However, caregivers who report feeling more prepared for the caregiving experience report lower levels of personal strain during cancer care [9,11]. Cancer caregivers experience greater burden than non-cancer caregivers in the U.S., and provide more hours of caregiving per week, and cancer caregivers need significantly more help making end of life decisions than do non-cancer caregivers [13].

Despite the turn toward the family caregiver and the serious demands they endure in the course of disease progression or survivorship, caregiving distress and need are rarely monitored or even asked about in the clinical setting [14]. A current study of cancer family caregivers of patients with incurable cancer had significantly high levels of depression, and their anxiety was twice the level of the patient partner. Caregivers of incurable patients that described their efforts as curative in care reported higher levels of depression [15].

With the needs of patients and family caregivers still so significant, scholars across social science disciplines are now using the language of palliative care and end of life to identify their specialties. It is not unusual to see applicants for academic jobs in public health, medical anthropology, professional and technical writing, health informatics, and population science to present a focus in palliative care and chronic conditions. For us, the communication studies discipline, in particular, has cultivated scholars in this new area of research as well. The growing breadth and depth of providers and researchers in this area is also exhibited by the growth of palliative care services available in healthcare.

The Center to Advance Palliative Care (CAPC) published its 2015 assessment reflecting a slow but steady change in the number of hospital palliative care teams in the United States, though the standard and definition of what constitutes a 'team' in palliative care remains ill-defined. Sixty-seven percent of 50+ bed hospitals in the US report a palliative care team service. This is a 5% increase from 2011 and a 14% increase from the 2008 CAPC report. Another point of measure is the CAPC state-by-state grade card; an A grade represents more than 80% of hospitals within a state reporting palliative care teams [16]. The 2015 Report Card included an increase from 3% to 17% of states graded at an A. Notable is that the 2015 assessment included zero F's for the first time (F = less than 20% of the state hospitals reporting palliative care teams) since the assessments began in 2008 [16].

We celebrate these advancements. But important gaps still remain. Despite the improving numbers of palliative care providers in care settings, still 1/3rd of 50+ bed hospitals do not claim any palliative care service, while another 1/3rd of the states received a grade of C (less than 60%) or D (less than 40%). The overall grade for the United States in 2015 was a B, unchanged from 2011 [16].

The National Hospice and Palliative Care Organization also tracks growth and change in the way we treat seriously ill and terminal patients in the US. In their assessment, agencies who participated in the study reported no change between 2006 and 2013 in the provision of formal pediatric palliative care services with specifically prepared staff nor the number of younger patients [17]. The odds of black and Hispanic children dying at home are far less than non-minority Americans indicating a lack of access to palliative and hospice care by this population [16].

These organizations demonstrate that where a person lives predicates his or her access to palliative care. The Northwest offers the greatest access to palliative care services. The south, the southwest, and non-urban care settings are far less likely to offer palliative care than urban locations [16]. The unfolding story of family loss without palliative or hospice care in my own neighborhood demonstrates the still-desperate need for this kind of care in the U. S.

Emma was Shelia's granddaughter, and my daughter's playmate. Emma brought word that her MiMi (Sheila) had been inpatient since the day after I saw her at the front door. Her days at the hospital stretched on, one into the next. The moment she went inpatient, Sheila—mother, grandmother, and family bank—ceased being the primary parent for a one, eight, and twenty four year old. Her daughter, Cass, was in free-fall to accommodate both little children. She had relied almost exclusively on Shelia to care for her children while she worked as a server at a nearby restaurant. Without Shelia, Cass missed work and did not take her 3rd grader to school. Her parenting partner was no longer there. Shelia's other daughter at the end of the street was less involved in her mom's illness, and had two children of her own. Between these two daughters, neither of them visited their mom during her hospital stay. Emma began staying with us. She talked about the day her MiMi would get better, and come home. Now the family started to hemorrhage significantly, financially and emotionally. The house of cards had fallen.

3. Palliative Care Communication Training

The National Consensus Project for Quality Palliative Care identifies the clinical practice of communication as central to palliative care, and calls for provider preparation for this particular clinical practice [18]. Healthcare governing bodies have also established communication competencies and education demands for current students and post graduate healthcare providers [16], and as such, a mounting number of training programs addressing communication in palliative care have been developed, marketed, revised, implemented, and sold.

Originating from the Communication discipline and grounded in communication theory, COMFORT Communication training has been offered regionally and nationally as a palliative care training for nurses, and palliative care team members since 2012. Unique to this training and the model, it is based on heavy integration of social science evidence, palliative care state of the science, and collaborative delivery crossing healthcare and academic disciplines [2,19]. The largest provider group receiving this training is nursing, followed by social work, medicine, and chaplaincy.

The Center to Advance Palliative Care (CAPC) began offering IPAL (Improving Palliative Care) in 2010—a central source of information for sharing expertise, evidence, tools and resources essential to the integration and improvement of palliative care in specific health care settings. IPAL has specific programming for EM (emergency), ICU (intensive care unit), and OP (outpatient). Only CAPC members can access resources, and the largest percentage of CAPC members is physicians. Relatedly, Palliative Care Leadership Centers selected by CAPC also model year-long mentoring for newly launched palliative care programs.

CAPC also supports VITAL Talk, a privatized communication-coaching model specific to patient and physician—as a training resource for communication in palliative care. Emerging from oncology, the coaches/trainers in this project rely heavily on physician experiences.

A simple Google search for palliative care communication training will produce institution-specific results for courses or certificates in aspects of palliative care at places like Stanford and Harvard medical centers, the University of Washington, Penn State, and Utah University, to name only a few. Countless resources are now available online that include podcasts, blogs, articles, and research exploring better pathways to get, use, and receive palliative care.

The installation of consult services and board certified healthcare providers widely defines what palliative care means to a healthcare system, while communication preparation and its impact on the quality of care lags behind in terms of strengthening processes and structures of those palliative care services [20,21]. Though we recognize the importance of training in palliative care and its impressive growth over the last decade, a shift in thinking about care and its quality involves still-needed compassionate action that moves beyond empathy, as well as attention to improved health literacy for patients, caregivers, communities, and care systems.

4. Health Literacy and Its Role in Quality Care

For Shelia, the closest thing to a family caregiver was Cass—her daughter, with little children, few skills to survive, and now a sudden need to provide for all of them. The impact of her mom's imminent dying accompanied by the silence around that reality created the perfect storm for her financial and emotional crash. Shelia remained in the hospital, and 8-year old Emma was lost and confused without her. Her life-long caregiver and bedmate had vanished. I stopped Cass in my yard as she dropped off Emma, and told her I thought Sheila was dying in the hospital.

Health literacy includes personal characteristics and social resources needed to access, understand, appraise, and use information and services to participate in decisions relating to the health and care of the patient. A deficit model has led the research and development of measures and interventions in the study of health literacy—identifying the shortcomings of the patient and sometimes family caregiver and their ability to seek, find, understand, and use health information. Both the Institutes of Medicine (IOM) and World Health Organization (WHO) define health literacy as involving not only patient/caregiver level characteristics, such as cognitive and functional skills, but also healthcare system processes, structures, and providers [3]. In accord with the IOM, nursing and health literacy researchers [22,23], the synergy among those receiving care, providing care, and the resources provided by health systems converge to either fortify or dissolve health literacy barriers.

Health systems rely on family caregivers manage adverse effects from disease and treatment in chronically and acutely-ill cancer patients [8]. As patients become sicker, higher levels of health literacy are demanded of family caregivers. Despite the demand for high-level health knowledge and decision-making, family caregivers often are unprepared and unable to navigate progressing disease [9]. Caregiver burden and distress are highest among those whose patient is living with increased symptom burden [10].

Yuen and colleagues posit that cancer caregiver health literacy skills extend beyond understanding and accessing information and include the caregiver's relationship and communication with the care recipient, relationships and communication with healthcare providers, communication within support systems, and managing the challenges of caregiving [23]. Models exploring oral health literacy [24], plain language use and understanding [25], as well as numeracy demands [26] are exciting additions to the growing number of applied examinations that are meant to improve the quality of care for patients and their family. Common among these new directions in health literacy is the awareness that conceptual understanding is not equivalent to word literacy; previous assumptions that linked the educational level of patients and caregivers with health literacy levels are no longer reliable [27,28].

Diane Meier, pioneer and leader in palliative care, has pointed at the health literacy challenges of providers and systems as key barriers in supplying high value care with simple solutions to the seriously ill [29]. Including all stakeholders (providers, communities, systems, patients, providers) in the health literacy problematic is an action that we believe will offer greater provision for improved care and quality of life. Palliative care is positioned to integrate health literacy improvement into its practice.

Health literacy that is informed and created by all who are participating in the acquisition, use, understanding, and communication about health decisions [22] may need to include the component of the relationships among participants to best be studied. Including the reality of the workload of health literacy to all participating, rather than measuring the deficits of those receiving care, promises to improve not only the tasks central to complex care, but more importantly the trust and commitment to improve outcomes across the board.

5. From Mutual Pretense (Empathy) to a Sustained Gaze (Compassion)

Cass and I were in the driveway. A moment passed after I told her I thought her mom was dying. She leaned in and we hugged. She shuddered and whispered "I know."

The ability to take another's perspective has long been identified as essential for patient/family centered care, which supersedes a biomedical or condition-guided focus to healthcare [30]. Concern for those who are suffering, whether the patient or the family of a patient, is the essence of empathy. Even though literature and anecdotal experiences plainly support the notion of empathy in healthcare training and practice, its translation into that training and practice remains unclear [31].

Empathic distress includes the feeling of immense care and concern, but also paralytic inaction; this kind of distress becomes focused on self. Distress, a product of empathy, can bring the focus back onto the provider, while "compassion leads to a focus on others" [32] (p. 201). Compassion is a feeling that emerges when facing suffering and being able to cope with that suffering (or to act in the midst of another's suffering) [32]. The conflation of empathy and compassion in the literature, as well as in casual references in the context of healthcare, and specifically palliative care, has confused the role of each. Recent studies demonstrate that patients experience empathy and compassion very differently from providers. Empathy emerges as a first stage of compassion, but then is followed by a motivation to change that suffering—and this is a second and distinct response that differs from empathy [33]. Compassion moves beyond empathy and includes a process of reacting, acknowledging, understanding, seeking help, performing actions aimed at a solution, and even receiving personal satisfaction [33]. Compassion departs from the empathy's response to acknowledge and understand suffering, and adds the distinct features of being motivated by action and seeking small, supererogatory acts of kindness [34].

So how might compassion serve this most challenging kind of care; palliative care? Are there ways that mutual pretense and empathy have partnered up unwittingly to deny patients and their families opportunities to act, to do, and engage the life that is present? Distress experienced by those around a dying person—whether family or provider—can paralyze if the fiction of cure and restoration is dramatized. This comes at the highest cost to the patient, who suffers alone in their false narrative of medical cure, and significant cost to the family who must live on knowing that better choices and more truthful communication could have changed the way a patient lived at the end of life.

Looking ahead to the next decade, we hope for increasing numbers of program announcements targeting palliative care research priorities, the family caregiver, and health literacy modeling. Rural and southern areas remain at a deficit for palliative care services, and the demand for programs and providers cannot keep pace. Innovative and integrated training models will be a pathway to educate providers, systems, as well as patients and caregivers about palliative care. Studies and implementations that include or are led by patient and caregiver stakeholders should become central to applied health communication and health literacy research.

As we wrote a decade ago, mutual pretense is eventually unsustainable. Today we do see progress in training, support for family caregivers, and for the dissemination of palliative care—all areas of concern in our early chapter. But the struggle of the patient and family, especially in non-urban settings, is all too resonant with our writings of 2008. Similar to my experience with Sheila and Cass, the mutual pretense collapses when conditions make its maintenance impossible. But the sustained gaze could be built on the actions of compassion; these actions move to acknowledge the reality of the patient's biomedical and psychosocial state, understand the needs of this person in the context of the life, seek help to fulfill the outstanding needs for the patient and family, and perform actions that supply small and large solutions. This can be the alternative to the internal stare produced by mutual pretense. Gazing directly into the face of suffering, and opting for sustained presence instead of pretense, moves providers, caregivers, and patient into the truly cloaked comfort of compassion.

Author Contributions: Joy Goldsmith and Sandra L. Ragan conceived and designed this conceptual work and wrote this article together.

Conflicts of Interest: The authors declare no conflict of interest.

References

1. Ragan, S.; Goldsmith, J. The ritual drama of pretense in the talk of dying patients and their doctors. In *Applied Health Communication*; Wright, K.B., Moore, S. D., Eds.; Hampton Press: Creskill, NJ, USA, 2008; pp. 207–227.
2. Wittenberg Lyles, E.; Goldsmith, J.; Ferrell, B.; Ragan, S.L. *Communication in Palliative Nursing*; Oxford University Press: New York, NY, USA, 2012.
3. Chou, S.W.-Y.; Gaysynsky, A.; Persoskie, A. Health Literacy and Communication in Palliative Care. In *Textbook of Palliative Care Communication*; Wittenberg, E., Ed.; Oxford University Press: New York, NY, USA, 2015.
4. Nuland, S. *How We Die: Reflections on Life's Final Chapter*; Alfred A Knopf: New York, NY, USA, 1993.
5. Frank, A. *The Wounded Storyteller: Body, Illness, and Ethics*; University of Chicago Press: Chicago, IL, USA, 1995.
6. Glaser, B.; Straus, A. *Awareness of Dying*; Aldine Publishing Company: Chicago, IL, USA, 1965.
7. Mischler, E. *The Discourse of Medicne: The Dialectics of Medical Interviews*; Ablex: Norwood, NJ, USA, 1984.
8. Family Caregiver Alliance. Available online: https://www.caregiver.org/selected-long-term-care-statistics (accessed on 6 January 2017).
9. Schumacher, K.L.; Stewart, B.J.; Archbold, P.G.; Caparro, M.; Mutale, F.; Agrawal, S. Effects of caregiving demand, mutuality, and preparedness on family caregiver outcomes during cancer treatment. *Oncol. Nurs. Forum* **2008**, *35*, 49–56. [CrossRef] [PubMed]
10. Palos, G.R.; Mendoza, T.R.; Liao, K.-P.; Anderson, K.; Garcia-Gonzalez, A.; Hahn, K.; Nazario, A.; Ramondetta, L.; Valero, V.; Lynch, G.; et al. Caregiver symptom burden: The risk of caring for an underserved patient with advanced cancer. *Cancer* **2011**, *117*, 1070–1079. [CrossRef] [PubMed]
11. Schumacher, K.L.; Stewart, B.J.; Archbold, P.G. Mutuality and preparedness moderate the effects of caregiving demand on cancer family caregiver outcomes. *Nurs. Res.* **2007**, *56*, 425–433. [CrossRef] [PubMed]
12. Given, B.; Wyatt, G.; Given, C.; Gift, A.; Sherwood, P.; DeVoss, D.; Mohamed, R. Burden and depression among caregivers of patients with cancer at the end of life. *Oncol. Nurs. Forum* **2004**, *31*, 1105–1117. [CrossRef] [PubMed]
13. Kent, E.; Longacre, M.; Weber-Raley, L.; Whiting, C.; Hunt, G. Cancer versus non-cancer caregivers: An analysis of communication needs from the 2015 Caregivers in the US study. *J. Clin. Oncol.* **2016**, *4* (Suppl. S4). [CrossRef]
14. Tanco, K.; Chan Park, J.; Cerana, A.; Sisson, A. A systematic review of instruments assessing dimensions of distress among caregivers of adult and pediatric cancer patients. *Palliat. Support. Care* **2017**, *15*, 110–124. [CrossRef] [PubMed]
15. Nipp, R.; El-Jawahri, A.; Fishbein, J.; Gallagher, E.; Stagl, J.; Park, E.; Jackson, V.; Pirl, W.; Greer, J.; Temel, J. Factors associated wtih depression and anxiety sysmptoms in family caregivers of patients with incurable cancer. *Ann. Oncol.* **2016**, *27*, 1607–1612. [CrossRef] [PubMed]
16. Center to Advance Palliative Care. *America's Care of Serious Illness: 2015 State-By-State Report Card on Access to Palliative Care in Our Nation's Hospitals*; Center to Advance Palliative Care: New York, NY, USA, 2015.
17. National Hospice and Palliative Care Organization. *NHPCO's Facts and Figures: Pediatric Palliative and Hospice Care in America*; National Hospice and Palliative Care Organization: Alexandria, VA, USA, 2015.

18. National Consensus Project for Quality Palliative Care. *Clinical Practice Guidelines for Quality Care*; National Consensus Project for Quality Palliative Care: Pittsburgh, PA, USA, 2013.
19. Goldsmith, J.; Ferrell, B.; Wittenberg Lyles, E.; Ragan, S. Palliative care communication in oncology nursing. *Clin. J. Oncol. Nurs.* **2013**, *17*, 164–167. [CrossRef] [PubMed]
20. Bainbridge, D.; Brazil, K.; Ploeg, J.; Krueger, P.; Taniguchi, A. Measuring healthcare integration: Operationalization of a framework for a systems evaluation of palliative care structures, processes, and outcomes. *Palliat. Med.* **2016**, *30*, 567–579. [CrossRef] [PubMed]
21. Wittenberg, E.; Ferrell, B.; Goldsmith, J. Assessment of a statewide palliative care team training course: COMFORT Communication for Palliative Care Teams. *J. Palliat. Med.* **2016**, *19*, 746–752. [CrossRef] [PubMed]
22. Young, A.J.; Stephens, E.; Goldsmith, J. Family caregiver communication in the ICU: Toward a relational view of health literacy. *J. Fam. Commun.* **2017**, *17*, 137–152. [CrossRef]
23. Yuen, E.; Dodson, S.; Batterham, R.; Knight, T.; Chirgwin, J.; Livingstone, P. Development of a conceptual model of cancer caregiver health literacy. *Eur. J. Cancer Care* **2015**, *25*, 294–306. [CrossRef] [PubMed]
24. Baker, D. The Meaning and the Measure of Health Literacy. *J. Gen. Int. Med.* **2006**, *21*, 878–883. [CrossRef] [PubMed]
25. McNeil, A.; Arena, R. The evolution of health literacy and communication: Introducitng Health Harmonics. *Prog. Cardiovasc. Dis.* **2017**, *59*, 463–470. [CrossRef] [PubMed]
26. Apter, A. Numeracy in health care: A clinician's perspective. In Proceedings of the Institute of Medicine Workshop on Health Literacy and Numeracy, Washington, DC, USA, 18 July 2015.
27. Weaver, N.; Wray, R.; Zellin, S.; Gautam, K.; Jupka, K. Advancing organization health literacy in health organizations serving high-needs populations: A case study. *J. Health Commun.* **2012**, *17*, 55–66. [CrossRef] [PubMed]
28. Pleasant, A.; Rudd, R.; O'Leary, C.; Paasche-Orlow, M.; Allen, M.; Alvarado, W.; Myers, L.; Parson, K.; Rosen, S. Considerations for a New Definition of Health Literacy. 2016. Available online: https://nam.edu/wp-content/uploads/2016/04/Considerations-for-a-New-Definition-of-Health-Literacy.pdf (accessed on 14 Febuary 2017).
29. Meier, D. *Communication: Palliative Care's Transformation Procedure*; Palliative Care and Health Literacy: Workshop Summary; The National Academies Press: Washington, DC, USA, 2015.
30. Maxwell, B. *Professional Ethics Education Studies in Compassionate Empathy*; Springer: New York, NY, USA, 2008.
31. Decety, J. Introduction. In *Empathy: From Bench to Bedside*; Decety, J., Ed.; MIT Press: Cambridge, UK, 2011; pp. vi–ix.
32. Wright, V.; Pendry, B. Compassion and its role in the clinical encounter—An argument for compassion training. *J. Herb. Med.* **2016**, *6*, 198–203. [CrossRef]
33. Perez-Bret, E.; Altisent, R.; Rocafort, J. Definition of compassion in healthcare: A systematic literature review. *Int. J. Palliat. Nurs.* **2016**, *22*, 599–606. [CrossRef] [PubMed]
34. Sinclair, S.; Beamer, K.; Hack, T.; McClement, S.; Raffin Bouchal, S.; Chochinov, H.M.; Hagen, N. Sympathy, empathy, and compassion: A grounded theory study of palliative care patients' understandings, experiences, and preferences. *Palliat. Med.* **2017**, *31*, 437–447. [CrossRef] [PubMed]

behavioral sciences

MDPI

Review

Still Searching: A Meta-Synthesis of a Good Death from the Bereaved Family Member Perspective

Kelly E. Tenzek [1,*] and Rachel Depner [2,3]

[1] Department of Communication, University at Buffalo, The State University of New York, Buffalo, NY 14260, USA

[2] Counseling, School, and Educational Psychology, University at Buffalo, The State University of New York, Buffalo, NY 14260, USA; rmpeloqu@buffalo.edu

[3] Center for Hospice and Palliative Care, Cheektowaga, NY 14227, USA

* Correspondence: kellyten@buffalo.edu; Tel.: +1-716-645-1514

Academic Editor: Maureen P. Keeley
Received: 3 March 2017; Accepted: 19 April 2017; Published: 25 April 2017

Abstract: The concept of a good death continues to receive attention in end-of-life (EOL) scholarship. We sought to continue this line of inquiry related to a good death by conducting a meta-synthesis of published qualitative research studies that examined a good death from the bereaved family member's perspective. Results of the meta-synthesis included 14 articles with 368 participants. Based on analysis, we present a conceptual model called *The Opportunity Model for Presence during the EOL Process*. The model is framed in socio-cultural factors, and major themes include EOL process engagement with categories of healthcare participants, communication and practical issues. The second theme, (dis)continuity of care, includes categories of place of care, knowledge of family member dying and moment of death. Both of these themes lead to perceptions of either a good or bad death, which influences the bereavement process. We argue the main contribution of the model is the ability to identify moments throughout the interaction where family members can be present to the EOL process. Recommendations for healthcare participants, including patients, family members and clinical care providers are offered to improve the quality of experience throughout the EOL process and limitations of the study are discussed.

Keywords: end of life communication; family; good death; bereavement; presence

1. Introduction

The thought of a good death seems contradictory in nature, but it continues to be researched and is of great value to healthcare participants. Hospice and end-of-life (EOL) care can be considered a paradox in that there is the possibility of beauty and quality living at EOL [1]. Paradoxes in EOL care can also come in the label of a good death, differences in desires for the EOL process and the idea that such a monumental moment for some is just another day for others [2]. There is a growing body of both quantitative and qualitative research on the topic of a good death [3–5], including work on a Good Death Inventory [6] and a Quality of Dying and Death scale [7]. Research on quality of death has focused on the perspective of clinical caregivers [8,9], the dying person [10,11] or a combination of healthcare participants [12–15]. Although there is not full consensus in the literature about what factors or qualities contribute to a good death, there are clear overlapping aspects to a good death, including "pain and symptom management, clear decision making, preparation for death, completion, contributing to others and affirmation of the whole person" [12] (p. 825). Many studies continue to find similar results that overlap with these categories [11,16,17]. Good death studies have also been conducted across disparate geographic locations, including rural developed and developing countries and different cultures such as Taiwanese widows, bereaved family members in Singapore, European countries, Japan, Kenya and Israeli community members [16–22].

Recently, two reviews of good death studies were published that focused on healthcare providers, patients and family members as they identified aspects of what a good death looks like [13,17]. The results illustrate consensus on certain ideas such as the importance of pain management, but there were also differences that indicate a highly individualized definition of a good death that included socio-cultural factors that defined quality of life [13,17]. Both reviews concluded with a call for more research [13,17]. More, specifically there was a call for healthcare participants at end of life to engage in more open, public dialogue surrounding death and dying [13]. In recent decades, research and clinical perspectives have shifted in focus with regard to viewing death as a pathological or medical phenomenon towards taking a more holistic and comprehensive perspective that values the positive aspects of death and dying [23]. This reconceptualization moves beyond the medical model of death and focuses on helping patients die at home and better quality of care in hospitals [24]. Recently, results of a systematic literature review illustrated that voices of rural participants at EOL have been marginalized and require attention because their needs are unique and present both challenges and benefits regarding the EOL experience in a rural setting [25]. Based on the results of this particular study, it is necessary for healthcare providers to understand the informational and medicinal needs of patients and family members in rural settings through communication and adequate dissemination of information [25]. While there are diverse contexts for EOL, it has been has considered a taboo topic, difficult for healthcare participants to bring up and engage in conversation [26]; if family members and patients know that the EOL is approaching, they have the opportunity to have meaningful conversations that promote a good death [27]. Therefore, we were interested in narrowing the focus to bereaved family member perspectives on going through the EOL process for a loved one. In doing so, we extend the EOL experience to continue to look past moment of death into bereavement experiences for survivors.

Family members have been noted to play numerous important roles with regard to the dying process as well as after the death of a loved one [25,28,29]. When an individual dies, it impacts the entire family and is noted as one of the most stressful life situations with regard to the family unit [30]. Additional research has found that quality of death may play a role in the manifestation of complicated bereavement. Particularly in a group of bereaved people, three aspects of quality of their loved one's death were associated with later complicated bereavement: (a) dissatisfaction with the explanation to the family about the patient's expected outcome; (b) the unreasonable cost of care; and (c) the family's perception that the deceased person had not achieved a sense of completion about his or her life [31]. This research highlights the unique relationship between how a person dies and what potential impact that death may have on his or her family. Furthermore, the role of communication has been noted as critical in EOL care and the grief and bereavement process [32,33]. While the line of inquiry specifically related to a good death from a family perspective is relatively new, more research is needed to understand the family perspective at end of life. Research with family members who experienced loss noted several comprehensive factors that contribute to quality of death. These include personal, relational, biomedical, psychological and spiritual factors [3].

We seek to continue this line of inquiry related to a good death by conducting a meta-synthesis of published qualitative research studies that examined a good death from the bereaved family member's perspective. A meta-synthesis allows for a more comprehensive understanding and conceptual or theoretical development that is not possible in one study alone [34,35]. We set out to engage in a systematic approach to research that included a literature search, description and screening for inclusion and exclusion criteria, quality assessment, data extraction and analysis [36–38]. Results of the meta-synthesis will be shared and discussed to better understand how family members experience the EOL process and the death of a loved one.

This meta-synthesis contributes to ongoing scholarly research and conversations related to EOL and a good death in three ways. First, we narrow the focus specifically to the perspective of the family members. Second, we expand the database search for articles, building upon the previous review [13], such that it is more inclusive of published articles. In doing so, we obtain a more comprehensive view of the literature. Finally, we will present a conceptual model in order to suggest future interventions that may be developed in order to help improve communication at EOL.

As our conceptualization of death continues to change towards a natural, developmental aspect of life, we must consider the communication processes within the family. No person dies in a vacuum and there are positive implications for reducing stigma, focusing on family bereavement interventions and encouraging more public dialogue for future family generations. Therefore, the guiding questions for the meta-synthesis were: What are bereaved family caregivers' experiences of going through EOL with a loved one, and how does the EOL experience contribute to a good or bad death?

2. Materials and Method

Meta-synthesis was used in this study to answer research questions regarding family caregivers' experiences of going through EOL and how that experience may contribute to a good or bad death. A meta-synthesis is a commitment of time and labor, but is beneficial for healthcare policy and practice [39]. We engaged in a four-step process for meta-synthesis that included (a) a literature search, (b) a quality appraisal, (c) classification and (d) synthesis [38,40].

2.1. Step 1: Literature Search Process

A comprehensive search was conducted, guided by key terms and the use of key databases. Then we eliminated duplicates and applied general search parameters to eliminate irrelevant search results. Once we had narrowed the results according to outlined general parameters, we prepared for full article review to determine study eligibility based on inclusion and exclusion criteria. The entire process is outlined below.

First, in an effort to expand the database search beyond [13], we included 14 databases for our search. Based on our guiding question for the study, we independently began our search using (a) PsycINFO, (b) Academic Search Complete, (c) MEDLINE with Full Text, (d) PsycARTICLES, (e) Psychology and Behavioral Sciences Collection, (f) PsycTESTS, (g) Social Sciences Full Text (H.W. Wilson), (h) Social Work Abstracts, (i) SocINDEX, (j) ALT Healthwatch, (k) CINAHL plus with full text, (l) Communication and Mass Media Complete, (m) Eric and (n) Health Source Nursing/Academic Edition. We carefully considered the key terms for our search rooted in relevant literature in the area of a good death and constructions of family. Therefore, examples of key terms included various combinations of: good death, end-of-life, family, bereavement, qualitative, hospice, quality death, caregivers and spouse. We independently searched for articles using the key terms through the databases outlined above and then came together multiple times to eliminate duplicates. Then we prepared for the next step, which was to set up the general parameters for our search and narrow down relevant articles that identified the topic of a good death, within the population of bereaved family members that had no restrictions on date or bereavement time. Our goal was to research a specific methodological approach to the EOL process, which was the "how", research was done and we looked at qualitative studies [38]. It was at this point that we also eliminated other meta-syntheses, article reviews, commentaries, editorial and dissertations. Furthermore, articles had to be in English.

2.1.1. Inclusion vs. Exclusion

Next, we met multiple times and discussed elements to guide the decision-making process for inclusion and exclusion criteria. In order to be included in the study, the articles were reviewed in full to identify the necessary components: (a) family members or loved ones of someone who was engaged in the dying process and/or passed away. The key here was the participant had to experience the loss of a loved one and the study was about that experience as opposed to a hypothetical loss; (b) mention good death at least once in the paper; (c) qualitative analysis/mixed methods were acceptable as long as the qualitative portion was clearly articulated; (d) the analysis had to provide results that portrayed the family perspective. For articles that combined healthcare participants, the family perspective had to be clearly articulated and represented equally in the analysis. If multiple healthcare participants were included and there was no differentiation between perspectives or there were not sufficient examples of family (i.e., quotes from the family were not equally represented among other perspectives) the article was excluded; (e) studies must have been reviewed and approved by an institutional review board. For our purposes, it was acceptable if a published study clearly articulated that an ethical review was conducted by an organization. We believed that, because of the enormity of the delicate time and topic in a family member's life, we wanted to ensure the study was held to the highest ethical standards. As we were going through the process, if we were unsure, we discussed the individual article together and came to a decision. While some studies claimed consent was gained, we felt this was not enough information to meet this criterion and therefore studies were not included; (f) finally, to be considered for inclusion, studies had to be published in a peer-reviewed journal outlet.

2.1.2. Search Results

Step 1 of the process is shown in Figure 1. The results from our independent search efforts, from October 2016 to the end of January 2017 combined, returned 1543 hits. Once all duplicates were removed there were 821 remaining hits. At this point, we began the title and abstract search according to the general parameters outlined above, which resulted in 134 articles for full review. We noticed that a common article in the literature surrounding good death did not appear in our search, so we manually incorporated that into our search, which then changed our total number of articles to 135 for full review. After full review, 14 articles remained after we eliminated 121 articles. See Figure 1.

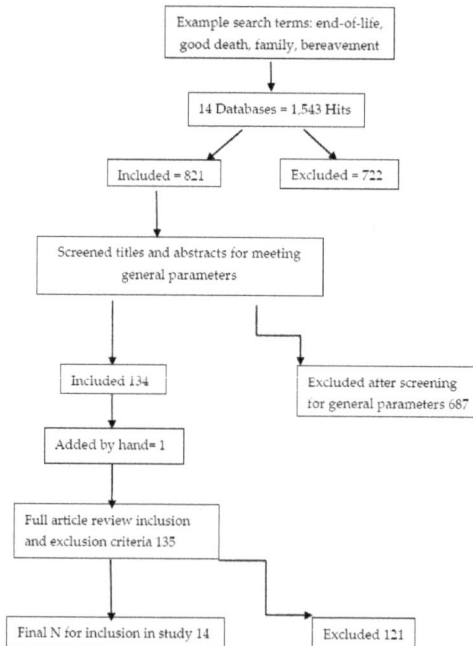

Figure 1. Search Results.

2.2. Step 2: Quality Appraisal

In order to address quality appraisal, we created a Microsoft Word coding document based on relevant criteria that examined the design and implementation of research using standards outlined by scholars [38,40–42]. We met to discuss each aspect of the coding sheet for quality appraisal and went through examples together until we had a shared understanding of what we believed quality to look like. We rated each article across key areas of demographic information, literature review, methodology, results and discussion. After completing the process for each article, we rated the quality of each article (e.g., 3 = high quality, 2 = moderate quality and 1 = low quality). As argued in previous research, if the article met the criteria for inclusion, they were not thrown out of analysis for low quality appraisal score [38,40].

2.3. Step 3: Classification Findings

Data were extracted by pulling information from the article to capture participant demographics and methodological details such as qualitative method, location of study, number of participants etc. We then also pulled the information directly from the results section from each article and placed this information into a Microsoft Word document to create our data set for coding purposes. We were able to then classify according to the Sandelwoski and Borroso system (no finding, topical, thematic, conceptual/thematic description, interpretive explanation) [38,43]. The results of this process are presented in Appendix A (Table A1).

2.4. Step 4: Data Abstraction and Synthesis

We were guided by [38]'s approach to meta-synthesis. In addition, while they argue that if classification results were no finding, topical, or thematic survey, then a meta-summary would be the more appropriate method, we argue, for the purposes of our study and moving scholarship forward, that an interpretive approach was appropriate. We wanted to begin to better understand bereaved family perspectives on a good death as a larger part of the EOL process and healthcare system. Furthermore, because there were no studies classified as no finding, only two were topical and a majority of studies were thematic, when the nature of qualitative work is to understand and make sense of phenomena through exploration and interpretation, an opportunity to truly integrate findings as opposed to comparing studies was presented [38].

We approached the data synthesis by combining taxonomic and constant targeted comparison grounded theory analysis [38,40]. We had not initially intended to use event timeline as an analytical tool, but because the conceptual elements aligned temporally, we also incorporated timeline into our analysis [36]. We followed a grounded theory approach by Charmaz [11]. The process entailed reading through the data to familiarize ourselves with the data and then began opening coding. Next we engaged in the processes of focused and axial coding, followed by diagramming. The results of this iterative process are showcased in the conceptual model presented in Figure 2.

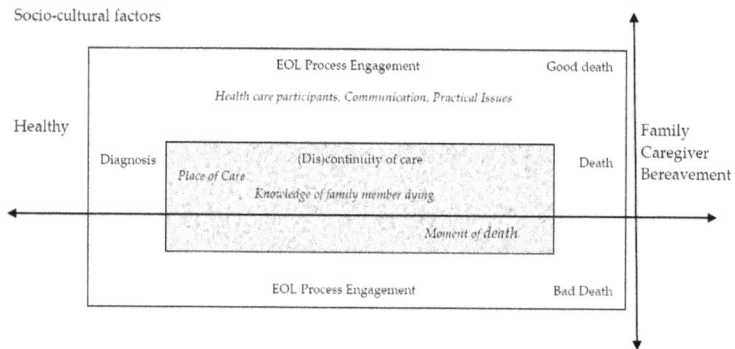

Figure 2. The Opportunity Model for Presence during the EOL Process.

2.5. Validity

As outlined by meta-synthesis scholars, the rigor and validity of the meta-synthesis is important. We took the following steps: (a) a detailed and thorough literature search; (b) collaborative discussion on appropriate inclusion and exclusion criteria; (c) quality appraisal by creating coding sheets guided by previous research; and (d) an audit trail of the collaborative process [38,40].

3. Results

Results of the meta-synthesis included 14 articles and are presented in Appendix A (Table A1). The 14 articles had quality appraisal scores ranging from 14 to 21, with an average score of 17.7. Results of the classification findings included eight thematic articles. Furthermore, three were conceptual, two were topical and one study was interpretive. None of the studies were classified as no findings. Results point to a complex and complicated process related to constructions of the EOL experience. There were a total of 368 participants that experienced a range of bereavement lengths when all studies were combined. The research questions that motivated the meta-synthesis were: what are bereaved family caregivers' experiences of going through EOL with a loved one, and how does the EOL experience contribute to a good or bad death? The results highlight that interpretation of death of a loved one included both unique and specific moments of care and overall recollections of the dying process. Ultimately, we observed that the EOL experience is influenced by multiple intertwined factors that may influence interaction at each new turning point or change within the patient's narrative as recalled by the family caregiver. When looking at the findings of the 14 studies as a whole, we found that the family caregivers who experienced positive engagement at one point or throughout the entire process had a better EOL experience. Conversely, family caregivers who experienced a negative moment(s) within the EOL care process expressed negative experiences. Based on the idea that there were critical moments recalled by family members that characterized the EOL experience and consequent labeling of a good death, we present a conceptual model, called *The Opportunity Model for Presence during the EOL Process*.

Analysis of the 14 studies taken in concert illustrated a progression through the dying experience as recalled by family caregivers. Therefore, we argue that a timeline emerged based on family caregiver's memory of events, starting from their loved one being healthy (not clearly dying, no idea it was a possible health outcome) continuing through the death of his or her loved one and into bereavement (see Figure 2). We do not mean to say that the timeline is linear and the events take place in the same order for all healthcare participants. Rather it is a dynamic timeline that fluctuates according to the EOL experience. At each stage of the timeline, there is an opportunity for engagement that allows the family member to be present to the EOL experience. When the opportunities for engagement are missed, the positive moments and experiences for quality and satisfying EOL care

are also missed. When this is the case, we argue negative experiences and low engagement result in labeling the experience as a bad death, leading to complicated bereavement.

Figure 2 illustrates a timeline that is immersed in (a) socio-cultural factors [19,20,45–47], and as the healthcare events and experiences progress, two themes emerge; (b) levels of engagement [19,45,48–51]; and (c) (dis)continuity of care [19,45,50,52,53]. These contribute to the EOL experience, which then is labeled as good or bad. The EOL experience does not end there however, as it extends into after-death experiences and shapes the bereavement process [45,48,50,54]. The results presented here compose a conceptual model that integrates diverse experiences throughout the EOL process. We remained grounded in the data as conceptual linkages emerged and we attempted to capture incredible nuance that showcased individual differences, but also provided clarity on elements that lead to a positive or negative EOL experience for family carers.

3.1. Socio-Cultural Factors

Based on the studies we defined socio-cultural factors as the different values, cultures, preferences and experiences that make up the environment for healthcare interactions. We include individual differences, patient-caregiver belief systems and past experiences in the socio-cultural factors. For example, definitions of EOL and bereavement experiences are incredibly diverse and different based on the family caregiver's experience, knowledge and media exposure [20,45,48,52].

Additionally, components of the socio-cultural elements that shape our environment include biomedical, psychosocial and spiritual components [19,48,55,56]. Finally, we argue language is part of the socio-cultural environment that healthcare participants bring with them into the EOL process. The use and understanding of language in part defines the environment. For caregivers, when they entered into the EOL process for their patient and interacted with doctors, the use of medical terminology worked socioculturally for the doctor in the medical context, but it did not work for the caregiver, who did not have the same language knowledge and experience [47]. The socio-cultural elements that make up peoples' environments are then carried with them as the timeline shifts from "healthy" to "diagnosis". The next section continues to discuss the EOL process from "diagnosis" to "death". We will first focus on the theme of EOL process engagement and subsequent categories of healthcare participants, communication and practical issues.

3.2. EOL Process Engagement

The theme of EOL process engagement identified the characters involved in EOL care known as healthcare participants, the type of interpersonal interactions that take place through communication and organizational or systematic issues that have the potential to influence how EOL care is perceived, which we refer to as practical issues.

3.2.1. Healthcare Participants

When the interaction moves forward into the healthcare scenario from healthy to initial diagnosis, certain participants entered into the EOL process in different roles. Clinical staff including doctors, nurses, hospice aides etc. began to fulfill clinical care needs. The familial healthcare participants include, spouses, children, siblings and grandparents who enact certain roles. For family members, that role could extend into healthcare provider or patient advocate. Some fulfilled this specific role because it was the morally appropriate thing to do [45,52,54]. There were also community members and religious or spiritual care providers who offered a certain type of care at EOL [19,49].

For family carers and participants in the studies, when care was needed and if it was administered and received properly (i.e., a smooth integration of care by provider), family carers felt good about the situation and were empowered [45,52,53]. This was also seen in family caregivers' desire for accommodation from medical staff/care facility to meet patients' needs. This also had to do with the carer knowing their loved one's history and preferences. One article illustrated that they had little understanding of how the medical care team worked. When working with specialized care teams, the roles were extremely complex [51]. When there was conflict between medical staff and family caregivers, the outcome was often feelings of frustration, isolation and powerlessness. For example, "if care was viewed as high quality, participants described a willingness to entrust the dying person's care to professional caregivers. If they were insecure about the quality of care, trust was lacking and they reported a need to be on guard as the dying person's advocate" [54] (p. 910). Role clarity was complicated by blurred lines between professional clinical caregiver roles and family caregiver roles, especially when the clinical staff had an expectation/assumption that the family caregiver knew and understood the biomedical nature of EOL processes. A thread that underlies the healthcare participant role and provision of care is communication. The next section delves into defining and explaining the communication portion of engagement during the EOL process.

3.2.2. Communication

We argue communication, or the interaction among healthcare participants during EOL care, is at the heart of the *Opportunity Model for Presence during the EOL Process*. Communication was comprised of elements such as social support, decision-making and relationships. Characteristics of interpersonal communication included trust, intimacy, empathy, trust and listening. The studies indicate a wide array of communication exchanges and experiences, and what we observed was that with the instances where the family caregiver perceived to be listened to, received kindness, social support and engaged in decision-making with other healthcare participants, the EOL process at that moment was positive [19,48,51,55]. When descriptions of healthcare encounters included a lack of involvement in decision-making, lack of listening, no kindness or empathy, family caregivers were frustrated, upset and had a negative perception of that EOL experience [47,50,52,54,56]. We argue here again that the negative examples due to communication were missed opportunities for a positive experience that can be addressed. The third component of EOL process engagement is practical issues throughout the EOL process.

3.2.3. Practical Issues

Practical issues emerged from the data set as tangible, concrete obstacles that influenced the quality of EOL process perceived by family caregivers, including spatial attributes, after death management and access to care and cost. First, in terms of spatial attributes, participants mentioned the set of hospital rooms, cleanliness of facilities and how these influenced the privacy or lack thereof during the EOL process [19,49]. We often think of the next step after death as funeral arrangements or cremation, or even grief and bereavement, but there are practical aspects that family caregivers mentioned they were not aware of and it influenced the EOL process immediately after their loved one had died [45]. Finally, there was not a strong thematic representation of access to care and care within the data set, but we argue it is such an important issue that it warranted mention as a practical barrier to even entering into the preferred type of EOL care and management of accessing health care and payments [54]. As we move both through the event timeline and concurrently address the sociocultural factors and levels of engagement, we now move deeper into the EOL process and address the theme of (dis)continuity of care. This theme has three categories that have the potential to oscillate back and forth between place of care, knowledge of family member dying and moment of death. We continue to thread the sociocultural factors through the model combined with engagement factors that simultaneously permeate the inner core of the model.

3.3. (Dis)continuity of Care

In the section of the model that addresses (dis)continuity of care, the data indicated that there was the potential for a lot of movement in the progression of the EOL process. Therefore, the overarching theme here is related to continuity of care through the process and identification of moments where there was either a smooth progression of care provided throughout the EOL process or a break in continuity, resulting in uncertainty or dissatisfaction. The section below discusses the categories of (dis)continuity of care.

3.3.1. Place of Care

Results of the analysis illustrate that the place of EOL care was a component to the EOL process [48,50,52,56]. Examples of place included: home, hospice, hospital and tertiary care facility. It was also evident that family caregiver experiences of place of care involved a combination of facilities and transfers among places of care or the missed opportunity to transition to a different type of care. Several studies noted that EOL care discussions occurred too late or were too ambiguous, which led to their loved one dying prior to receiving the change in care [56]. This, at times, created stress for the family caregiver because they realized their loved one could have died in a different way or in a different setting. The place of EOL care was noted and linked to the type of care accessed (dying at home versus dying in a hospital) and subsequently utilized (whether a transfer was discussed, secured or not addressed), as well as the family member's overall perception of the dying process. The last-minute nature of EOL discussions relating to plan of care required flexibility in that, even if the desires of patient were known, the biomedical needs of that patient may shift and change options for receiving EOL care [52,56].

3.3.2. Knowledge of Family Member Dying

The place of care was complicated by family caregiver knowledge of where their loved one was in the dying process. There is a range of possible combinations for knowledge and understanding of the reality of the loved one dying. For example, the family may not know their loved one was at EOL and it was a complete shock. This may be because they were not told of the biomedical status of patient [50] or they may have been told, but they did not/could not accept that. Another possibility could be that the family member knew and it was communicated so much that it became offensive. Another study noted the importance of preparing for the death of their loved one through awareness and understanding, indicating it is best if patients and family members know and understand that their loved one is dying [45]. The data also note the importance of the family members having anticipatory time to reflect on and begin to make sense of their loved one's death prior to the moment of death, compared to individuals that had an ambiguous understanding of their loved one's situation who reported the moment of death as more traumatic or complicated due to the unexpected nature of the situation. The place of death and knowledge further complicated the moment of death.

3.3.3. Moment of Death

While (dis)continuity of care is the primary theme for this portion of the conceptual model, we know that these factors are oscillating and we see the categories of place of care and knowledge level go back and forth as the loved one's health changes. This extends into the moment of death. Here we see conflict arise when a patient did not die in the place they wanted, the family caregiver was unaware that their loved one was dying and when a family caregiver was not present for the death of a loved one. While a family member could not have knowledge regarding the imminent death, this also means that they were not prepared for the actual moment of death and this shaped the experience of losing a loved one. The biomedical option of sedation was also discussed as an option for EOL care that may be administered for patients in different physical locations at various points in the EOL process, but when death was near, it could complicate the exact moment of death. This example had particular relevance to understanding the palliative sedation intervention, which can lead to distress [20]. If we continue along the timeline enmeshed with sociocultural and EOL engagement and proceed until after the moment of death, we arrive at this reflective space of labeling the EOL experience ranging from a good death with high engagement to a bad death with low engagement.

3.4. Good vs. Bad Death Experiences

Based on our findings, while a good death had to be mentioned at least once in the paper, not all studies used the label good or bad death to describe their experiences. What we see are examples of peaceful death, beautiful death, death quality etc. [46,49,55] as well as traumatic or stressful deaths [45,48,50,53–55]. What our model illustrates is that the entire process is made up of many turning points or moments of opportunity. These moments of opportunity are particularly salient when the family caregiver felt there were barriers to care, a discontinuity of care, if the death came as a shock or if the patient's needs were not fulfilled, because this left family caregivers with negative feelings of low engagement and powerlessness [48–51,53,54,56]. Once the death has happened, the timeline pushes out of engagement and (dis)continuity of care into family carer bereavement.

Results illustrate that it is an incredibly difficult experience to lose a loved one. Authors of one of the studies conceptualized the grief trajectory as including three main stages: (a) the initial loss or gap left from the death of a loved one; (b) the acute or intense grief following the death; and, finally, (c) a stepped journey towards bereavement recovery [56]. The dynamic and overlapping nature of both the end-of-life process and bereavement of the family member can be difficult to disentangle from one another. However, it became clear how important it was for family caregivers to spend the EOL engagement and (dis)continuity of care portions of the timeline present with the loved one, being active and living to the fullest at EOL. Therefore, the final section discusses the overarching conceptual component that drives the theoretical model: presence.

3.5. Presence

Based on the studies, we define presence in part as being physically present with the patient, if that was desired, and, more holistically, being focused and aware [19,46,49,53,55] of what was happening at each step in the timeline. We do not mean that being physically present for every family member will determine a positive or negative EOL experience. However, being present and aware of what patient wanted along with knowing what options were available to the patient and family become necessary so that an informed decision can be made. This creates positive opportunities for high engagement. We argue when the family member had the opportunity to be present and engage in a variety of ways, by (a) awareness of the illness' trajectory, (b) saying an appropriate goodbye, (c) negotiating the plan of care with the clinical staff, (d) being an advocate for the patient and (e) experiencing kindness, empathy and support, then a quality EOL experience was possible [20,45,49,53,54]. These opportunities for presence do not happen in isolation. Being fully present to the EOL experience requires collaboration with all healthcare participants and an awareness of sociocultural factors and engagement levels. Finally, we argue that the bereavement experience is cyclical and loops back to the beginning of the timeline healthy, when the caregiver begins the process again for a loved one or they receive a diagnosis and enter into the process model. The relational nature of death, dying and loss cannot be fully explicated from one another. Each represents an opportunity for the reconceptualization of these experiences. This is particularly noted by one of the articles as the authors write that "bereavement was found to be an individualized, contextualized and multifaceted experience ... with subthemes of positive assistance or of being hampered by factors both before and after death" [48] (p. 263). These results stress the importance of expanding the conceptualization of bereavement to include an anticipatory period that encompasses the cyclical and cumulative nature of grief after the death of a loved one.

4. Discussion

The guiding questions for this meta-synthesis were (a) what are bereaved family caregivers' experiences of going through EOL with a loved one and (b) how does the EOL experience contribute to a good or bad death? Results indicate that the experiences of caregivers going through the EOL process with a loved one are incredibly mixed. There were both good and bad experiences, good moments and terrible narratives of the poor communication that left a negative imprint on the family member's EOL experience and grieving process. In terms of what components made up the good death experience, the results closely align with previous scholarship in the good death literature, including pain and symptom management, clear decision-making, preparation for death and communication [6,7,12,14, 17,57,58]. Furthermore, the results align with an earlier meta-synthesis of EOL care from the family perspective that reported the necessity of quality communication among healthcare participants and clinicians being open about imminent death [30]. While the review discussed the importance of advance care directives to the feeling of being prepared, advance care planning was not strongly represented within our data set. However, we believe that the process nature of EOL and making changes to the sociocultural factors, such as normalizing death through advanced care directives, can really improve the care provided throughout the EOL process. The importance of support throughout the entire process is crucial, including continued support after the loss of a loved one, as times of grief and sadness require a reconstruction of life without the loved one [45,48,59]. Although loss is challenging in any circumstance, we argue the loss of a child is extremely difficult and changes the lives of the surviving bereaved [60]. While much of the good death literature focuses on the natural progression to EOL, the importance of bereavement when parents and siblings lose a loved one, the biopsychosocial and spiritual factors, communication and decision-making are even more important because the bereavement experience becomes part of the sociocultural factors that will influence the family's next experience with EOL.

It became clear that no one entered into the diagnosis phase and the EOL process intending to have negative experiences, but nonetheless this was often the case. We argue that with the use of the *Opportunity Model for Presence during the EOL Process*, if family members are aware of the process of EOL then they can be more aware of being present to and advocating for the care their loved one desires at EOL. As previously stated, we believe that quality communication is essential for providing and experiencing care at EOL. As the following quote explains, it is not just about dying, but living throughout the entire process: "The pivotal role of good communication is the route to ensuring that issues are addressed, with hope maintained for the patient to live as well as possible until they die, and that patients' quality of life is maximized" [61] (p. 91). If we can maximize the quality of life while the patient is alive with the knowledge, understanding and acceptance that the loved one will pass away, all of the healthcare participants can become engaged, present and continue to make memories. These memories become what the family member will have with them after their loved one dies. We do not imply this is an easy process, but we do emphasize the importance of capturing the opportunities to be present throughout the EOL process will have a positive influence on bereavement.

Recommendations are offered in the latest Institute of Medicine report to continue to address barriers to quality and individualized EOL care including (a) care delivery, (b) clinician-patient communication and advance care planning, (c) professional education and development, (d) policies and payment systems and (e) public education and engagement [62] (p. 3). While we believe each of these aspects can be applied to the current study, we want to offer two recommendations for moving research in the area of EOL processes. We argue that specifically related to concepts of a "good death", family caregivers and bereavement in this study align with the recommendations from IOM for communication, professional education and development and public education and engagement. First, with the model, we propose there are areas for interventions to be developed to help healthcare participants communicate about EOL. Research illustrates that healthcare participants struggle with engaging in EOL conversations [26,62,63]. Methods and models currently exist to help clinicians interact with patients and family members: SPIKES [64], COMFORT [65], PREPARED [66] and BATHE [67]. We argue these conversations need to continue to be integrated into medical education through curriculum development and continuing education for medical professionals, wherein the focus on palliative care and hospice become more prevalent. However, we do not mean to imply that the enormity of engaging in the EOL conversation should only fall on the doctors. Patients and family members need to be their own advocate as well throughout the EOL process and be involved in conversations related to advance care planning and team meetings [62]. We argue that being more open about experiences of losing a loved one in the past and integrating EOL conversations into conversations much earlier in the educational system would create the opportunity to naturalize EOL and continue the dialogue regarding death and dying [13]. We argue more classes at the college level, not only for medical students but as courses offered in communication, social work and nursing departments, would be extremely beneficial.

Secondly, while the timeline we propose in the model is not linear in nature, there is an opportunity for a "presence check" at all stages of the EOL process. According to the IOM report, achieving the goal of affordable care that is sustainable for people with advanced illness is possible and requires, "the provision of quality care that offers patients and families both compassion and choice" [62] (p. 22). As healthcare providers and scholars, we must continue to ask questions such as "how are the relationships, how is the communication, and what practical barriers are in the way of achieving the goals for EOL interaction?" This may be something as mundane as the cleanliness and ease of maneuvering the facility and greeting fellow healthcare participants with a smile. We realize that communication and relationships take work and there are certain organizational constraints, but the results of this meta-synthesis illustrate how meaningful and powerful the positive aspects of communication can be on EOL processes including listening, involvement in decision-making, appropriate touch and support throughout the EOL process. Familiar faces from diagnosis to bereavement seemed to be significant. By combining clinical competence through interpersonal communication skills and knowledge as defined by the IOM with "presence checks" for healthcare participants we can further provide quality care through compassion and choice [62].

Limited by search parameters, we intentionally searched broadly to capture articles that fit our search criteria, but then we also had specific inclusion and exclusion criteria that narrowed the scope. We feel this is both a boon and a bane when it comes to obtaining a holistic picture of the context we were searching to understand. Secondly, methodologically, a meta-synthesis calls for synthesis of findings within the articles, but without the use of original participant quotations. The meta-summary however, is more quantifiable and focuses on frequencies at a surface level of understanding and interpretation [38]. We felt that our articles for inclusion were more on the thematic side of the scale but, because of the rich nature of experiences and deeply emotional topic area, they warranted a more in-depth look beyond categorizing by frequencies of information analysis. Therefore, the conceptual model is proposed to help healthcare participants understand the process in front of them during EOL and create the opportunities for presence checks, but should be taken as something that needs further investigation for nuances that may have been lost in the meta-synthesis in order to see the bigger picture of good death and family bereavement. We want to continue research efforts to apply the model in future studies and create interventions at different timelines where the findings indicate there is a window of opportunity for high engagement.

5. Conclusions

We argue the meta-synthesis contributes to ongoing scholarly research and conversations related to EOL and a good death in three ways. First, we narrowed the focus specifically to the perspective of the family members. Second, we expanded the database search for articles from the previous review [38] to be more inclusive of published articles and obtain a more comprehensive view of the literature. Finally, we proposed a conceptual model in order to help healthcare participants have more positive EOL experiences. We look forward to continued efforts in this area of EOL communication to help healthcare participants, especially bereaved family members, achieve a good death.

Conflicts of Interest: The authors declare no conflict of interest.

Appendix A

Table A1. Step 3 Classification of data.

Source/Country	Aim/Purpose	Methods/Data Collection	Sample N	Bereavement Period	Classification and QA Score
Holdsworth, (2015) [45] United Kingdom	"The aim of this article is to describe the end-of-life experience from the point of view of bereaved family carers with particular reference to the role that care providers play in shaping this experience" [45] (p. 835).	Interviews	45	6–10 months	Thematic/21
Wilson, MacLeod, & Houttekier, (2016) [48] Canada	"As it does not appear that research has focused on a linkage between death quality and the intensity of bereavement grief, we conducted a mixed-methods research study to determine if this relationship exists and for evidence-based insights into any connections between bereavement grief and death quality" [48] (p. 261).	Interviews	41	5 months–8 years	Thematic/18
Nelson, Schrader, & Eidsness, (2009) [54] United States	"The aim of this study was to explore end-of-life (EOL) experiences of South Dakotans who had experienced the death of a loved one in the last 5 years" [54] (p. 905).	Interviews	35	Within 5 years	Topical/14
Lee, Woo, & Goh, (2013) [19] Singapore	"The aim of this study was to examine the concept of a good death from the perspectives of both the dying person and the family caregiver, as perceived by bereaved family caregivers of advanced cancer patients" [19] (p. 37).	5 focus groups, 1 interview	18	6–18 months	Thematic/16
Kongsuwan, Chaipetch, & Matchim, (2012) [55] Thailand	"The purpose of the study was to describe the concept of a peaceful death in ICUs from Thai Buddhist family members' perspectives" [55] (p. 152).	Interviews	9	2–12 months	Conceptual/20
Abib El Halal, Piva, Lago, El Halal, Cabral, Nilson, & Garcia, 2013 [47] Brazil	"The aim of this study was to explore parents' perspectives of the quality of the care offered to them and their terminally ill child in the child's last days of life in two Brazilian PICUs" [47] (p. 496).	Semi-structured interview	15	6–12 months	Thematic/16
Donnelly & Battley, (2010) [49] Ireland	"To describe the contemporary experience of relatives in a tertiary referral hospital. of the moment of death, traditionally a very significant event" [49] (p. 96).	Interviews	24	Unclear	Topical/18

Table A1. *Cont.*

Source/Country	Aim/Purpose	Methods/Data Collection	Sample N	Bereavement Period	Classification and QA Score
Robert, Zhukovsky, Mauricio, Gilmore, Morrison, & Palos; (2012) [51] United States	"To understand the needs and experiences of bereaved parents whose child had received care at one National Cancer Institute–designated comprehensive cancer center. The investigators were particularly interested in the parents' perceptions of the care received by their child, their expectations of palliative care, and recommendations on how best to improve palliative care for children with cancer and their parents" [51] (p. 318).	Focus groups	14	Lost a loved one a minimum of one year before study	Thematic/20
Evans, Cutson, Steinhauser, & Tulsky (2006) [52] United States	"To describe caregivers' reasons for transfer from home hospice to inpatient facilities, preferences for site of care and death, and their experiences during these transfers" [52] (p. 100).	Interviews	18	Contacted about study at least four weeks after patient death	Thematic/17
Jack, O'Brien, Scrutton, Baldry, & Groves, (2015) [53] United Kingdom	"To explore bereaved family carers' perceptions and experiences of a hospice at home service" [53] (p. 131).	Interviews	20	At least 3 months	Conceptual/20
Williams, Bailey, Noh, Woodby, Wittich & Burgio (2015) [56] United States	"The purpose of this qualitative study was to explore the personal and interpersonal context of next-of-kin's discussions with clinicians regarding discharge planning to home hospice or inpatient palliative care service for hospitalized veterans" [56] (p. 51).	Participant obser-vation, focus groups, and interviews	78	3–6 months	Interpretive/17
Wilches-Gutiérrez, Arenas-Monreal, Paulo-Maya, Peláez-Ballestas, & Idrovo, (2012) [46] Mexico	"To ascertain the elements comprising the health/illness /death process in the context of a holiday in this municipality (Yautepec, Morelos, Mexico)" [46] (p. 775).	Interviews	7	Loss within the last four years	Conceptual/18
Bruinsma, Brown, van der Heide, Deliens, Anquinet, Payne, Seymour, & Rietjens, (2014) [20] Belgium, United Kingdom, Netherlands	"The purpose of the study was to explore relatives' descriptions and experiences of continuous sedation in end-of-life care for cancer patients and to identify and explain differences between respondents from the Netherlands, Belgium, and the UK" [20] (p. 3243).	Interviews	38	3–18 months	Thematic/18
Workman & Mann, (2007) [50] Canada	"To identify areas for improvement in delivering high quality end-of-life care on the medical teaching unit" [50] (p. 433).	Interviews	6	6 months	Thematic/15

References

1. Twycross, R. Patient care: Past, Present, and Future. *Omega J. Death Dying* **2007**, *56*, 7–19. [CrossRef]
2. Masson, J.D. Non-Professional Perceptions of 'Good Death': A Study of the Views of Hospice Care Patients and Relatives of Deceased Hospice Care Patients. *Mortality* **2002**, *7*, 191–209. [CrossRef]
3. Van Gennip, I.E.; Pasman, H.R.W.; Kaspers, P.J.; Oosterveld-Vlug, M.G.; Willems, D.L.; Deeg, D.J.H.; Onwuteaka-Philipsen, B.D. Death with Dignity from the Perspective of the Surviving Family: A Survey Study Among Family Caregivers of Deceased Older Adults. *Palliat. Med.* **2013**, *27*, 616–624. [CrossRef] [PubMed]
4. Good, M.J.D.; Gadmer, N.M.; Ruopp, P.; Lakoma, M.; Sullivan, A.M.; Redinbaugh, E.; Arnold, R.M.; Block, S.D. Narrative Nuances on Good and Bad Deaths: Internists' Tales from High-Technology Work Places. *Soc. Sci. Med.* **2004**, *58*, 939–953. [CrossRef]
5. Lee, H.J.; Jo, K.H.; Chee, K.H.; Lee, Y.J. The Perception of Good Death among Human Services Students in South Korea: A Q-methodological Approach. *Death Stud.* **2008**, *32*, 870–890. [CrossRef] [PubMed]
6. Miyashita, M.; Morita, T.; Sato, K.; Hirai, K.; Shima, Y.; Uchitomi, Y. Good Death Inventory: A Measure for Evaluating Good Death from the Bereaved Family Member's Perspective. *J. Pain Symptom Manag.* **2008**, *35*, 486–498. [CrossRef] [PubMed]
7. Patrick, D.L.; Engelberg, R.A.; Curtis, J.R. Evaluating the Quality of Dying and Death. *J. Pain Symptom Manag.* **2001**, *22*, 717–726. [CrossRef]
8. Griggs, C. Community Nurses' Perceptions of a Good death: A Qualitative Exploratory Study. *Int. J. Palliat. Nurs.* **2010**, *16*, 140–149. [CrossRef] [PubMed]
9. Cipolletta, S.; Oprandi, N. What is a Good Death? Health Care Professionals' Narrations on End-of-Life Care. *Death Stud.* **2014**, *38*, 20–27. [CrossRef] [PubMed]
10. Cheng, S.-Y.; Hu, W.-Y.; Liu, W.-J.; Yao, C.-A.; Chen, C.-Y.; Chiu, T.-Y. Good Death Study of Elderly Patients with Terminal Cancer in Taiwan. *Palliat. Med.* **2008**, *22*, 626–632. [CrossRef] [PubMed]
11. Granda-Cameron, C.; Houldin, A. Concept Analysis of Good Death in Terminally ill Patients. *Am. J. Hosp. Palliat. Med.* **2012**, *29*, 632–639. [CrossRef] [PubMed]
12. Steinhauser, K.E.; Clipp, E.C.; McNeilly, M.; Christakis, N.A.; McIntyre, L.M.; Tulsky, J.A. In Search of a Good Death: Observations of Patients, Families, and Providers. *Ann. Intern. Med.* **2000**, *132*, 825–832. [CrossRef] [PubMed]
13. Meier, E.A.; Gallegos, J.V.; Montross-Thomas, L.P.; Depp, C.A.; Irwin, S.A.; Jeste, D.V. Defining a Good Death (Successful Dying): Literature Review and a Call for Research and Public Dialogue. *Am. J. Geriatr. Psychiatry* **2016**, *24*, 261–271. [CrossRef] [PubMed]
14. Munn, J.C.; Dobbs, D.; Meier, A.; Williams, C.S.; Biola, H.; Zimmerman, S. The End-of-Life Experience in Long-Term Care: Five Themes Identified from Focus Groups with Residents, Family Members, and Staff. *Gerontologist* **2008**, *48*, 485–494. [CrossRef] [PubMed]
15. Pattison, N.; Carr, S.M.; Turnock, C.; Dolan, S. 'Viewing in Slow Motion': Patients', Families', Nurses' and Doctors' Perspectives on End-of-Life Care in Critical Care. *J. Clin. Nurs.* **2013**, *22*, 1442–1454. [CrossRef] [PubMed]
16. Leichtentritt, R.D.; Rettig, K.D. The Good Death: Reaching an Inductive Understanding. *Omega* **2000**, *41*, 221–248. [CrossRef] [PubMed]
17. Rainsford, S.; MacLeod, R.D.; Glasgow, N.J.; Wilson, D.M.; Phillips, C.B.; Wiles, R.B. Rural Residents' Perspectives on the Rural "Good Death": A Scoping Review. *Health Soc. Care Community* **2016**. [CrossRef] [PubMed]
18. Hsu, M.; Kahn, D.L.; Hsu, M. A Single Leaf Orchid: Meaning of a Husband's Death for Taiwanese Widows. *Ethos* **2002**, *30*, 306–326. [CrossRef]
19. Lee, G.L.; Woo, I.M.H.; Goh, C. Understanding the Concept of a Good Death among Bereaved Family Caregivers of Cancer Patients in Singapore. *Palliat. Support. Care* **2013**, *11*, 37–46. [CrossRef] [PubMed]
20. Bruinsma, S.M.; Brown, J.; van der Heide, A.; Deliens, L.; Anquinet, L.; Payne, S. Making Sense of Continuous Sedation in End-of-Life Care for Cancer Patients: An Interview Study with Bereaved Relatives in Three European Countries. *Support. Care Cancer* **2014**, *22*, 3243–3252. [CrossRef] [PubMed]
21. Hirai, K.; Miyashita, M.; Morita, T.; Sanjo, M.; Uchitomi, Y. Good Death in Japanese Cancer care: A Qualitative Study. *J. Pain Symptom Manag.* **2006**, *31*, 140–147. [CrossRef] [PubMed]

22. Grant, E.; Murray, S.A.; Grant, A.; Brown, J. A Good Death in Rural Kenya? Listening to Meru Patients and their Families Talk about Care Needs at the End of Life. *J. Palliat. Care* **2003**, *19*, 159–167. [PubMed]

23. Carr, D. A "Good Death" for Whom? Quality of Spouse's Death and Psychological Distress among Older Widowed Persons. *J. Health Soc. Behav.* **2003**, *44*, 215–232. [CrossRef] [PubMed]

24. Maeda, I.; Miyashita, M.; Yamagishi, A.; Kinoshita, H.; Shirahige, Y.; Izumi, N.; Yamaguchi, T.; Igarashi, M.; Kato, M.; Morita, T. Changes in Relatives' Perspectives on Quality of Death, quality of Care, Pain Relief, and Caregiving Burden Before and After a Region-Based Palliative Care Intervention. *J. Pain Symptom Manag.* **2016**, *52*, 637–645. [CrossRef] [PubMed]

25. Rainsford, S.; MacLeod, R.D.; Glasgow, N.J.; Wilson, D.M.; Phillips, C.B.; Wiles, R.B. Rural End-of-Life Care from the Experiences and Perspectives of Patients and Family Caregivers: A Systematic Literature Review. *Palliat. Med.* **2017**. [CrossRef] [PubMed]

26. Quill, T.E. Initiating End-of-Life Discussions with Seriously Ill Patients: Addressing the Elephant in the Room. *J. Am. Med. Assoc. (JAMA)* **2000**, *284*, 2502–2507. [CrossRef]

27. Pecchioni, L.L.; Overton, C.B.; Thompson, T. Families communicating about health. In *The Sage Handbook of Family Communication*; Turner, L.H., West, R., Eds.; Sage: Los Angeles, CA, USA, 2015; pp. 306–319.

28. Stajduhar, K.I.; Funk, L.; Outcalt, L. Family Caregiver Learning-How Family Caregivers Learn to Provide Care at the End of Life: A Qualitative Secondary Analysis of Four Datasets. *Palliat. Med.* **2013**, *27*, 657–664. [CrossRef] [PubMed]

29. Linderholm, M.; Friedrichsen, M. A Desire to Be Seen: Family Caregivers' Experiences of their Caring Role in Palliative Home Care. *Cancer Nurs.* **2010**, *33*, 28–36. [CrossRef] [PubMed]

30. Gladding, S.T. *Family Therapy: History, Theory, and Practice*, 5th ed.; Pearson Education, Inc.: Upper Saddle River, NY, USA, 2011.

31. Miyajima, K.; Fujisawa, D.; Yoshimura, K.; Ito, M.; Nakajima, S.; Shirahase, J.; Mimura, M.; Miyashita, M. Association Between Quality of End-of-Life Care and Possible Complicated Grief Among Bereaved Family Members. *J. Palliat. Med.* **2014**, *17*, 1025–1031. [CrossRef] [PubMed]

32. Jackson, J.; Derderian, L.; White, P.; Ayotte, J.; Fiorini, J.; Hall, R.O.; Shay, J.T. Family Perspectives on End-of-Life Care: A Metasynthesis. *J. Hosp. Palliat. Nurs.* **2012**, *14*, 303–311. [CrossRef]

33. Bosticco, C.; Thompson, T. The Role of Communication and Storytelling in the Family Grieving System. *J. Fam. Commun.* **2005**, *5*, 255–278. [CrossRef]

34. Campbell, R.; Pound, P.; Pope, C.; Britten, N.; Pill, R.; Morgan, M.; Donovan, J. Evaluating Meta-Ethnography: A Synthesis of Qualitative Research on Lay Experiences of Diabetes and Diabetes Care. *Soc. Sci. Med.* **2003**, *56*, 671–684. [CrossRef]

35. Hammell, K. Quality of Life after Spinal Cord Injury: A Meta-Synthesis of Qualitative Findings. *Spinal Cord* **2007**, *45*, 124–139. [CrossRef] [PubMed]

36. Evans, C.J.; Harding, R.; Higginson, I.J. 'Best practice' in Developing and Evaluating Palliative and End-of-Life Care Services: A Meta-Synthesis of Research Methods for the MORECare Project. *Palliat. Med.* **2013**, *27*, 885–898. [CrossRef] [PubMed]

37. May, C.R.; Masters, J.; Welch, L.; Hunt, K.; Pope, C.; Myall, M.; Griffiths, P.; Roderick, P.; Glanville, J.; Richardson, A. EXPERTS 1-Experiences of Long-Term Life-Limiting Conditions Among Patients and Carers: Protocol for a Qualitative Meta-Synthesis and Conceptual Modelling Study. *BMJ Open* **2015**, *5*, e007372. [CrossRef] [PubMed]

38. Sandelowski, M.; Barroso, J. *Handbook for Synthesizing Qualitative Research*; Sandelowski, M., Barroso, J., Eds.; Springer Publishing Company: New York, NY, USA, 2007. Available online: http://ebookcentral.proquest.com/lib/buffalo/detail.action?docID=423305 (accessed on 23 January 2017).

39. Mohammed, M.; Moles, R.; Chen, T. Meta-Synthesis of Qualitative Research: The Challenges and Opportunities. *Int. J. Clin. Pharm.* **2016**, *38*, 695–704. [PubMed]

40. Duggleby, W.; Hicks, D.; Nekolaichuk, C.; Holtslander, L.; Williams, A.; Chambers, T.; Eby, J. Hope, Older Adults, and Chronic Illness: A Meta-Synthesis of Qualitative Research. *J. Adv. Nurs.* **2012**, *68*, 1211–1223. [CrossRef] [PubMed]

41. Hammell, K.W. Informing Client-Centred Practice through Qualitative Inquiry: Evaluating the Quality of Qualitative Research. *Br. J. Occup. Ther.* **2002**, *65*, 175–184. [CrossRef]

42. Critical Appraisal Skills Programme (CASP). 10 Questions to Help You Make Sense of Qualitative Research. 2013. Available online: http://media.wix.com/ugd/dded87_29c5b002d99342f788c6ac670e49f274.pdf (accessed on 24 January 2017).

43. Sandelowski, M.; Barroso, J. Classifying the Findings in Qualitative Studies. *Qual. Health Res.* **2003**, *13*, 905–923. [CrossRef] [PubMed]

44. Charmaz, K. *Constructing Grounded Theory: A Practical Guide through Qualitative Analysis*, 2nd ed.; Sage: Los Angeles, CA, USA, 2014.

45. Holdsworth, L.M. Bereaved Carers' Accounts of the End of Life and the Role of Care Providers in a 'Good Death': A Qualitative Study. *Palliat. Med.* **2015**, *29*, 834–841. [CrossRef] [PubMed]

46. Wilches-Gutiérrez, J.L.; Arenas-Monreal, L.; Paulo-Maya, A.; Peláez-Ballestas, I.; Idrovo, A.J. A 'Beautiful Death': Mortality, Death, and Holidays in a Mexican Municipality. *Soc. Sci. Med.* **2012**, *74*, 775–782. [CrossRef] [PubMed]

47. Abib El Halal, G.M.C.; Piva, J.P.; Lago, P.M.; El Halal, M.G.; Cabral, F.C.; Nilson, C.; Garcia, P.C. Parents' Perspectives on the Deaths of their Children in Two Brazilian Pediatric Intensive Care Units. *Int. J. Palliat. Nurs.* **2013**, *19*, 495–502. [CrossRef] [PubMed]

48. Wilson, D.M.; MacLeod, R.; Houttekier, D. Examining Linkages between Bereavement Grief Intensity and Perceived Death Quality: Qualitative findings. *OMEGA J. Death Dying* **2016**, *74*, 260–274. [CrossRef]

49. Donnelly, S.; Battley, J. Relatives' Experience of the Moment of Death in a Tertiary Referral Hospital. *Mortality* **2010**, *15*, 81–100. [CrossRef]

50. Workman, S.; Mann, O.E. 'No Control Whatsoever': End-of-Life Care on a Medical Teaching Unit from the Perspective of Family Members. *QJM Q. J. Med.* **2007**, *100*, 433–440. [CrossRef] [PubMed]

51. Robert, R.; Zhukovsky, D.S.; Mauricio, R.; Gilmore, K.; Morrison, S.; Palos, G.R. Bereaved Parents' Perspectives on Pediatric Palliative Care. *J. Soc. Work End-of-Life Palliat. Care* **2012**, *8*, 316–338. [CrossRef] [PubMed]

52. Evans, W.G.; Cutson, T.M.; Steinhauser, K.E.; Tulsky, J.A. Is there No Place like Home? Caregivers Recall Reasons for and Experience upon Transfer from Home Hospice to Inpatient Facilities. *J. Palliat. Med.* **2006**, *9*, 100–110. [CrossRef] [PubMed]

53. Jack, B.A.; O'Brien, M.R.; Scrutton, J.; Baldry, C.R.; Groves, K.E. Supporting Family Carers Providing End-of-Life Home Care: A Qualitative Study on the Impact of a Hospice at Home Service. *J. Clin. Nurs.* **2015**, *24*, 131–140. [CrossRef] [PubMed]

54. Nelson, M.L.; Schrader, S.L.; Eidsness, L.M. "South Dakota's dying to Know": Personal Experiences with End-of-Life Care. *J. Palliat. Med.* **2009**, *12*, 905–913. [CrossRef] [PubMed]

55. Kongsuwan, W.; Chaipetch, O.; Matchim, Y. Thai Buddhist Families' Perspective of a Peaceful Death in ICUs. *Nurs. Crit. Care* **2012**, *17*, 151–159. [CrossRef] [PubMed]

56. Williams, B.R.; Bailey, F.A.; Noh, H.; Woodby, L.L.; Wittich, A.R.; Burgio, K.L. "I was Ready to Take Him Home": Next-of-Kin's Accounts of Loved One's Death During Hospice and Palliative Care Discussions in Veterans Affairs Medical Centers. *J. Soc. Work End-of-Life Palliat. Care* **2015**, *11*, 50–73. [CrossRef] [PubMed]

57. Emanuel, L.L.; Emanuel, E.J. The Promise of a Good Death. *J. Lancet* **1998**, *351*, SII21–SII29. [CrossRef]

58. Payne, S.; Burton, C.; Addington-Hall, J.; Jones, A. End-of-Life Issues in Acute Stroke Care: A Qualitative Study of the Experiences and Preferences of Patients and Families. *Palliat. Med.* **2010**, *24*, 146–153. [CrossRef] [PubMed]

59. Naef, R.; Ward, R.; Mahrer-Imhof, R.; Grande, G. Characteristics of the Bereavement Experience of Older Persons after Spousal Loss: An Integrative Review. *Int. J. Nurs. Stud.* **2013**, *50*, 1108–1121. [CrossRef] [PubMed]

60. Hinds, P.S.; Schum, L.; Baker, J.N.; Wolfe, J. Key factors affecting dying children and their families. *J. Palliat. Med.* **2005**, *8*, S-70–S-78. [CrossRef] [PubMed]

61. Finlay, I.G. Quality of Life to the End. *Commun. Med.* **2005**, *2*, 91–95. [CrossRef] [PubMed]

62. Institute of Medicine; Committee on Approaching Death: Addressing Key End of Life Issues. *Dying in America: Improving Quality and Honoring Individual Preferences near the End of Life*; National Academies Press: Washington, DC, USA, 2015. Available online: https://www.nap.edu/read/18748/chapter/1 (accessed on 16 April 2017).

63. Casarett, D.J.; Quill, T.E. "I'm Not Ready for Hospice": Strategies for Timely and Effective Hospice Discussions. *Ann. Intern. Med.* **2007**, *146*, 443–449. [CrossRef] [PubMed]

64. Baile, W.F.; Buckman, R.; Lenzi, R.; Glober, G.; Beale, E.A.; Kudelka, A.P. SPIKES—A Six-Step Protocol for Delivering Bad News: Application to the Patient with Cancer. *Oncologist* **2000**, *5*, 302–311. [CrossRef] [PubMed]

65. Villigran, M.; Goldsmith, J.; Wittenberg-Lyles, E.; Baldwin, P. Creating COMFORT: A Communication-Based Model for Breaking Bad News. *Commun. Educ.* **2010**, *59*, 220–234. [CrossRef]

66. Clayton, J.M.; Hancock, K.M.; Butow, P.N.; Tattersall, M.H.N.; Currow, D.C. Clinical Practice Guidelines for Communicating Prognosis and End-of-Life Issues with Adults in the Advanced Stages of A Life-Limiting Illness, and Their Caregivers. *Med. J. Aust.* **2007**, *186*, 77–108.

67. Lieberman, J.A.; Stuart, M.R. The BATHE method: Incorporating counseling and psychotherapy into the everyday management of patients. *Prim. Care Companion J. Clin. Psychiatry* **1999**, *1*, 35–38. [CrossRef] [PubMed]

behavioral sciences

MDPI

Article

Communicatively Constructing the Bright and Dark Sides of Hope: Family Caregivers' Experiences during End of Life Cancer Care

Jody Koenig Kellas [1,*], Katherine M. Castle [1], Alexis Johnson [2] and Marlene Z. Cohen [3]

[1] Department of Communication Studies, University of Nebraska-Lincoln, Lincoln, NE 68588-0329, USA; kcastle4@unl.edu
[2] Department of Communication and Journalism, Arkansas Tech University, Russellville, AR 72801, USA; ajohnson93@atu.edu
[3] Center for Nursing Science, University of Nebraska Medical Center, Omaha, NE 68198, USA; mzcohen@unmc.edu
* Correspondence: jkellas2@unl.edu

Academic Editor: Maureen P. Keeley
Received: 1 March 2017; Accepted: 9 May 2017; Published: 15 May 2017

Abstract: (1) Background: The communication of hope is complicated, particularly for family caregivers in the context of cancer who struggle to maintain hope for themselves and their loved ones in the face of terminality. In order to understand these complexities, the current study examines the bright and dark sides of how hope is communicated across the cancer journey from the vantage point of bereaved family caregivers; (2) Methods: We analyzed interviews with bereaved family caregivers using qualitative thematic and case oriented strategies to identify patterns in the positive and negative lived experiences when communicating about hope at the end of life; (3) Results: Two overarching patterns of hope emerged. Those who experienced hope as particularized (focused on cure) cited communication about false hope, performing (faking it), and avoidance. Those who transitioned from particularized to generalized hope (hope for a good death) reported acceptance, the communication of hope as social support, prioritizing family, and balancing hope and honesty; (4) Conclusion: Family caregivers face myriad complexities in managing the bright and dark sides of hope. Interventions should encourage concurrent oncological and palliative care, increased perspective-taking among family members, and encourage the transition from particularized to generalized hope.

Keywords: hope; palliative care; cancer; communication; family caregiver; bereaved

1. Introduction

The tension between hope for a cure and the reality of terminality [1] presents a communicative paradox for family caregivers in the context of cancer. Babrow, Kasch, and Ford [2] explain that illness is ripe with uncertainty. Family caregivers must help patients combat loneliness [3] and maintain their quality of life [4] as patients face their own terminality. Hope can influence what patients chose to disclose to family caregivers, and may hinder coping if the patient feels compelled to remain positive about their illness [4,5]. Thus, family caregivers play a vital role in helping patients move from hoping for recovery to hoping for a dignified death [6,7]. This endeavor is complicated, however, by family dynamics, as well as caregivers' own needs, fears, burdens, and stressors. In short, a myriad of responsibilities may fall on the shoulders of family caregivers as they help patients and the larger family system negotiate hope at the end of life.

These responsibilities, as well as societal expectations, render hope particularly important for those facing serious illness [8], such as cancer. Indeed, hope plays a significant role in modern

Behav. Sci. **2017**, *7*, 33

scripts for healthcare and the recovery process [8]. Hope is a vital component of what Frank [9] refers to as the restitution narrative, the dominant narrative of health and illness in which the body is viewed as starting in good health, descending into illness, and ultimately returning to good health. Illness is perceived as a bodily breakdown that physicians and patients must work to repair, positioning the physician as the active hero in the recovery process [9]. Hope, then, is an essential construct in maintaining the legitimacy and credibility of the medical model [10] situated within this master narrative.

Hope is also an important psychological resource at the end of life for cancer patients and caregivers. Hope can be a life-affirming [11] coping mechanism [12,13], giving meaning and protecting against despair [13]. Despite this, positioning hope as a welcome component of cancer care may be oversimplifying what is not only a psychological resource, but also a *communicative* construction, which must be negotiated by patients and caregivers who share in the cancer journey from differing vantage points.

Maintaining hope is complicated in the context of cancer, and patients and caregivers often have reported different experiences and needs. For example, Koenig Kellas, Castle, Johnson, and Cohen [14] found that whereas patients told cancer stories focused on themes of positivity in hope, and palliative and hospice providers worked to help families reframe cancer stories from curative to focused on everyday happiness, 40% of family caregivers in their sample experienced isolated cancer journeys marked by false hope and denial. The disproportionate number of family caregivers experiencing negativity and chaos in the cancer journey seems to support research on the stressors associated with caregiver burden [12] and made Koenig Kellas and colleagues reason that family caregivers may be particularly prone to experience isolation during cancer care. Indeed, while medical practitioners often postpone the severity of illness diagnoses in the context of cancer [15] and patients often avoid communication in the endeavor of protective buffering (i.e., protecting family members from psychological burden, [16]), family caregivers must increasingly bear the brunt of physical and emotional care. With this, family caregivers must broker the communication and negotiation of hope in an environment of shifting diagnoses, managing tension between patients and medical providers, keeping support networks and children appropriately apprised of the patients' well-being, and providing needed levels of physical and psychological support.

Toward the end of life, when curative measures are no longer possible, family caregivers may experience tensions in shifting between hoping for a cure and accepting terminality. In the former, families hope that setbacks in patients' illnesses are temporary and often focus on alleviating the symptoms that the patient faces [5]. As the disease progresses, family caregivers may move from a framework of particularized hope to one of generalized hope [17] shifting their focus from finding a cure to hoping for a good death [4,6] or a theologically/spiritually focused hope [15]. Generalized hope is a state of being that gives life meaning, while particularized hope is geared toward specific outcomes. Pattison and Lee [6] argue that, in the face of death, there is hope for a good afterlife. Family caregivers may turn to spiritual dedication or spiritual hope as a way of coping with illness and loss [18]. This transition can be difficult, however, and studies have shown that patients lament when their loved ones avoided discussing this transition and the realities of their illness, thereby hindering coping and well-being [19]. Denial can lead to false optimism [20] and to ill-advised treatment decisions [15].

Despite this, we know little about how hope is communicated in the face of cancer care, particularly in the experience of family caregivers. Understanding how family caregivers negotiate this tension is vitally important for their own and their family members' well-being and end-of-life coping. Knowing the ways in which family caregivers experience and communicate hope during the cancer journey and at the end of life can lend insight into best and worst practices that may help others prepare for the immense responsibility of family caregiving and coping. Investigating these processes also acknowledges the potential functional ambivalence [21] of hope. In other words, hope is a construct typically regarded as positive, but, when considered in the complex context of cancer care and communicatively negotiated among the larger cancer caregiving system and family, can function with dispreferred outcomes. For example, family caregivers may be so focused on popularized notions that hope facilitates better patient outcomes (i.e., people who are hopeful beat cancer or live longer) that they may neglect the signs that patients are ready to move to generalized hope and prepare for death. Thus, in the current study, we were also interested in exploring the potentially bright and dark sides of hope as it is communicated in families in the context of cancer.

Through interviews with bereaved family caregivers, we investigated these positive and negative lived experiences with communicating about hope. Specifically, we posed the following research questions:

RQ1: How do family caregivers experience hope over the course of the cancer journey?

RQ2: How was hope communicated—by family caregivers and others—over the course of the cancer journey?

2. Materials and Methods

Participants were required to be at least 19 years of age and self-identify as a family caregiver for a patient in the context of cancer care. After receiving human subjects approval from the Institutional Review Board (IRB), we engaged in purposive sampling typical in health communication research [22] as well as snowball sampling [23]. First, flyers were distributed in palliative care clinics, local hospitals and oncology clinics, and at local community cancer events. Second, we posted the call for the study on social media (e.g., Facebook) and invited people to share the link to the recruitment materials.

The sample for the current study included 10 bereaved family caregivers who had provided primary or secondary care to their loved ones over the course of the cancer journey. Although this manuscript is part of a larger study in which we also recruited and interviewed cancer patients and medical practitioners, the current analysis focuses only on bereaved family caregivers so that we can best understand family communication of hope at the end of life. Interviews were conducted until theoretical saturation was reached on the two overarching themes described in the results. Participants included eight females and two males who ranged in age from 23 to 74 (M = 56.00, SD = 17.34). Participants were White and primarily middle class. They lived across a variety of Midwestern and Western states. Six of the participants were spouses of the cancer patients, one was a son, one was a daughter, one was a daughter-in-law, and one was a sister.

Interviews took place in person at a location of the participants' choosing (e.g., the social interaction lab, coffee shops, office conference rooms, homes) or over the phone. They ranged in length from 18 to 115 min (M = 62.84, SD = 29.64) and resulted in 136 single spaced pages of transcription. After obtaining informed consent, one of the first three authors interviewed participants about their story of the cancer journey, questions about hope (e.g., "How has hope been present for you?" "Has anyone communicated hopeful messages to you over the course of the cancer journey and if so, what did they say, how did you feel, how did you respond?" "Has the communication of hope ever been unwelcome or negative?"), and questions about communication and relational challenges not relevant to the current analysis (see [7]). To ensure uniformity of the interviews, each of the first three authors met after our initial interviews to discuss the process and adjust the interview protocol and follow-up questions. The majority of changes were made to a portion of the interview protocol not relevant to the current study.

Interviews were transcribed verbatim and pseudonyms were provided to mask participant identity. We analyzed the data using a combination of qualitative case-oriented and variable-oriented strategies [24]. Specifically, we began by analyzing the data to answer RQ1 and RQ2 using thematic analysis guidelines offered by Braun and Clark [25]. We inductively identified themes, moving back and forth between the data and the emerging analysis. In order to get familiar with the data, we transcribed the interviews and then reviewed each transcription in depth. This process resulted in an initial list of categories relevant to the experience and communication of hope. We then coded the data and organized it into meaningful groups. This process yielded themes across cases for how bereaved family caregivers experienced hope (RQ1) and how they felt hope was communicated by and to them over the course of the cancer journey (RQ2). We then used a matrix approach to synthesize and compare individual cases in order to look for patterns in the data. This process of stacking comparable cases [24] (see Table 1) enabled us to examine the ways in which the interpretive recurring themes across cases justified creating two overarching types of hope experiences. These types of experiences—*Particularized* and *Particularized to Generalized*—were characterized by differing forms of communication of hope as presented in the Results below.

3. Results

The results of the thematic analysis revealed that participants experienced hope (RQ1) and communicated hope (RQ2) in both positive and negative ways. Indeed, the findings support the functionally ambivalent nature of hope in the context of cancer and end-of-life care. The results of the cross-case analysis revealed two overarching types of hope experiences that differed based on the experience of hope and the communication of hope across that experience. In what follows, we present the results of the thematic analyses organized according to these two emergent types of experiences: *Particularized* experiences of hope and hope that moved from *Particularized to Generalized*.

3.1. Particularized Hope

Research Question 1 asked about how bereaved family caregivers experienced hope over the course of the cancer journey. Consistent with previous literature on hope at the end of life [11], we found that bereaved family caregivers defined hope as either particularized—in which hope is geared toward a specific outcome (e.g., treatment, cure)—or as generalized—in which hope is geared toward some broadly defined future event (e.g., a good death, no pain). Particularized hope was illustrated by Ashley who described stages of hope that "kept not working out" (line 234). Ashley's husband had pancreatic cancer and the family experienced a series of hopeful moments in treatment, including surgery followed by a clinical trial. She explains, "[There was hope] in the clinical trial. Um, there was hope that maybe that would work for him. And um it was hopeful for him, it was hopeful for me, it was hopeful for our kids. And, um, that made life a little easier to know that there was a grasp of hope" (lines 243–245). Whereas Ashley described stages of hope, Jackson described hope as a series of let downs. He described hope as particularized when he said, "Well everybody tries to give you hope and they tell you this might work. We have something new. And, you know, hope is a series of let downs. And nothing is a permanent cure, it just might get you a few more months, a year, who knows" (lines 46–48).

Some participants seemed in denial about the possibility of their loved one's death from cancer, thereby keeping them in the stage of experiencing hope only as particularized. For example, Michelle never gave up on the idea of a cure for her mother's lung cancer. Even after a surgery was cancelled due to complications, Michelle was unwilling to give up hope: "[The doctor said], 'We're not going to be able to do that procedure . . . we can't do chemo...' So, no chemo, no procedure. Nothing. They were just like we're going to do what we can do to make her comfortable. So you know, I heard that, but I said, *you guys are going to fix her*" (lines 162–167, emphasis added).

Others seemed to want to move from a focus on hope as cure to hope for a good death (i.e., to move from particularized to generalized hope), but were unable to because of the unwillingness of other family members. For example, two wives in the sample—Karen and Sylvia—both discussed wanting to talk to their husbands about dying, but their husbands refused to give up hope that they would beat the cancer. Thus, although the family caregivers hoped to transition between stages of hope, their efforts were stymied by false hope and refusals from other family members, including patients.

Results of the cross-case data analysis (see Table 1) revealed that those who experienced hope as solely or primarily particularized also experienced the communication of hope similarly across the cancer journey. Specifically, in the current sample, 50% of the participants' interviews and cancer stories were characterized only by the experience of particularized hope in which they hoped for a cure or the possibilities of treatment exclusively or until the very end of life. When they described how hope was communicated during their family's cancer journey, their interviews were dominated by the communication of *false hope and minimizing, avoidance/denial,* and *performing (fake) hope.*

Table 1. Cross-Case analysis of hope experienced and the communication of hope.

Participant	Hope Experienced	Communication of Hope
Jackson	Particularized	Performing False Hope
Brian	Particularized	Performing False Hope
Sylvia	Particularized	Performing False Hope Avoidance/Denial
Karen	Particularized	False Hope Avoidance/Denial
Michelle	Particularized	Performing False Hope Avoidance/Denial
Julia	Particularized → Generalized	Acceptance Prioritizing Family
Ashley	Particularized → Generalized	Acceptance Prioritizing Family Social Support
Sally	Particularized → Generalized	Acceptance Social Support Balancing Hope & Honesty Performing
Lauren	Particularized → Generalized	Acceptance Social Support Balancing Hope & Honesty Performing
Diane	Particularized → Generalized	Social Support Prioritizing Family

3.1.1. The Communication of False Hope

Participants experienced the *communication of false hope* from medical practitioners, patients, and social network members. For example, Karen complained, "Oh practitioners always gave us hope I felt was very honestly … misleading, very misleading. I wish they would have been more up front about the progression of the disease … " (lines 171–173). Brian's mother, during her battle with breast cancer tried to communicate hope to Brian: "My mom would always say, 'It's gonna be ok, I'm gonna be fine, you know this one's gonna, this treatment's gonna do it.' And after the fifth or sixth treatment I realized that this wasn't probably gonna work. So, I had no hope, pretty much" (lines 40–42). Finally, social network members communicated a type of false hope to participants when they minimized family caregivers' expressed worry. Jackson explained, "Until there's really a cure, you try to stay positive as you can, but you know, at first the people saying 'You know everything's going to be OK.' The reassuring you helps, but then after a while it becomes white noise" (lines 116–118). False hope was experienced negatively by participants in the particularized group, but they were still not able to overcome it in the endeavor of moving to generalized hope.

3.1.2. Performing Particularized Hope

Whereas others gave them false hope, family caregivers who remained primarily in a state of particularized hope also reported faking hope to others, something we coded as *Performing*. Performing entailed putting on a bright and positive face for others. Sometimes, this was embraced as part of a larger life attitude as in the case of Michelle who said, "I've always been hopeful of everything anyway, whether it's been my mom's situation or someone else's. You know I've always been that person that says 'Oh, everything will be fine. They are going to get through it because they are strong. It's going to be OK' ... with my mom, I fell off of that a little bit and blamed myself for her being ill and me not being able to fix things like I normally do. Since then, I've gotten back on track. And I've gotten back on hope lane and I'm back down that positive journey again" (lines 436–442). In turn, Michelle's mother also performed for her. She said, "I would always tell my mom to stay positive and stay strong. As caregivers, we kind of have to be empathetic towards what they are going through ... [but] I was selfish. Because I didn't care that chemo was destroying her and making her miserable. I just wanted her to do it. And in the end she told my husband that she did it for me. Because she was tired. She told my husband that she was so tired. She said, 'I'm doing this for Michelle'" (lines 403–408). Michelle's mom performed for her long after she was ready to give up knowing it would keep Michelle's hope alive.

Other participants put on a happy face for those around them as Jackson articulated, "Well, yeah, you know I tried to give hope to the actual patient, my wife. And tried to keep positive because what else can you do? Friends and family you also try to make less of it. You know you don't want people hanging around thinking you know with long faces going, 'Oh, I'm so sorry for you,' um, you know, you want them upbeat. And you want them ... happy around her that there is hope" (lines 62–66). Thus, particularized participants had to maintain (the illusion of) hope in order to maintain their particularized narrative of a cure.

3.1.3. Avoidance/Denial

Finally, family caregivers who experienced hope as particularized reported the avoidance of communication about terminality or other difficult topics associated with end of life cancer. Sylvia, for example, lamented, "There were so many times I wanted to talk to him about how he felt about knowing he was going to die ... but I just couldn't because I knew he had this hope ... and you know I never wanted to ... discourage that because I thought, 'you never know'" (lines 376–387). Karen also could not talk to her husband about death, but she also experienced avoidance from her extended family, including her husband's brother who experience tremendous regret about his denial that his brother could die and the ensuing missed opportunity for communication. Moreover, her own parents refused to move from particularized to generalized hope in their communication. She notes, "My parents were one of these that didn't talk about dying ... .I don't know if it feared [sic] them that it might upset me, but I need it, I needed people to talk to. I needed people to understand what I was going through and what I feared" (lines 286–293). Karen's needs were never met and her cancer journey was dominated by family avoidance and practitioner false hope.

3.1.4. Summary

In short, half of the bereaved caregivers in the current study told stories and described hope in the context of end-of-life cancer as dominated by a particularized experience of hope. This experience was focused on cure and treatment. Therefore, in the endeavor of preserving hope, end-of-life family communication was dominated in these interviews by the communication of false hope (particularly by practitioners and social network members); the performance by family caregivers and other members to stay positive; and the avoidance of communication about death in the effort of preserving particularized hope.

3.2. Particularized to Generalized Hope

Unlike those whose journeys remained particularized, the other half of our sample told stories and described family end-of-life communication that was characterized by a shift between particularized and generalized hope. These participants hoped that treatment would cure their loved one's cancer, but after realizing that the cancer was terminal, shifted their focus to hope for a good death, comfort, minimized pain, and/or an afterlife. The participants who experienced this shift too faced the communication of false hope and performing during the particularized phase of hope, but they also had interviews dominated by *acceptance* and the communication of hope in the forms of *social support* and the *prioritizing of family communication* as their experience shifted to generalized hope. Communication that was characterized as *performing* in those participants whose experiences stayed particularized, was softened by a shift to generalized hope for the other half of the sample. We coded this communication as the *Hope-Honesty Dialectic*.

3.2.1. Acceptance

When participants shifted from particularized to generalized hope, they communicated a level of acceptance that was missing from the interviews of those whose hope remained particularized. Julia and her husband—who was diagnosed with esophageal cancer and lived for eight months—tried to be accepting of his prognosis from the very beginning, only experiencing the tension between particularized and generalized hope in their communication with extended family. Although she and her husband "struggled with family members over hope ... presenting us with opportunities that in our mind offered false hope ... We didn't see it that way. We saw it as making the best of what time he had left" (lines 151–160). Julia communicated acceptance by supporting Josh's decisions: "I remember the hope I gave Josh was that I would support the decision that he wants ... I will not try to argue you out or into some kind of medical procedure ... and be 100% with him in the decisions that we made together" (lines 217–226). Other caregivers held on to particularized hope longer, but eventually moved toward a generalized, more spiritual hope. When asked how hope was communicated in the family, Ashely said, "Well, I guess we just all talked about it and thought [treatment] would happen. And, uh, everybody was elated, but you know the stages kept not working out. So, I guess ... everybody passes on eventually. And that this was just his time. And that nothing medically could prevent it. And we just kind of had to accept it. And not that it was easy, it wasn't. We didn't want to lose him. But, um, hope in that there is an afterlife" (lines 233–237). The move from particularized to generalized hope was enabled by an acceptance of terminality.

3.2.2. The Communication of Hopeful Social Support

This kind of acceptance was facilitated in part by hopeful social support that family caregivers both gave and received. As one of her father-in-law's caregivers, Sally communicated social support to her husband and mother-in-law as they negotiated the move from particularized to generalized hope. She remembered: "I don't remember particular messages, but just reassuring them that it was okay for them to feel whatever they were feeling it was okay for them to be grieving, it was normal and they shouldn't be feeling badly about feeling bad" (lines 219–222). Sally also received social support from her parents who she described as "huge in providing hope and encouragement for us [in that] they had just gone through this with my grandma ... it was hopeful for us to know that ... we weren't abnormal in ... what we were feeling ... and also the hope that it was going to get better and easier" (lines 191–197). Lauren also described "a tremendous support system with my children ... [and grandchildren]" telling the story of how their grandson would "go in and kneel by his grandfather's bed and pray for him by the hour. Just holding his hand and wouldn't let him go and telling him don't give up. I think Jacob probably gave Ron the most hope of anyone, um, just because his faith was so strong ... " (lines 373–376). Thus, when participants shifted from particularized to generalized hope, communication was characterized by hopeful messages of support.

3.2.3. Prioritizing Open Family Communication at the End-of-Life

Participants whose hope journeys moved from particularized to generalized also had interviews dominated by intentional moves to prioritize open communication among family members and the connection it facilitated during cancer care. Diane traveled across several states to care for her brother at the end of his life and spent many hours talking to him, singing, and reminiscing about family. Ashley contrasted the difficulty in the transition from particularized hope to the hopeful communication that characterized generalized hope: " ... Telling the kids that there was no more hope. It was difficult and it was difficult for them, of course. Um, but we were all together and ... [crying] ... our communication with each other was wonderful. I mean there wasn't anything held back. We talked about everything and shared our opinions, and our advice, and our concerns" (lines 293–301). Julia, whose family resisted the move from particularized to generalized hope prioritized family communication when they finally came around: "The people that were the most helpful when his family finally came around and said, 'OK we are embracing your plan and that means we're going to come down and spend a weekend with you and we're just going to have a really good time. And we're going to talk about everything we want to talk about.' And so those are the times that we really had a lot of hope that these were positive things that could come from his being sick and dying. You know, conversations he would have never had with people if he wasn't dying that, you know, will never forget" (lines 200–206, emphasis added). At the transition of hope, open family communication was valued, prioritized, and facilitated closeness.

3.2.4. Balancing Hope and Honesty

Finally, like those participants situated in the particularized experience of hope, those that moved from particularized to generalized hope also experienced the tension of wanting to *perform* positivity and hope for others. Their articulation emerged differently, however into what we coded as the balancing hope and honesty. This was the struggle between being situated with the acceptance of hope as generalized (i.e., being honest about the reality of death) as a family and maintaining a strong sense of positivity and hope, often for the dying loved one. Lauren stressed this in how she communicated the diagnosis with her children: "I think it's very important to be as honest as you can be without saying that there's no hope, but you do have to say this is a very serious situation. And, that prepares them, you know?" She also articulated this tension in how she evaluated patient–provider communication ("So there was always a glimmer of hope, but it was also I think very important for the doctor to be very honest and candid ... there was always hope ... prayer is powerful and faith will get you through. But reality has to be part of that picture of hope as well" lines 320–323). Finally, she directed family communication for her husband based on the hope–honesty dialectic: "I think that's the one thing I did ask of all the children and grandchildren. When you visit with your grandfather don't show him sadness if you can help it. Show him strength so that he'll be able to let go and know that you'll be OK" (lines 394–397). Sally also managed the hope–honesty dialectic in her communication with the larger support network. She explained, "I was the one sharing messages about ok, this is what happened at the doctor's appointments, and I tried ... to do it in a hopeful way. And I remember I would try to be positive no matter how bad the news was" (lines 214–217). Staying positive and hopeful even in the reality of facing death characterized the communication of those who transitioned in their journey of hope from cure to acceptance. It was less about performing and more about reframing and accepting death as inevitable and hopeful at the same time.

3.2.5. Summary

In summary, one half of our participants moved from a particularized focus on treatment and cure to a hope that was generalized—focused on a good death, afterlife, and enjoying the time family members had left together. The experience of these participants was qualitatively different than the experience of those who remained in a particularized stage of hope as their communication was characterized by hope as social support, close family communication, and maintaining hope in the face of acceptance.

4. Discussion

The current analysis used a combination of thematic and case-oriented strategies [24] to identify two trajectories of hope for bereaved family caregivers. The two experiences—particularized and particularized to generalized hope—supports previous research that shows that many people move from hope for a cure to hope for a good death [6]. Our findings add to the literature in two important ways. First, our results provide an initial portrait of the communication that characterizes hope in families' end-of-life cancer journeys. Participants who stayed in the particularized stage of hope experienced the communication of false hope, were required to perform, or "fake," hope for others, and experienced avoidance and denial from family members in communication that may have allowed them to move from particularized to generalized experiences of hope. Those that did make the transition, on the other hand, experienced acceptance and hopeful communication in the forms of social support, prioritizing family communication, and negotiating the dialectic between honesty and communicating hope.

Although previous research examines the move between particularized and generalized hope, in hope theory, hope is conceptualized as a psychological construct independent of a relational context. McNulty and Fincham [26] (pp. 103–104) call for a more contextualized understanding of psychological constructs because "whether optimism or expectancies for desirable outcomes have beneficial or harmful implications depends on the context in which they occur". This is particularly true when considering hope in the context of palliative care, and is further compounded when you consider the *communication* of hope given that communication constitutes lived experiences and relationships. After all, human existence is relational [27], and meaning is constructed between communicators [28]. People construct the meaning of hope together through communication, making the relational context of utmost importance in understanding hope. Whereas hope theory recognizes that interpersonal relationships are central to maintaining hope [29], it fails to recognize that hope itself is negotiated through interpersonal relationships wrought with tensions in understanding and experiencing hope. The current study lends texture to our understanding of hope as a communicated construct in families at the end of life.

Second, the current study illuminates the bright and dark sides of hope communication at the end-of-life. False hope has been characterized in previous research as problematic. When false hope is fostered by medical providers, for example, it can be especially damaging to the patient's ability to adapt positively to their situation and importantly, to re-construct their identities in the face of their changing circumstances [13]. Additionally, it can influence their ability to be responsive to and engaged in their own care given that their goals and expectations of medical provider recommendations may be curative as opposed to palliative [30]. Previous research, however, focuses primarily on the effects of false hope on patients. The current study shows that family caregivers have much to balance in the effort of maintaining, not only medically-dictated but also family- and patient-dictated forms of false, particularized hope. Hope is a precarious balance for caregivers. Previous research reveals the beliefs that talking about cancer erodes hope thereby fueling silence [31]. This was seen in the avoidance strategies of particularized participants in our study. Strategies such as mutual topic avoidance and demand-withdraw patterns of conflict are inversely associated with marital satisfaction and predict psychosocial distress [32]. Thus, understanding the dark side of communicating hope and the inability to transition from particularized to generalized hope at the end of life has consequential outcomes for family health. In the current study, when the participants transitioned from particularized to generalized hope, they did seem more able to experience the brighter sides of hope communication—including deep connection with family members, affirming social support, and the ability to maintain positivity while still accepting the reality of their loved one's terminality.

Despite the positive sides of hope, the amount of competing communication demands that family caregivers must manage in the practice of maintaining hope signals a paradox in the communication of hope at the end of life. Talking about moving from particularized to generalized hope (e.g., accepting the likelihood of terminality and facing death together) can erode hope associated with the restitution narrative [9]. Talking about moving from generalized to particularized hope (e.g., arguing for treatment by family members to patients or couples who have accepted terminality) may erode hope in narratives of acceptance. Not talking about the transition between types of hope precludes the potential hope offered by more biospychosocial approaches to supportive, family-based care—namely, palliative care.

Koenig Kellas and colleagues [14] argued for the need for concurrent oncological and palliative care and palliative family communication interventions focused on bridging the gaps between patients, health, and family caregivers. Although palliative care is intended for patients and their families at all stages of serious illness, the adoption of palliative care and biopsychosocial, patient-centered models of care still lag behind biomedical models [19]. This is unfortunate because cancer patients and their families experience reciprocal suffering that can be alleviated in palliative care [33]. Palliative care focuses on both curative and comfort care and on the spiritual, psychosocial, familial, and emotional needs of patients in addition to their physical needs [34] by taking a team-based approach to care—ideally from the time of diagnosis to death. The concurrent delivery of oncological and palliative care is in demand and supported by the American Society of Clinical Oncology's Provisional Clinical Opinion for the combination of oncology and palliative care [35]. This sentiment is echoed by the Institute of Medicine (IOM)'s [36] recommendations for patient-centered care, developing caregiving competencies of the surrounding workforce, and the need for palliative care, psychosocial support, and family caregiver support across oncological care in its recent report, *Delivering High Quality Cancer Care: Charting a New Course for a System in Crisis*. The results of the current study suggest that some of those competencies may involve the negotiation of hope in a complex system of interpersonal and professional relationships. The path between particularized and generalized hope in the context of end-of-life palliative care is not always linear and family caregivers need guidance for their own and their families' well-being. Palliative interventions are needed that encourage communication competence and the experience of cancer as communal (see [7]). In the current study, the communication of hope facilitated acceptance when generalized, through social support, and through the prioritization of family communication. These skills can be facilitated and improved among families in the context of cancer and other life-limiting illnesses.

Finally, the move from particularized to generalized hope seems to enable the possibility of effective, life affirming final conversations [37]. These conversations have been shown to benefit families, bringing closure and increasing closeness at the end of life. Family caregivers must help manage hope, but given its paradox, they must also receive training in conceptualizing, communicating, and reframing hope to enable family connection and individual well-being at the end of life. Future research should test the connections between managing hope and psychosocial health with larger samples than were possible in the collection of the current data.

5. Conclusions

Family caregivers face myriad complexities in managing the bright and dark sides of hope. Interventions should encourage concurrent oncological and palliative care, increase perspective-taking among family members, and encourage the transition from particularized to generalized hope.

Acknowledgments: This research was supported through a Revisions Award granted from the Office of Research and Economic Development at the University of Nebraska-Lincoln and an Enhancing Research Excellence Grant from the College of Arts and Sciences at the University of Nebraska-Lincoln.

Author Contributions: Jody Koenig Kellas, Kathy Castle, and Alexis Johnson conceived and designed the study and performed the interviews; all four authors, including Marlene Cohen, analyzed the data; and Jody Koenig Kellas, Kathy Castle, and Alexis Johnson wrote the paper.

Conflicts of Interest: The authors declare no conflict of interest.

References

1. Philip, J.; Gold, M.; Brand, C.; Douglass, J.; Miller, B.; Sundararajan, V. Negotiating hope with chronic obstructive pulmonary disease patients: A qualitative study of patients and healthcare professionals. *Int. Med. J.* **2011**, *42*, 816–819. [CrossRef] [PubMed]
2. Babrow, A.S.; Kasch, C.R.; Ford, L.A. The many meanings of 'uncertainty' in illness: Toward a systematic accounting. *Health Commun.* **1998**, *10*, 1–24. [CrossRef] [PubMed]
3. Segrin, C.; Passalacqua, S.A. Functions of loneliness, social support, health behaviors, and stress in association with poor health. *Health Commun.* **2010**, *25*, 312–322. [CrossRef] [PubMed]
4. Benzein, E.G.; Berg, A.C. The level of and relation between hope, hopelessness and fatigue in patients and family members in palliative care. *Palliat. Med.* **2005**, *19*, 234–240. [CrossRef] [PubMed]
5. Benkel, I.; Wijk, H.; Molander, U. Using coping strategies in not denial: Helping loved ones adjust to living with a patient with a palliative diagnosis. *J. Palliat. Med.* **2010**, *13*, 1119–1123. [CrossRef] [PubMed]
6. Pattison, N.A.; Lee, C. Hope Against Hope in Cancer at the End of Life. *J. Relig. Health* **2011**, *50*, 731–742. [CrossRef] [PubMed]
7. Chang, E.C.; Sanna, L.J. Optimism, accumulated life stress, and psychological and physical adjustment: Is it always adaptive to expect the best? *J. Soc. Clin. Psychol.* **2003**, *22*, 97–115. [CrossRef]
8. Reinke, L.F.; Shannon, S.E.; Engelberg, R.A.; Young, J.P.; Curtis, J.R. Supporting hope and prognostic information: Nurses' perspectives on their role when patients have life-limiting prognoses. *J. Pain Symptom Manag.* **2010**, *39*, 982–992. [CrossRef] [PubMed]
9. Frank, A. *The Wounded Storyteller: Body, Illness and Ethics*; The University of Chicago Press: Chicago, IL, USA, 1995.
10. Perakyla, A. Hope work in the care of seriously ill patients. *Qual. Health Res.* **1991**, *1*, 402–433. [CrossRef]
11. Gibson, M.; Gorman, E. Long-term care residents with cancer and their health care providers reflect on hope. *Can. J. Aging* **2012**, *31*, 285–293. [CrossRef] [PubMed]
12. Duggleby, W.; Hicks, D.; Nekolaichuk, C.; Holtslander, L.; Williams, A.; Chambers, T.; Eby, J. Hope, older adults, and chronic illness: A metasynthesis of qualitative research. *J. Adv. Nurs.* **2012**, *68*, 1211–1223. [CrossRef] [PubMed]
13. Wiles, R.; Cott, C.; Gibson, B.E. Hope, expectations and recovery from illness: A narrative synthesis of qualitative research. *J. Nurs.* **2008**, *64*, 564–573. [CrossRef] [PubMed]
14. Koenig Kellas, J.; Castle, K.M.; Johnson, A.; Cohen, M. *Cancer as Communal: Understanding Communication and Relationships from the Perspectives of Patients, Survivors, Family Caregivers, and Health Care Providers*; Paper Presented to the Family Communication Division of the National Communication Association: Philadelphia, PA, USA, 2016.
15. Garrard, E.; Wrigley, A. Hope and terminal illness: False hope versus absolute hope. *Clin. Eth.* **2009**, *4*, 38–43. [CrossRef]
16. Foxwell, K.R.; Scott, S.E. Coping together and apart: Exploring how patients and their caregivers manage terminal head and neck cancer. *J. Psychosoc. Oncol.* **2011**, *29*, 308–326. [CrossRef] [PubMed]
17. Mok, E.; Lau, K.; Phil, M.; Lam, W.; Chan, L.; Ng, J.; Chan, K. Health-care professionals' perspective on hope in the palliative care setting. *J. Palliat. Med.* **2010**, *13*, 877–883. [CrossRef] [PubMed]
18. Grbich, C; Parker, D.; Maddocks, I. The emotions and coping strategies of caregivers of family members with a terminal illness. *Palliat. Care* **2001**, *17*, 30–36.
19. Goldsmith, D.J.; Miller, L.E.; Caughlin, J.P. Openness and avoidance in couples communicating about cancer. *Commun. Yearb.* **2008**, *31*, 62–119. [CrossRef]
20. Planalp, S.; Trost, M.R. Communication issues at the end of life: Reports from hospice volunteers. *Health Commun.* **2008**, *23*, 222–233. [CrossRef] [PubMed]
21. Spitzberg, B.H.; Cupach, W.R. Introduction. In *The Dark Side of Close Relationships (pp. xi-xxii)*; Spitzberg, B.H., Cupach, W.R., Eds.; Lawrence Erlbaum: Mahwah, NJ, USA, 1998.
22. Devers, K.J.; Frankel, R.M. Study design in qualitative research 2: Sampling and data collection strategies. *Educ. Health* **2000**, *13*, 263–271. [CrossRef]
23. Lindlof, T.R.; Taylor, B.C. *Qualitative Communication Research Methods*; Sage: Thousand Oaks, CA, USA, 2002.

24. Miles, M.B.; Huberman, A.M.; Saldana, J. *Qualitative Data Analysis: A Methods Sourcebook*; Sage: Thousand Oaks, CA, USA, 2014.
25. Braun, V.; Clarke, V. Using thematic analysis in psychology. *Qual. Res. Psychol.* **2006**, *3*, 77–101. [CrossRef]
26. McNulty, J.K.; Fincham, F.D. Beyond positive psychology? Toward a contextual view of psychological processes and well-being. *Am. Psychol.* **2012**, *67*, 101–110. [CrossRef] [PubMed]
27. Arnett, R.C. Situating a dialogic ethics. In *The Handbook of Communication Ethics*; Cheney, G., Munshi, S., Munshi, D., Eds.; Routledge: New York, NY, USA, 2011.
28. Buber, M. *I And Thou*; Charles Scribner's Sons: New York, NY, USA, 1970.
29. Snyder, C.R.; Rand, K.L.; King, E.A.; Feldman, D.B.; Woodward, J.T. "False" hope. *J. Clin. Psychol.* **2002**, *58*, 1003–1022. [CrossRef] [PubMed]
30. Kersten, C.; Cameron, M.G.; Oldenburg, J. Truth in Hope and Hope in Truth. *J. Palliat. Med.* **2012**, *15*, 128–129. [CrossRef] [PubMed]
31. Zhang, A.Y.; Siminoff, L.A. Silence and cancer: Why do families and patients fail to communicate? *Health Commun.* **2003**, *15*, 415–429. [CrossRef] [PubMed]
32. Manne, S.; Badr, H. Intimacy and relationship processes in couples' psychosocial adaptation to cancer. *Cancer* **2008**, *112*, 2541–2555. [CrossRef] [PubMed]
33. Sherman, D.W. Reciprocal suffering: The need to improve family caregivers' quality of life through palliative care. *J. Palliat. Med.* **1998**, *1*, 357–366. [CrossRef] [PubMed]
34. Kamal, A.H.; Bull, J.; Kavalieratos, D.; Taylor, D.H., Jr.; Downey, W.; Abernethy, A.P. Palliative care needs of patients with cancer living in the community. *J. Oncol. Pract.* **2011**, *7*, 382–388. [CrossRef] [PubMed]
35. Smith, T.J.; Temin, S.; Alesi, E.R.; Abernethy, A.P.; Balboni, T.A.; Basch, E.M.; Ferrell, B.R.; Loscalzo, M.; Meier, D.E.; Paice, J.A.; et al. American Society of Clinical Oncology provisional clinical opinion: The integration of palliative care into standard oncology care. *J. Clin. Oncol.* **2012**, *30*, 880–887. [CrossRef] [PubMed]
36. IOM (Institute of Medicine). *Delivering High-Quality Cancer Care: Charting a New Course for a System in Crisis*; The National Academies Press: Washington, DC, USA, 2013.
37. Keeley, M.P.; Yingling, J.M. *Final Conversations: Helping the Living and Dying Talk to Each Other*; VanderWyk & Burnham: Acton, MA, USA, 2007.

behavioral sciences

MDPI

Essay
Death of an Ex-Spouse: Lessons in Family Communication about Disenfranchised Grief

Jillian A. Tullis

Department of Communication Studies, University of San Diego, 5998 Alcalá Park, Camino Hall 126, San Diego, CA 92110, USA; jtullis@sandiego.edu; Tel.: +1-619-260-6897

Academic Editor: Maureen Keeley
Received: 28 February 2017; Accepted: 21 March 2017; Published: 24 March 2017

Abstract: The death of a loved one is an emotional-laden experience, and while grief and mourning rituals are less formal today in many communities, there remain some social norms for individuals to process loss. The death of an ex-family member, such as a former spouse, is more complicated and expectations for how to respond are fraught with uncertainty. While grief has been studied and is primarily understood as an individual cognitive process, scholars in sociology and communication are considering the ways in which grief and mourning are social and take place in dialogue with others. This manuscript explores Kenneth Doka's concept of disenfranchised grief, which is "grief that is experienced when loss cannot be openly acknowledged, socially sanctioned, or publicly mourned" through the author's experience of the death of her ex-husband. The narrative will recount how the author learned about her ex-husband's death (via text message), and will challenge definitions of family and family communication about death and grief, particularly the communication strategies used to cope with this unique type of loss.

Keywords: autoethnography; loss; narrative; text message

---

1. Introduction

"Did you hear that Tim P passed away yesterday?"
What the fuck?!?! I thought to myself. My ex-husband is dead.

So yeah, that was the moment I learned about the death of my former spouse. By text message. On a Sunday morning while I was lying in bed reading the news as I do most Sundays, with the dog nestled close to me. I had forgotten all about the pending message from my friend Pam, who was at my wedding 13 years ago. And there it was. Not even ten words situated in that familiar green text message bubble. Pam and I only talk on the phone a couple of times a year and until this Sunday in September the last time we spoke was in November around Thanksgiving. What the hell! I mean I always knew this day would come since Tim was more than two decades older than me. I had contemplated his dying, his death, and being a young widow. Once we were divorced, though, I had not given as much thought to what this moment would feel like. Any concerns I had about his death were only practical since we had one lingering financial tie. So I just stood in my bedroom, I was out of the bed by now, my mind racing. Looking back, I wish I had sat down, grounded myself a bit before making my next move. But I just stood there staring at my phone as if standing there would help this news make more sense. I replied to the text message:

"No. I didn't. I hadn't talked to him in years. Thanks for letting me know."

But I was not thankful. I felt irritated. Why do people think it is okay to share this kind of news via text? I did what I normally do in these moments of shock and uncertainty. I called my mom.

2. Background and Methods

I study how people talk about dying and death and teach classes about how we communicate at the end of life. Not only am I infinitely fascinated by the subject, but I find it very life affirming. It gives me perspective and it teaches me so much about dying, but also about living and what makes a good life. Since this is my specialty, I have heard more than my share of stories about how people cope when their loved one dies. The narrative or story above, which I will return to in a moment, is one of those tales. It is a story about death and grief, but a particular type of grief, disenfranchised grief. It is also a story about families, how we define family and how we communicate in families about bereavement and the grief, or reactions that follow a loss. Grief is generally investigated and understood as an individual cognitive process, yet scholars in other fields of study investigate the ways in which grief and mourning are social and take place in conversation with others [1]. With this in mind, I use my own story to process this death, and to examine and understand communication with family about grief.

Before I return to the story about my reaction to the death of my ex-husband, I should explain a few things about how I present my story, also known in scholarly settings as autoethnography [2]. This approach to writing and research uses personal experience to understand aspects of culture. To accomplish this, the researcher or writer combines existing research about a topic with their personal story to offer new insights. Autoethnography, while useful and accessible to a broad audience, does not guarantee the same protections as other types of research. Therefore, names have been changed to protect the confidentiality of the people I write about. I have also fictionalized the story. This means that while the story really happened, I have changed other details in addition to the names, such as where people live, what kind of work they do, and their hobbies to further conceal their identities. While one of the major characters in this story is dead, I am still obligated to protect him and loved ones who are still alive and could read this article. Third, since I did not take notes during this experience, I have used my memory to recreate phone calls, text messages and face-to-face conversations. I have done my best to be as accurate as possible [3]. Now that I have explained my ethical obligations, some of the methodological issues, and how I have addressed them, let me return to the story.

3. Story Continues

"So, Tim P died", I say stoically to my mom. I did not know how to say it so I just said it. "My ex-husband", I added, because she did not respond immediately.

"Oh no!" I could hear her start to cry—a familiar response. It is almost the exact reaction she had when I told her one of my mentors had died suddenly. Instead of sympathizing with my mother's feelings, I began to feel insecure and thought, 'Oh shit! Maybe I'm supposed to be crying. Why am I not crying?' Some tears welled up, as I stood in my bedroom talking with my mom, but they never fell. Crying just did not feel authentic; they would have been reactionary, a response to my mother's emotions. She and my ex-husband were also closer in age than I was to Timothy, so I think it felt like a peer had died. I, on the other hand, could not feel much more than shock. Despite being in his early 60s, his death only seemed unexpected. And while I knew intellectually this was a tragedy, especially for his family, it did not feel that way emotionally for me. I figured whatever the circumstances, his death felt premature. Yet, I did not feel the sadness that comes with realizing someone you know and care about is permanently gone from your life because they have died.

"What happened?" she asked. "I shouldn't be crying. He was your husband. I don't even know why I'm crying."

"It's okay", I said. I was actually glad one of us had some clear feelings about this news because I really did not. "I don't know." Truth be told, I had some guesses, but I was really afraid to say them aloud. An accident? I wondered. Cancer? Maybe he killed himself? No. No. No. He would not do that, I thought. Has to be something else. "Pam told me by text. I don't know anything other than that he died yesterday."

Behav. Sci. **2017**, *7*, 16

"Well that's a crappy thing to do", my mom said, referring to the text message. Her tone had changed and she was in full Mom-Mode, protective of her child's emotional well-being and trying to take care of me by taking charge and giving me direction. "Call her. Find out what she knows. And call me back."

"Okay."

"Love you."

"Love you too." I end the call with my mom and search my contacts to dial Pam's number. I feel a small sense of dread as the phone rings. She picks up by the second ring and sounds like she is expecting my call, which made me even more annoyed that she did not just ring me in the first place.

"Hey", Pam said quietly with a knowing tone.

"Hey", I said, trying to match her tone. "So, any idea what I happened?" I asked, hoping Pam could quell my worries that my ex-husband, the man I was partnered with for 12 years, did not die in a traumatic way. I realized, as Pam recounted what she knew, that this was my primary concern. The fact that my ex-husband was dead did not really seem like the most pressing issue, but how he died was my worry. This was the information I needed because it would help me know what his final days were like. I wanted to determine if he was suffering emotionally or physically, if he knew his death was coming, or if it was sudden. I think that because my work is driven by the desire to minimize people's suffering at the end of life, I was more interested in having these details. Apparently, Pam was looped in on an email thread among some of our former co-workers, which helped me pull things together. It sounded like cancer.

My analytical, scholar brain kicked in as I contemplated the death of my ex-husband. Disenfranchised grief came immediately to mind. Kenneth Doka, a professor of gerontology, describes disenfranchised grief as "the grief that is experienced when a loss cannot be openly acknowledged, socially sanctioned, or publicly mourned" [4] (p. 160). He goes on to say that there are three ways this can occur. One is that the relationship between the deceased and the griever is not recognized. Consider, for example, the spouse who has dementia and does not always remember their partner and is not told about the death because they may not understand. In this case, the griever is perceived as incapable of experiencing the loss. The second is that the loss is not recognized as legitimate. Charles Corr (1999), a retired professor of philosophical studies, describes the death of a pet or a miscarriage that occurs early in a pregnancy as two types of loss that some might not view as real and worthy of strong emotions [5]. A third type of disenfranchised grief focuses on those relationships that are dismissed or not recognized. Divorced spouses are one example and this is why I wondered how I should communicate with others about this loss and how they would respond to me. The problem with disenfranchised grief, which is not present in those deaths that are socially and culturally recognized, is that problems can arise for the griever because there are few sources of support available to help facilitate mourning. Depression and prolonged grief are both concerns. Support groups for people whose ex-spouse has died are not abundant, in part because it is not socially acceptable or expected to grieve the death of someone they divorced. My experience fit into the third type of disenfranchised grief; following my ex-husband's death, my relationship, our history together, was not recognized by my former in-laws and the possibility of disenfranchised grief only seemed more likely because I never felt like we reconciled once our marriage ended.

Now that I had some sense about what may have happened to Tim, that he had some illness that preceded his death, I started to wonder about the appropriate response to this news. Before I got off the phone with Pam, I asked her to pass along any information she might learn about a funeral, but not even Pam and her husband were sure they would attend. She was always more of my friend and had no contact with Tim after we split. I called my mom back and shared this new information and together we reflected on my life with Timothy.

By the time I got off the phone with my mom the second time, the feeling of shock had subsided some and I just started to feel sad for Tim. I think he was afraid to die because in all the years we were together he never seemed to accept his mortality. Despite the death of family members, Timothy never seemed interested in confronting the reality of his own death. In fact, the death of a niece may have contributed to his fear of dying. While we would occasionally talk about my research interests, Tim never seemed comfortable with the subject. Looking back, I suspect that embracing mortality would also require Tim to acknowledge the ways in which his behavior could contribute to an early death. If Tim were to accept that he would die, he might also feel compelled to reprioritize his goals and behavior. Since Tim seemed fearful, I was also really worried about him dying alone despite having a big family. I guess I was also worried he did not have a girlfriend in his life. If there were one term I would use to describe Tim it would be *serial monogamist*. As soon as I started to think about his family, my heart started to ache for his brother, who he was very close to, and his parents, who were both in their 90s. To bury your younger brother and your son was not right. I knew they would be heartbroken. I knew I would not attend any funeral or memorial service because there were too many unknowns, but moreover, my appearance after seven years apart would just detract from rather than comfort Tim's family. I decided I would at least send a card to his parents expressing my condolences to them and my ex-brother and sisters in-law.

One week after first learning of Tim's death, I had managed to gather a few more details from a woman Tim and I met at the NASCAR track we visited annually while we were married. Based upon what Deborah told me, I gathered that Tim had a growth on his neck and had surgery, but the cancer came back and by the time he was actively dying he was not able to talk and was eating through a tube. This was a special kind of punch to the gut.

In the last year of my doctoral program, I worked on a project with people who had terminal head or neck cancer. One morning I drove to the cancer center to interview a man whose cancer was advanced, his lips were so swollen from the disease that he was unable to speak for himself. His life partner, a woman he had been with for years, but was not married to, communicated on the man's behalf. The efforts this couple made to participate in the study, driving early in the morning to meet with me before his appointment, moved me deeply. I encouraged everyone I saw to appreciate their ability to talk and smile. Later that night, after an emotionally taxing day, Tim locked me out of the house. This was really the beginning of the end of our marriage. I know this is probably going to sound strange, but in some weird way, Tim's death seemed like the alternative ending to the movie of my life with him. While I could not have predicted how or when Timothy would die, I did expect to be with him in health and sickness until death.

After a week and no word from anyone in Tim's family, I decided to do nothing. I did not even send a card to his parents. I talked with my brother about what to do, whether I should have any contact with Tim's kids or one of his siblings and that is when it occurred to me that Tim's family would support each other and it was the job of my family and friends to support me. While my mom, dad, and brother offered condolences and helped me process this strange life event, some of my friends were less available. I would call them, leave a generic message—I did not want to text or leave a voicemail announcing a death—and they just never called back. The majority of my other friends were thankfully very supportive, acknowledged and therefore validated that this was a legitimate loss that I might have significant, albeit conflicted emotions. Of the people I did speak with who knew Tim, none were surprised that he was dead. Sad for him and his family, but not really surprised. He lived a rough life. He smoked, he drank too much, and the drinking was a vicious cycle he could not break from, not even after we split. In fact, when I called the friend who was the best man at our wedding to tell him Tim had died, he confessed they had not kept in touch, in part because Tim was rarely sober. It is hard to stay friends or married to someone who is frequently intoxicated. Yet the loss of his marriage and friends did not appear to change his drinking behavior. So, while I felt some small comfort in knowing I was not the only one who could not make our made-family work, I still felt really ambivalent because we never reconciled. Tim never came around to seeing why our marriage ended. Even up until just weeks before our divorce was final, he was still talking about our family. The four of us: our two dogs and the two of us. Maybe it sounds naïve to say, but until he died, I had hoped he might call me and say he was sorry and that he finally realized his drinking was a problem.

Finding out someone you once cared about deeply has died via text message prompts a reaction of shock. Texting is a cold flat channel to receive such powerful information. I was worried about how I would feel as time passed. I wondered if I would eventually have a deep emotional breakdown or if I would feel ostracized and long for recognition if my former in-laws never contacted me. By the time an obituary was published, which my mom shared with me over the phone, attending any of the planned formal rituals that generally follow the death of an (current or former) intimate other was not feasible. This prompted additional questions about what exactly I should do to not only mourn the death of my ex-husband, but also get the closure I needed to further process the end of my marriage since the apology I hoped to receive was never going to come.

Tim's death and the fact that no one from his family contacted me also raised questions about the meaning of family and how families communicate about dying and death. Friends and family members shape and legitimize romantic relationships and those in relationships look for affirmation from friends and family. I was surely a full-fledged member of Tim's family at one time. They welcomed me and I cared about them, yet few family members had any contact with me when Tim and I split. In fact, when one family member called me during our separation and said, "You knew how he was when you married him", I realized I could not count on his family to support me in any way during our separation or divorce. It was clear to me then, and again in his death, that despite more than a decade together, they would fully support Tim to my exclusion. The lack of contact in the years following our split seemed appropriate—they were *Team Tim P.*—but not reaching out to me after his death felt like an erasure—as if I never existed in the larger story of Tim's life. His obituary offers another perspective and some insight into why this might have been the case. According to the obituary, published in his hometown paper, Tim had a girlfriend at the time of his death. It is also possible, that because Tim and I never reconciled, that his family simply honored his wishes to keep strict boundaries. I may never know. And in the absence of any contact with his family and any opportunity to participate in formal death rituals like a funeral, I would have to find my own path to grieving and mourning the death of my ex-husband.

It has been six months since I was notified, via text, of my ex-husband's death. I talk freely about Tim when my life as a married person comes up and if people inquire about him today, I volunteer that he died. While I did visit his gravesite with my mom when I was home for Thanksgiving, I am still trying to come up with a ritual that would acknowledge and honor our relationship, as well as mark the end of Tim's life. But this does not feel as urgent as it did six months ago. Perhaps this is the benefit of time. I did take one step towards catharsis. I rewrote Tim's obituary. "Did the person who wrote this even know Tim!?" I lamented after my mom read the paltry sentences. The blurb was completely unsatisfying and it offered none of Timothy's personality because it was just a listing of facts, none of which truly celebrated his life. So I rewrote it, in the form of a eulogy, partially to make up for the lack of flare, but in hopes of finding some conclusion. Here is an excerpt:

> Timothy Patterson, known to many as Tim P, the man who declared at the age of 47 that he had consumed one million Budweisers, has died at the age of 61. He was most proud of having been a single father to his daughters and loved his granddaughters dearly. He also had a niece he was very close to, who was like a third daughter. Tim loved NASCAR, was mechanically inclined, and could fix anything. No one made better ribs than him and he had what I will call a very creative vocabulary. *Mofo* was one of his favorite words for those he loved and those he hated. To listen to Tim talk with his brother was like listening to two people speaking a foreign language. He was a reluctant dog owner when we were together, but only because he understood the pain of losing a pet. Nevertheless, he loved our pitbulls, Amber and Gus, so fully.

To be honest, in the days following the news that my ex-husband had died, I reflected on many positive memories, but as I looked over a few old photos I realized that the man I had some fond memories of had changed. I could see those changes in his face in those pictures. In older images of our first years together, Tim's face conveyed a tranquil demeanor. In the later photos, Tim appeared less at peace and more distressed. Perhaps this look was the result of more daily drinking, unacknowledged depression following his retirement, or anxiety about our marriage. Maybe it was a confluence of these things, but it is clear now that I will likely never know. What is clear is that the first guy I wanted to know and the second not at all. So I knew that my reminiscing was not out of love. He had changed too much and I did not like the changes. Too many years had passed since my ex and I had any contact and the interactions we had in the years since our divorce were unpleasant, at least for me. In fact, they were crude reminders why we were no longer together. I knew I did not still love him. Perhaps this is the silver lining in the grey cloud of his death. I could truly move on and I did not need his family to affirm our life together any more than I needed them to help me mourn.

4. Discussion

According to the American Psychological Association, 40%–50% of married couples divorce [6]. While divorce is common, our rituals for grieving a divorced spouse are not clear. The role of families and how families communicate with us about our romantic relationships effect the development, maintenance, and dissolution of those relationships. They also have a deep influence on how we process loss through death. Families and friends can mean the difference between appropriate grief or a complicated, disenfranchised grieving experience. Despite the lack of contact with Tim's family, I took steps to minimize my pain and process my feelings of loss through rewriting his obituary, talking with my family and friends (some who also knew Tim), and eventually visiting his grave. When we are able to support our friends and family whose grief runs the risk of being disenfranchised, we can best help them by offering them a listening ear. Talking and listening to the details of the relationship, its meaning, its challenges, and its triumphs are helpful to process a death. This is especially true if others are intentionally or unintentionally disenfranchising a griever through their messages or lack of communication. We can counter efforts to disenfranchise grief by listening when someone shares his or her story rather than shut down conversations that dismiss the relationship solely because it ended years earlier in divorce. Another suggestion is to offer to help that person create and participate in some ritual of closure. This could include visiting the deceased's grave or creating some other event that formally signals an end. Given the variations on what constitutes "family" today, the possibility that grief could be disenfranchised is great and it is best to be prepared to offer support.

5. Conclusions

Death, whether sudden or expected, produces a range of emotions from shock to sadness to anger. How we learn about a death, although not well understood, seems to contribute to those reactions. In the last five years, I have received more bad news via social media and text message than ever before and I wonder what the implications are for my and others ability to grieve. While these communication technologies help us feel connected when we are alone, I cannot help but question if they offer the same quality of support as telephone or face-to-face interactions. The death of my ex-spouse illuminated these concerns, and prompted me to question the role of family in the grieving process, while challenging my thinking about how we define family. My goal in sharing my personal experience with the death of an ex-spouse and disenfranchised grief is to challenge our thinking about how we communicate about loss, but also encourage each of us to find effective ways support others when grief looms.

Acknowledgments: The author would like to thank Tasha Dunn for her invaluable assistance with the development of this manuscript.

Conflicts of Interest: The author declares no conflict of interest.

References

1.   Vera, M.I. Social dimensions of grief. In *Handbook of Death and Dying*; Bryant, C.D., Ed.; Sage Publications, Inc.: Thousand Oaks, CA, USA, 2003; Volume 2, pp. 838–846.

2. Ellis, C.; Adams, T.E.; Bochner, A.P. Autoethnography: An overview. *Hist. Soc. Res.* **2011**, *36*, 273–290.
3. Tullis, J.A.; McRae, C.J.; Adams, T.E.; Vitale, A. Truth Troubles. *Qual. Inquiry* **2009**, *15*, 178–200. [CrossRef]
4. Doka, K. Disenfranchised grief. In *Living with Grief: Loss in Later Life*; Doka, K.J., Ed.; Hospice Foundation of America: Washington, DC, USA, 2002; pp. 159–168.
5. Corr, C.A. Enhancing the concept of disenfranchised grief. *OMEGA-J. Death Dying* **1999**, *38*, 1–20. [CrossRef]
6. Marriage and Divorce. Available online: http://www.apa.org/topics/divorce/ (accessed on 20 February 2017).

behavioral
sciences

MDPI

Article

Final Conversations: Overview and Practical Implications for Patients, Families, and Healthcare Workers

Maureen P. Keeley [1],* and Mark A. Generous [2]

[1] Department of Communication Studies, Texas State University, 601 University Drive, San Marcos, TX 78666, USA
[2] Department of Communication, Saint Mary's College of California, 1928 St. Mary's Road, Moraga, CA 94575, USA; mag31@stmarys-ca.edu
* Correspondence: mk09@txstate.edu or Maureen.keeley@txstate.edu; Tel.: +1-512-245-3133

Academic Editor: Scott J. Hunter
Received: 31 January 2017; Accepted: 30 March 2017; Published: 5 April 2017

Abstract: The current paper presents a summary of a 12-year body of research on final conversations, which will be useful for healthcare providers who work with patients and family nearing the end-of-life, as well as for patients and their family members. Final conversations encompass any and all conversations that occur between individuals with a terminal diagnosis and their family members (all participants are aware that their loved one is in the midst of the death journey). Final conversations take the family member's perspective and highlights what are their memorable messages with the terminally ill loved one. In this paper the authors highlight the message themes present at the end-of-life for both adults and children, the functions each message theme serves for family members, and lastly, the communicative challenges of final conversations. Additionally, the authors discuss the current nature and future of final conversations research, with special attention paid to practical implications for healthcare providers, patients, and family members; also, scholarly challenges and future research endeavors are explored.

Keywords: final conversations; end-of-life communication; family communication; death and dying

1. Introduction

Close relationships are critical to the end-of-life (EOL) journey, both for terminally ill people and their family members [1]. In particular, it is the communication between these two parties at the end-of-life that has been shown to have a profound impact on the EOL journey [1,2]. Here, the focus will be one aspect of EOL communication known as final conversations, which include all interactions, verbal and nonverbal, that an individual has with another who is terminally ill from the moment of a terminal diagnosis to the point of death [1]. Final conversations may involve only one conversation, but they can also be (and often are) a series of conversations [2]. Final conversations research has focused on the themes, functions and impacts of communication at the end-of-life from the perspective of the family members, close friends, and other individuals that are allowed within the inner sanctum of a terminally ill person's life, which until recently, was an understudied perspective in the EOL literature [2]. The current manuscript seeks to summarize this body of research, while also addressing three primary insights gleaned from this work: practical implications for healthcare providers, patients, and families; scholarly challenges; and, future research directions.

2. Summary of Final Conversations Research

Prior to 2004, scholars exploring familial interactions in the midst of death and dying primarily focused on the perspective of the terminally ill person [2]. It is only within the last fourteen years that a focus on the "other" person (i.e., family members or close others), through the participation in final conversations, has been explored [3]. Findings suggest that final conversations have the potential to have a tremendous impact on family relationships (biological, legal, or chosen families) [1,4]. Specifically, the realization that time is limited because of a terminal illness increases the urgency for both the terminally ill person and family members to say final goodbyes, and to try to make amends if necessary in their relationships; it also creates a window of opportunity for people to make time in their busy lives to focus on the relationship with the terminally ill person through their participation in final conversations [1]. Final conversations often give terminally ill people the opportunity to help their family members move forward after the death by providing advice, direction and permission to move on, as well as creating a sense of closure and completion of the relationship [1,2]. It is only through communication that terminally ill people and their family members can work together to achieve greater meaning about life, death, and their relationships [3].

2.1. A Brief Overview of Methodology

The final conversations body of research uses both qualitative and quantitative methodologies. The data was collected in three phases over a fourteen year period. Specifically, Phase I and Phase II of data collection consisted of in-depth retrospective interviews with adults (Phase I) and children/adolescents (Phase II) [2,4]. Retrospective accounts have proven to be especially clear for family members reflecting back on their EOL communication with the terminally ill person [2,4]. A sampling of the questions of the interviews that led to the most substantive findings include: "Would you share with me your recollection of your final conversation or conversations with your loved one?"; "What was the most meaningful conversation that you had with this person?"; "Why was it the most meaningful to you?"; "What sorts of nonverbal experiences stick out in your mind from this time period?"; and, "What did each of these nonverbal experiences mean to you?" The language of the questions was appropriately adapted according to the age of the participants. Phase I had a total of 85 adults (age range: 21–85) and Phase II had a total of 65 children/adolescents (age range: 5–18). Interviews were collected until saturation was reached, meaning that no new information was being revealed. An interpretive paradigm was used to analyze the data to ensure that the themes captured the authentic and significant experiences of EOL communication from the family members' perspectives, which facilitated the categories to emerge from the data.

Phase III employed a cross-sectional survey design in order to create and test initial validation of a Final Conversations Scale [5]. The scale was developed based on past literature, as well as findings from the previous qualitative phases (see [5] for the scale and findings). One-hundred fifty-two participants completed the survey by retrospectively recalling their final conversations.

2.2. Final Conversations Themes and Functions

Five overarching themes emerged from Phase I and Phase II: love, identity, religious/spiritual messages, everyday talk, and difficult relationship talk [2,4]. These five themes—with the exception of difficult relationship talk, which was not found in a children/adolescent sample—emerged in both adult and children/adolescent samples. These messages include both verbal and nonverbal messages [2]. Nonverbal communication is a critical aspect of final conversations, because as death nears, the ability to talk and verbalize words often becomes more challenging and limited for the terminally ill person [6]. Not all themes are present in every final conversation, although often two or three themes can exist within the same conversation; at the same time, in some relationships, one theme will take precedence and be the focal point of the entire conversation, which highlights the importance of contextual elements on the enactment of final conversations [1].

The first theme—messages of love—is the most prominent theme for adults to communicate with the terminally ill family member at the end-of-life [7]. Love is communicated both verbally through words, as well as nonverbally via hugs, looks, hand holds, kisses, or other expressions of love [1]. There is not a right or wrong way to communicate love, it is simply important for individuals to communicate it in a way that the other person will understand. Adults and children/adolescents note that messages of love helped to validate and strengthen relational bonds with the terminally ill family member [2,4].

The second theme is verbal messages related to individual and relational identity [2]. Identity messages signify the statements that represent the assessment or formation of the self [8]. These messages may contain new information for the family member (e.g., advice, messages of insight and confirmation) [1], or they may highlight known (but perhaps previously downplayed) attributes [2]. When faced with the impending death of a loved one, individuals often take the opportunity to examine, reevaluate, and even redefine themselves because of their final conversations, which was a common function of identity-related messages articulated by participants [2].

The third theme centered on religious/spiritual messages, which may be direct affirmations of their faith or spiritual experiences [9,10]. Religious messages often incorporated doctrinal and denominational experiences that include specific behaviors, beliefs, or rituals of a system of worship from a specific religious group that the terminally ill person or family members identified with or shared [9,10]. Spiritual experiences are a phenomenon described as a transcendent occurrence that has deep meaning for the individuals and greatly impacts their belief in an afterlife [9,10]. These spiritual experiences might be encountered by the terminally ill person or a family member prior to their final conversations, or during the EOL journey. Religious/spiritual messages functionally help validate individuals' beliefs in a higher power and their expectation that they will meet again someday in heaven or whatever comes after this life [9]. In addition, religious/spiritual messages provide comfort and solace for terminally ill people and family members during an often chaotic, uncertainty-inducing time [2,9,10].

The fourth theme, everyday talk and routine interactions, focuses on the ordinary, commonplace conversations and repeated types of daily interactions (e.g., discussing daily activities, talking about television and movies, reminiscing, sharing stories, etc.) [1,2,4]. This was the most prominent theme that emerged from children/adolescents interviews about final conversations [4]. Everyday communication performs numerous and simultaneous purposes within families, including: building bonds, coordinating interactions, structuring time and sharing histories [2]. At the end-of-life, all of these functions are critical for the family members, as they give a sense of normalcy and control in the midst of chaos that an impending death often brings to the situation [4].

The fifth memorable theme is difficult relationship talk, which often includes an account of the challenges in the relationship between the terminally ill person and the family member prior to the illness, as well as the struggle that the family member had in talking with the dying person [2]. Difficult relationship talk includes messages that revealed attempts at understanding, accepting, or beginning the forgiveness process towards the terminally ill person [2]. For the individuals that have these challenging relationships, they often report that difficult relationship talk was the most important to them during their final conversations. Additionally, family members highlight that they have to find the right time and the resolve to engage in the conversation, and they hope to finally have a positive interaction with the dying loved one before death. Individuals are hoping to find a way to release pent up anger and frustrations so as not to be left holding these negative emotions following the death [2]. At the same time, some individuals also talk about avoiding certain conversations so as not to make their relationship worse [11]. It is also important to note that interviews with children and adolescents did not uncover the theme of difficult relationship talk. Perhaps the absence of difficult relationship talk from children/adolescent's interviews is because they don't realize how challenging the relationships are yet, or because they don't have the cognitive and communicative ability to participate in difficult relationship talk [4].

We were interested in quantitatively validating the aforementioned themes via the construction of the Final Conversations Scale [5]. While constructing the scale, the a priori decision was made to include scale items that measured instrumental talk, which includes discussions regarding the death and dying process (e.g., discussions about the illness, funerals, chores to be completed after the death, etc.). Although this theme did not emerge during the qualitative interviews, we argued that this theme is an important, yet potentially neglected topic of conversation during the EOL journey [3]. A possible explanation for why instrumental talk did not emerge during in-depth interviews is because participants did not recall those conversations as memorable or significant to the relationship. Previous research examining EOL communication highlights the significance of this topic for terminally ill people and reveals that instrumental death talk is occurring [12], yet may not be the most memorable messages for the family members upon reflection and recall. Instrumental talk messages are functionally important, as they can help family members and patients discuss and negotiate needs, desires, and advanced directives [13]. Analyses of the quantitative survey conducted in Phase III revealed a five-factor scale that included messages of love, spiritual/religious messages, difficult relationship talk, everyday talk, and instrumental death talk [5]. Due to possible inadequate operationalization, identity did not emerge as a meaningful factor in the quantitative analyses; however, we are currently working to revise the operationalization of identity, as well as replicate and confirm the aforementioned themes. Specifically, we returned to the qualitative analyses to create more behaviorally concrete scale items to measure the identity dimension of the Final Conversations Scale.

Overall, Keeley and her associates' findings revealed that communication at the end-of-life is as important for the family members as it is for those that are dying [1–3]. This conclusion however should not imply that participating in final conversations is an easy task. On the contrary, communicating in the midst of grief, fear, and uncertainty can be an overwhelming endeavor for both the terminally ill person and family members [1]. High emotions frequently complicate and often interfere with effective communication [1]. In addition, many individuals have never seen or been a part of final conversations and feel ill-equipped for communication at the end-of-life [1,2]. Some of the communication issues include: how to begin the conversations, what topics should and should not be talked about at the end-of-life, who is in charge of leading the conversation, and how much emotion can be displayed during the interaction [1]. Consequently, family members can find the task daunting with many challenges to overcome [14], or they simply choose to avoid certain topics altogether [11].

2.3. Challenges

Due to the fact that final conversations usually occur in private, and most individuals have little to no experience with communication at the end-of-life, people are uncertain about the right timing for these important conversations [2]. In addition, family members often face certain tensions and apprehensions about what and how to talk with the terminally ill person [14]. The following section summarizes the communicative challenges and difficulties noted by individuals who have engaged in final conversations.

The first challenge, which also influences the manifestation of other communicative difficulties, is time; specifically, in previous articles we discuss the issue of terminal time, which we define as all moments that occur between the terminal diagnosis and death of the terminally ill person [1,14]. Time creates both the impetus for final conversations, as well as the framework for the communicative context at the end-of-life [1,14]. The framework for EOL communication comes from terminal time which constructs a structure, agenda, and background that are fundamental parts of final conversations. At the end-of-life, time creates a structure for the conversations in that there are hard boundaries surrounding the conversations because there is a beginning (i.e., diagnosis of terminal illness) and an end (i.e., death) regarding the availability for the conversation. It also can create an agenda for the conversations (i.e., What do I want or need to say to the terminally ill person before their death?). Lastly, it establishes the background for every conversation (i.e., How is the terminally ill person emotionally feeling and physically looking today? Are they in pain? Do they have enough energy to participate in a conversation? Am I ready for this conversation?) [1]. For some, the diagnosis of a terminal illness creates urgency and awareness that time may be running out for opportunities to communicate and interact with the terminally ill person [14]. Unfortunately for others, they wait too long to participate in final conversations. As death nears, terminally ill people often suffer from extreme physical fatigue, difficulty in speaking and even mental deterioration, which can make it nearly impossible to have any substantial communication with them during the later stages of the dying process [12]. Thus, the physical and mental state of the terminally ill person may provide a tangible barrier to effective, open communication [11].

The remaining challenges related to final conversations can be understood via relational dialectics theory [15]. Dialectical tensions refer to the "dynamic interplay of opposing forces or contradictions", which are illustrated by dialogue between relational partners [15] (p. 3). Three dialectical tensions relevant at the end-of-life include: the acceptance-denial of the impending death; openness-closedness regarding how honest and revealing they are with each other on a wide variety of topics; and, the expression-concealment of emotion that occurs during the death journey [14].

The tension of acceptance-denial highlights the struggle that many individuals deal with when faced with the news that their loved one has a terminal illness [14]. Some individuals refuse to accept the terminal diagnosis because it causes them anguish and anxiety [16]. For others, it may simply be that they are afraid that if they accept the diagnosis, that they are giving up hope, and in part, inducing a faster death [14]. By accepting the impending death, individuals are able to face the truth of the situation, thereby allowing them to make the most of the time that they have left with their dying loved one [1].

The tension of openness-closedness represents individuals' struggle with the desire to self-disclose information to the terminally ill person, but also to keep some information private [14]. For instance, some families have norms regarding what should and should not be talked about based on their family history, such as personal and private information about themselves, or negative relationship issues. This avoidance may be a way to manage potentially negative emotional responses (i.e., self-protection and other-protection) [11].

In addition, some people worry that various topics could upset the terminally ill person, therefore causing unnecessary burden [11,14]. In fact, both family members and the terminally ill individuals may avoid topics and act positive in the midst of the death journey as a way to protect each other, because they believe the other to be too vulnerable to have honest and open conversations about death and dying [17]. Even more problematic is that sometimes both the terminally ill person and family members mistakenly think the other person doesn't want to talk about the difficult experience of death and dying, when in reality they do, which leads to a missed opportunity for dialogue and connection [18].

The tension of expression-concealment of emotions highlights the struggle to show the emotions they are experiencing juxtaposed with the desire or expectation to be strong and hide their true feelings at the end-of-life [11]. Strong negative emotions such as sadness, fear, or anger are inevitable at the end-of-life and most people are not good at expressing negative emotions [19]. From childhood through adulthood, many of the responses to the expression of negative emotions are gender based. For instance, boys are socialized not to show sadness by telling them "big boys don't cry", or they are congratulated for "being a strong and brave little man" [19]. Women are chastised for showing anger and are often called negative names for displaying their anger; this is so common that many women report trouble communicating their anger and instead they cry [19]. Culture also plays a big role in the display of all emotions, especially negative emotions because they are a bigger threat to the positive image of the individual or the larger community depending on the values of the society [19]. Finally, some families have expectations that they are supposed to be strong for one another and not display emotions related to sadness, anxiety, and distress [11,14].

3. Practical Implications

The research summarized above has implications for healthcare and palliative care providers, as well as the terminally ill person and their family members. First, final conversations research has helped us understand the interpersonal scripts between terminally ill patients and their family members that accompany the EOL journey [2]. Interpersonal scripts are important to consider in any communicative context, as they represent working models of individuals' communication behaviors and choices [20]; but, this concept is especially poignant in the context of family communication at the end-of-life. The US, and Western culture broadly, tends to view death as uncertainty-inducing and scary, which could potentially lead to an underdeveloped interpersonal script and avoidance surrounding the EOL context [11]. If, however, people become more aware of final conversations, see examples of what they look like, and begin developing their own scripts concerning the end-of-life, then people will potentially begin the conversations sooner with more fulfilling outcomes. Why is this? Because currently, many family members wait until the very end to have these conversations, and by then it is too late because terminally ill people are in the active stages of dying, where they are often not physically capable of verbal interactions [6].

Second, raising family members' awareness about final conversations can help facilitate dialogue regarding needs and desires of the terminally ill person and family members related to EOL communication. Providing examples and giving encouragement to participate in final conversations earlier in the death journey may enable participants to have a better EOL experience. Participating in communication at the end-of-life could also help decrease individuals' fear of the death process and help to change the culture of silence and uncertainty surrounding death [1].

We have argued that individual needs regarding communication at the end-of-life vary from person to person and from context to context [3]. It is the task of healthcare and palliative care professionals to use the tools available to them to help families articulate their communicative needs. For instance, the Final Conversations Scale is available, which is a measure of EOL relational communication that assesses verbal and nonverbal messages that occur at the end-of-life (see [5] for scale). Although this scale was originally designed to assess retrospective accounts of EOL communication for research goals, it can be adapted as a checklist to capture communicative needs of family members currently engaged in final conversations, as well as to help generate new scripts for both the terminally ill person and their family members. For example, palliative care professionals can adapt the scale's wording to present tense and change the scale's numeric anchors to assess needs (e.g., 1 = I do not want to talk about this; 7 = I want to talk about this). Furthermore, dialoguing with terminally ill people and their family members can help healthcare providers understand the needs, fears, and desires concerning their EOL journey.

Finally, the issue of children and adolescents' engagement in final conversations should be addressed with regard to practical implications, as this population is frequently shielded from the death and dying process by family members in an effort to protect them [3]. We analyzed messages of advice from children/adolescents to other children/adolescents and adults regarding final conversations [21]. (Mainly, these participants advised individuals to focus on confirming the relationship between the terminally ill patient and child/adolescent, as well as family members talking sooner rather than later with the children/adolescents [21]. In addition, these conversations need to be candid, open and honest regarding the patient's status and progress. Children/adolescents are not clueless and can often see that something serious is occurring between family members. Thus, by talking sooner rather than later, children/adolescents are given the chance to participate in final conversations on their own terms and in their own time. From the interviews we discovered a slight paradox—family members tend to believe that children/adolescents are too young and fragile to handle final conversations and death, but the children/adolescents desire more transparency from family members [21]. Thus, we advocate for a collaborative communicative approach to talking with children and adolescents about final conversations and death: Ask, Look, and Listen (ALL) [21]. In particular, family members should Ask children and adolescents about what they have seen, heard, and already know about what is happening regarding the terminally ill family member. Look at how the child/adolescent communicates by paying attention to nonverbal behaviors like body language, facial cues, and tone of voice, all of which will provide cues to the child/adolescent's comfort level. Additionally, individuals should Listen actively to what the child/adolescent says verbally by paraphrasing their words, asking for clarification, and remaining nonverbally responsive and calm. Children and adolescents deserve to be part of final conversations and have their questions addressed openly in a way that they can understand [21]. There is still much work to be done with regard to children/adolescents and the death and dying process, but open communication is a good place for families to start.

4. Scholarly Challenges and Future Directions

It is critical to discuss the challenges scholars face when conducting research within the final conversations context. To begin, final conversations research is emotionally arousing for participants, as the EOL journey is wrought with novel, challenging emotional experiences. Because of this, we have encountered particular limitations in our research. For instance, our samples are almost always predominantly female, which could be a reflection of societal gender norms that dissuade men from discussing emotionally-charged topics, or could be because women are often tasked to be the primary caregivers at the end-of-life [2,5]. Participants also tend to be predominantly Caucasian, which raises questions about cultural variation in how final conversations manifest within families [22], which is a critical component healthcare providers must consider when handling EOL issues with patients and families. Additionally, from an anecdotal standpoint, we have noticed a tendency for participants' retrospective accounts of final conversations to be mainly positive [2]. While we have heard some of the final conversations that were challenging and difficult, we are aware that there are many people who choose to avoid the situation completely or who have had such negative final conversations that they may have chosen not to share their experiences with us. There is much more to be learned about this aspect of final conversations. Less homogenous and more representative samples are needed. We call upon researchers with access to understudied populations and contexts to address this salient gap in the literature.

The familial context, and its influence on final conversations, needs to be further explored [3]. Specifically, scholars could seek to understand how communicative beliefs and norms, as well as relational dynamics within the family influence the frequency and quality of final conversations during the end of life. In addition, researchers might examine how family members (e.g., siblings, spouses) collaboratively narrate their final conversations experiences with a loved one after death, as well as how family relationships outside of the terminally ill person are affected by final conversations.

Finally, longitudinal work on final conversations would help establish causal links between relational messages exchanged at the end-of-life, their antecedents, and outcomes. In particular, it would be revealing to explore how the frequency and quality of final conversations potentially influences post-death social, psychological and physiological well-being outcomes (e.g., bereavement, grief, personal growth, support network outreach, stress, depression, etc.), and this influence would be best studied via longitudinal analysis. Longitudinal research could also help researchers understand the causal influence of particular antecedents, like family communication norms and beliefs, on the frequency and quality of final conversations during the EOL journey. To move forward, scholars could employ a longitudinal design in three phases: (1) survey members of families at the onset of a family member's terminal diagnosis in order to assess family communication environments, religious orientation, and relationship quality among family members; (2) survey participants again post-death about their final conversation experiences prior to death, as these memories would be especially poignant; (3) survey participants a final time two to three years later to assess variables related to social, psychological and physical well-being.

Behav. Sci. **2017**, *7*, 17

5. Conclusions

This manuscript has outlined the findings from the body of research on final conversations. In addition, we have provided healthcare and palliative care professionals, as well as family members, practical implications to assist in the EOL journey. Understanding final conversations and their impact on families is of crucial importance to the academic and professional healthcare communities, as well as to individuals and their families as they face an impending death. Fortunately, the surface of EOL family communication research has been scratched, thanks in part to the dedicated scholars who aim to help individuals through the EOL journey, and also to those who have opened their lives as participants in research. We are confident these findings will be useful to many, but we are also aware that more questions remain unanswered; thus, while we have come a far way, more work is still needed.

Acknowledgments: No funding was used to write this manuscript. The authors would like to thank the over 300 participants over the years who have been generous enough to share their final conversation stories with us.

Author Contributions: Maureen P. Keeley and Mark A. Generous shared equal responsibility in writing this manuscript.

Conflicts of Interest: The authors declare no conflicts of interest.

References

1. Keeley, M.P.; Yingling, J. *Final Conversations: Helping the Living and the Dying Talk to Each Other*; VanderWyk & Burnham: Acton, MA, USA, 2007.
2. Keeley, M.P. "Turning toward death together": The functions of messages during final conversations in close relationships. *J. Soc. Pers. Relatsh.* **2007**, *24*, 225–253. [CrossRef]
3. Keeley, M.P. Invited article: Family communication at the end of life. *J. Fam. Commun.* **2016**, *16*, 189–197. [CrossRef]
4. Keeley, M.P.; Generous, M.; Baldwin, P. Exploring children's final conversations with dying family members. *J. Fam. Commun.* **2014**, *14*, 208–229. [CrossRef]
5. Generous, M.A.; Keeley, M.P. Creating the Final Conversations (FCs) Scale: A measure of end of life relational communication with terminally ill individuals. *J. Soc. Work End Life Palliat. Care* **2014**, *10*, 257–289. [CrossRef] [PubMed]
6. Manusov, V.; Keeley, M.P. When talking is difficult: Nonverbal communication at the end of life. *J. Fam. Commun.* **2015**, *15*, 387–409. [CrossRef]
7. Keeley, M.P. Final conversations: Messages of love. *Qual. Res. Rep.* **2004**, *5*, 34–40.
8. Brockmeier, J.; Carbaugh, D. Introduction. In *Narrative and Identity: Studies in Autobiography, Self and Culture*; Brockmeier, J., Carbaugh, D., Eds.; John Benjamins Publishing Company: Amsterdam, The Netherlands, 2001; pp. 1–22.
9. Keeley, M.P. Final conversations: Survivors' memorable messages, concerning religious faith and spirituality. *Health Commun.* **2004**, *16*, 87–104. [CrossRef] [PubMed]
10. Keeley, M.P. Comfort and community: Two emergent communication themes of religious faith and spirituality evident during final conversations. In *Speaking of Spirituality: Perspectives on Health from the Religious to the Numinous*; Wills, M., Ed.; Health Communication Series; Hampton Press: Creskill, NJ, USA, 2009; pp. 227–248.
11. Generous, M.A.; Keeley, M.P. Wished for and avoided conversations with terminally ill individuals during final conversations. *Death Stud.* **2016**, *40*. [CrossRef] [PubMed]
12. Wittenberg-Lyles, E. *Dying with Comfort: Family Illness Narratives and Early Palliative Care*; Hampton Press: Cresskill, NJ, USA, 2010.
13. Cherlin, E.; Fried, T.; Prigerson, H.G.; Schulman-Green, D.; Johnson-Hurzeler, R.; Bradley, E.H. Communication between physicians and family caregivers about care at the end of life. When do discussions occur and what is said? *J. Palliat. Med.* **2005**, *8*, 1176–1185. [PubMed]

14. Keeley, M.P.; Generous, M.A. The challenges of final conversations: Dialectical tensions during end-of-life family communication from survivors' retrospective accounts. *South. Commun. J.* **2015**, *80*, 377–387. [CrossRef]

15. Baxter, L.A.; Braithwaite, D.O. Social Dialectics: The Contradictions of Relating. In *Contemporary Communication Theories and Exemplars*; Whaley, B., Samter, W., Eds.; Erlbaum: Mahwah, NJ, USA, 2006; pp. 275–292.

16. Moller, D.W. *Confronting Death: Values, Institutions, & Human Morality*; Oxford University Press: New York, NY, USA, 1996.

17. Bluebond-Langner, M.; Nordquist Schwallie, M. "It's back": Children with cancer talking about their illness when cure is not likely. In *Healing the World's Children: Interdisciplinary Perspectives on Child Health in the Twentieth Century*; Commachio, C., Golden, J., Witz, G., Eds.; Mcrill-Queen's University Press: Montreal, QC, Canada, 2008; pp. 161–175.

18. Goldsmith, J.; Wittenberg-Lyles, E.; Ragan, S.; Nussbaum, J.F. Lifespan and End-of-Life Health Communication. In *The Routledge Handbook of Health Communication*; Thompson, T.L., Parrott, R., Nussbaum, J.F., Eds.; Routledge: New York, NY, USA, 2011; pp. 441–454.

19. Fischer, A.H. *Gender and Emotion: Social Psychological Perspectives*; Cambridge University Press: Cambridge, UK, 2000.

20. Koerner, A.F.; Fitzpatrick, M.A. Toward a theory of family communication. *Commun. Theory* **2002**, *12*, 70–91. [CrossRef]

21. Keeley, M.P.; Generous, M.A. Advice from children and adolescents on final conversations with dying loved ones. *Death Stud.* **2014**, *38*, 308–314. [CrossRef] [PubMed]

22. Aiken, L.A. *Death, Dying, and Bereavement*; Lawrence Erlbaum: Mahwah, NJ, USA, 2001.

MDPI AG

St. Alban-Anlage 66

4052 Basel, Switzerland

Tel. +41 61 683 77 34

Fax +41 61 302 89 18

http://www.mdpi.com

Behavioral Sciences Editorial Office

E-mail: behavsci@mdpi.com

http://www.mdpi.com/journal/behavsci

www.ingramcontent.com/pod-product-compliance
Lightning Source LLC
Chambersburg PA
CBHW051315020426

42333CB00028B/3346